Manager's Guide to the Sarbanes-Oxley Act

Manager's Guide to the Sarbanes-Oxley Act

Improving Internal Controls to Prevent Fraud

SCOTT GREEN

WILEY

John Wiley & Sons, Inc.

Published by John Wiley & Sons, Inc., Hoboken, New Jersey

Published simultaneously in Canada

For general information on our other products and services, or technical support, please contact our Customer Care Department within the United States at 800-762-2974, outside the United States at 317-572-3993 or fax 317-572-4002.

Wiley also publishes its books in a variety of electronic formats. Some content that appears in print may not be available in electronic books.

For more information about Wiley products, visit our Web site at *www.wiley.com*.

Library of Congress Cataloging-in-Publication Data:

Green, Scott, 1962–
  Manager's guide to the Sarbanes-Oxley Act : improving internal
controls to prevent fraud / Scott Green.
       p. cm.
Includes bibliographical references and index.
  ISBN 0-471-56975-5 (CLOTH)
  1. Corporations—Accounting. 2. Corporations—Corrupt practices. 3. Corporations—
Accounting—Law and legislation. 4. Disclosure of information—Law and legislation. I. Title.
  HF5686.C7G5687 2004
  658.4'73—dc22

                                                    2003020250

Printed in the United States of America

10 9 8 7 6 5 4 3

To my wife Gabriella. Your support and untiring efforts on my behalf made this work a reality.

Contents

Foreword

BY IRA MILLSTEIN

The corporate scandals of 2001 and 2002 have been referred to as the "perfect storm." Everything that could go wrong at a few of our nation's largest public corporations did. At the eye of the storm was the classic agency problem: the risk that managers and directors may not always subordinate their own self-interests to the interests of the shareholders on whose behalf they are supposed to be acting. The risk is heightened when countervailing pressures from auditors, legal counsel, analysts, and other gatekeepers are absent.

Such was the case in many of the public corporations that made headlines. Agents and gatekeepers failed shareholders by putting their own self-interests first or passively allowing the status quo of management power to go unquestioned and, hence, unchecked. I expect that most agents and gatekeepers are honest people who try to do the right thing. For many caught up in these scandals, it may have been a matter of not having access to the information required to detect poor behavior. Structural and cultural barriers may have blocked the flow of important information, or may have impeded an understanding of the context that made the information important. We saw how self-interest—heightened by rich stock options in a boom economy, the opportunity of additional business or business flow to related entities, and a prevailing culture of relatively unfettered CEO power—can result in otherwise honest people acting badly.

Regardless of the extent to which the corporate governance system failed, the result seriously wounded public confidence in our financial markets. When the public can't trust agents and gatekeepers to provide effective oversight of assets provided by investors, the public, in their own self-interest, will decline to invest. Therefore, restoring investor confidence in the summer of 2002 was vital. In addition to expanding regulatory oversight and providing guidance for auditors, analysts, and lawyers, the Sarbanes-Oxley Act of 2002, interpreted by the SEC through implementing rules, with a new set of listing standards from the New York Stock Exchange and the NASDAQ, addresses many of the structural and cultural issues that arguably impeded the flow of information to directors and investors.

Now the tough part begins as managers and directors and those who advise them work to implement the provisions of the act, especially the provisions that relate to internal controls and implicate the board's role in risk assessment and information flow. *Manager's Guide to the Sarbanes-Oxley Act* provides valuable insights and guidance, backed by real-life examples, for managers, directors, and counselors working to design and implement controls, create monitoring tools to help identify poor behavior, take self-correcting action before they take hold in an organization, and otherwise meet the act's requirements.

Legislation, regulation, listing rules, or ethical norms will not restrain individuals who are intent on fraud. However, diligent independent directors who are properly led, informed, and assisted can circumscribe the agency problem. As our corporate governance models self-correct to emerging threats, confidence in our nation's public corporations and the financial markets will return. These improvements will incrementally and persistently sap strength from the perfect storm until it dissipates and is replaced by fair weather. The storm will then become another survival story to pass on to future generations, impressively told by those of us that lived through it.

Ira Millstein is a senior partner in the international law firm of Weil, Gotshal & Manges LLP. He is an internationally renowned authority on corporate governance and regularly counsels corporate boards, managers, and investors on various corporate governance and regulatory matters. His views on various governance-related issues have been solicited by the U.S. Congress and Securities & Exchange Commission, as well as by the World Bank, the Organisation for Cooperation and Development, and other domestic and international policy-setting bodies. He has taught graduate business school courses on corporate governance at Yale, Harvard, and Columbia.

Preface

Regard your good name as the richest jewel you can possibly be possessed of—for credit is like fire; when once you have kindled it you may easily preserve it, but if you once extinguish it, you will find it an arduous task to rekindle it again. The way to gain a good reputation is to endeavor to be what you desire to appear.

—Socrates, 469 B.C.–399 B.C.

A recent CBS poll revealed that, as a result of corporate scandals at Enron, WorldCom, Adelphia Communications, and others, a whopping two-thirds of Americans believe that corporate executives are dishonest. This overall assessment is even worse now than during the last financial crises, the savings and loan debacle of the 1980s. Congress has responded to public outrage by passing the Sarbanes-Oxley Act. The act has far-reaching consequences for every manager who works in a public company. It will not prevent fraud or operational losses, but it will make a manager responsible for one occurring on his or her watch. It requires senior managers to certify that their company has an operational system of internal controls over financial reporting. In business, everything flows down the chain of command. Virtually all managers will be required to maintain a system of internal control and will be held accountable if a fraud occurs.

Now more than ever, managers need to understand that they are fighting a war. The threats come from within their own ranks and from outside their world of influence. The enemy is intelligent, better financed, and more dangerous than ever before. It seems as if the front line is everywhere. Though fraud can originate from negative forces outside the organization by those positioned to quickly test and take advantage of a company's control structure, more often than not, fraud will originate from employees within an enterprise. These employees are often trusted, long tenured, and know the company well enough to conceal fraudulent activities for years. The most damaging schemes are likely to be committed by senior executives. Experienced managers conduct frauds that are 28 times more harmful to companies than their junior counterparts. The latest trend is that a company's own senior management "cooks the books" without the knowledge of the board of directors.

To the average investor, it appeared that Enron went from the seventh largest corporation in the United States to bankruptcy in a matter of a few weeks. In reality, Enron began its descent as early as 1997, when it began filing inaccurate financial statements. Related party transactions that eventually helped to destroy the company enriched long-serving, trusted senior management. All this was done in the full view of the firm's attorneys and accountants, who helped set up the investment vehicles and blessed the financial statements. The company had a distinguished and savvy board whose members seemed largely unaware of their perilous position. The Enron story is not only one of fraud, but of understanding the ethical makeup of a management team, the culture fostered with the rank-and-file employees, and the absence of an internal control structure.

From time to time, well-publicized events such as the accounting fraud at Enron raise awareness of the importance of a strong control environment, at which point the demand for control advisory services takes off, only to fall back to earth again when the public outrage wanes. We are now in a period of unprecedented corporate scandal. It has cost many pensioners crippling losses, damaged corporate credibility, and resulted in the elimination of thousands of jobs, both internal and external to the bankrupt companies. As a result, this time, it appears that the focus on internal controls will not fade away. New legislation will hold a company's managers accountable, and they must respond or face stiff penalties and even prison.

The reasons the focus on controls has been so transitory are many, but one of the most compelling is that there have been no simple tools available to apply to a business. The most complete publication currently available is a comprehensive study prepared by the Committee of Sponsoring Organizations of the Treadway Commission (COSO) called "Internal Control-Integrated Framework." As an auditor, I, as do many professional accountants and CFOs, use this framework to assess controls at the entity level. In fact, the SEC has specifically accepted the COSO framework for purposes of complying with Sarbanes-Oxley. But the two-volume tome contains material that is technical and difficult to understand for all but accountants, CFOs, and general auditors of major corporations. Even for them, some of the material can be arcane and difficult to apply. Every possible risk is contemplated, but most managers will not be in a position to take responsibility for many risks inherent in a company. This is particularly true for entity, or top-level, controls designed to address specific risks that exist far from most managers' area of influence. For instance, most managers do not have decision rights pertaining to the maintenance of corporate liquidity, nor do they need to understand concepts such as value-at-risk or Monte Carlo simulation. The CFO, treasurer, or a risk manager will normally be tasked to address liquidity, subject the company's resources to stress-testing to ensure the financial viability of the organization, and regularly report the results to the CEO. Nevertheless, the management of these and other risks requiring highly trained specialists were appropriately contemplated in the COSO publication. Consequently, for most managers, the vast majority of the publication does not apply to them in a practical way. If the framework were dropped on the desk of most general managers who are untrained in the art of internal control with instructions to implement it, they would not know where to begin. The same holds true for many control self-assessment workbooks. The idea is worthy: Provide a template that managers can use to perform an assessment of how well their business is controlled. However, most are written by accountants in a language that is difficult to digest.

On the other extreme are publications by authoritative bodies such as the American Institute of Certified Public Accountants (AICPA) and the Institute of Internal Auditors (IIA). Many of these excellent books and pamphlets provide guidance for conducting audits of complex processes and direction for addressing esoteric accounting issues. But the majority of these too are for accountants and auditors, and are not practically useful to most managers—unless they are in need of a sedative.

Control advisory has been a constant part of my professional life. I am a certified public accountant with over 15 years experience in the field, and I recognized early on that all managers—not just auditors and accountants—need to add control assessment skills to their set of business tools. So, over time, I developed the Control Smart approach to enable general managers to easily assess their own control structure. I continue empowering managers with this framework today. I am currently the director of audit for Weil, Gotshal and Manges, one of the largest law firms in the world and a leader in the practice of corporate governance, where I have global responsibility for evaluating the firm's control structure. I previously worked as a managing director of operations at ING Barings, the global investment bank, as well as at Goldman Sachs, Deloitte & Touche, and Boise Cascade Corporation, where I also helped both internal and external clients wrestle with control issues. I have advised managers on many diverse subjects, from executive compensation and reengineering initiatives to due diligence on potential target companies. But no job is more vital to me than advising management on how to set up strong, cost-effective internal controls, not only because it is the right thing for the company and its shareholders, but also because it is the best course of action to protect and preserve the jobs of managers and the livelihood of their employees.

By writing this book, I hope to bring this exciting and unique approach to general managers everywhere. The Control Smart approach enables managers to identify the risk types affecting all businesses—and their owners—and to focus their energy on those areas where they can make a difference. Moreover, Control Smart helps them to identify control gaps, or procedural voids, in their business process that threaten the organization and to design process-level controls.

To put these threats into context and help you avoid similar pitfalls, the book contains numerous examples, most ripped from the headlines of our national media. You will come to understand how to apply the lessons learned from the embezzlement at Harvard University's Hasty Pudding Theatricals, the fraud at Adelphia Communications, or the massive operational losses experienced by Firestone to your own business. Case studies will give you insight into the personalities at Enron and Tyco, which enabled a fraudulent culture, as well as read what one person did right to surface the smoke-and-mirrors accounting at WorldCom. Once the framework is implemented, you will have a method to monitor the operational risks inherent in your business. Information and knowledge are empowering tools, and the ability to easily monitor operational risk will enable you to identify whether controls are working. Armed with this data, you can prevent or obtain early detection of fraud and operational loss. Knowing that your business is well controlled, you can focus on serving internal or external customers and developing your career.

Regardless of public perception, most executives are honest and want to do the right thing for their shareholders, employees, and other stakeholders. The lack of readily available management tools, combined with the urgency created by the Sarbanes-Oxley Act, have sent managers and board members scurrying back to school to bone up on accounting principles. However, a recent article in the *New York Times* indicates that this approach is not effective, but the landscape has changed and managers are doing what they can to adjust. What managers at all levels need is a simple, practical template to help them assess operational risk, arguably the one risk that all managers must address. This need is met by *Manager's Guide to the Sarbanes-Oxley Act: Improving Internal Controls to Prevent Fraud* and the Control Smart approach, which is a powerful tool that will provide managers at all levels, from the board room to department management, with a template to prevent and detect fraud, embezzlement, and operational losses on their watch. More important, the approach has been developed to complement the COSO framework; to that end, it contains its basic components (control environment, risk assessment, control activities, information and communications, and monitoring) as it relates to most managers, and is presented in language that is comprehensible to nearly all managers. Put another way, Control Smart does not *replace* COSO, which addresses specific entity-level control activities, processes, and risks normally managed by specialists that are not relevant to the majority of managers. Rather, the Control Smart approach supports, and is intended to be used in conjunction with, the COSO framework by providing general managers with an easy-to-use, complementary tool that can be applied at the process level. I expect that most public companies will adopt COSO as their internal control framework. By implementing the Control Smart approach, a manager will be able to identify, evaluate, and monitor controls for those processes under his or her watch, prepare many of the deliverables required by COSO and similar frameworks, demonstrate compliance with the intent and spirit of the Sarbanes-Oxley regulations as they relate to his or her operations, and, ultimately, sleep better at night. The by-product of this tool is the protection of a manager's reputation, job security for his or her employees, and demonstration of fiduciary responsibility on behalf of shareholders.

I have endeavored to ensure this work is as up to date as possible. That said, inevitably, the outcome of many cases currently being litigated may impact the effectiveness of current legislation. There are credible movements afoot to water down certain provisions of the Sarbanes–Oxley Act; however, the final rule for management's report on internal control over financial reporting has been issued by the SEC and will go into effect for most companies on or after June 15, 2004 (April 15, 2005 for companies with a market capitalization under $75 million). As such, every CEO and manager should expect that they will be called on to attest to the strength of their control environment. Whether a manager likes it or not, he or she will be held accountable for a fraud or operational loss occurring on his or her watch. A material control break or fraud can seriously damage and even end a career. The time to address this risk is now.

Whether you are a board member, senior executive, or a middle manager, this book is relevant to you. It will help you understand internal control, design a strong structure, and make certain that a major fraud or operational loss does not occur to a function under your charge and derail your career.

Acknowledgments

This work is really a collaboration—a collection of advice, opinions, and revisions. In fact, so many have affected this work in so many ways, that I apologize in advance for anyone I have forgotten to mention.

A special note of thanks to my executive editor, Sheck Cho, and my agent, Richard Curtis, for guiding me through the maze called the publishing business.

I am also deeply grateful for the support of the partners and employees of Weil, Gotshal & Manges. In particular, I thank Stephen Dannhauser, Richard Davis, Norman LaCroix, Katherine D'Urso, and Deborah Cinque. I also must highlight the timely advice and collaboration of Ira Millstein, Holly Gregory, Robert Messineo, David Murgio, and Kevin Curtin which provided much needed momentum to this project.

I would be remiss for not identifying those who substantially contributed and/or edited the manuscript, including: Mark Chimsky, Harold Gibson, Jim Balsillie, John Duffy, Linda Orlando, Michelle Werner, Scott Foushee, J.J. L'Eplattenier, Dane Bonn, John Egan, Orval Hansen, Allan Shaw, Dr. Cliff Green, Dr. Herman Berliner, and Arnold Ross.

And thank you to the many whose advice, whether about the book, publishing, or internal controls, made the work better for their effort. These include: Ivar Nelson, John Cirrito, Dave Allocco, Dr. Magda Polenz, Rob Mastrandrea, Lori Leach, Dr. Jan Salisbury, Terry Mulry, Dr. Andrew Spieler, George Gordon, Dr. Byron Dangerfield, Karen Page, Amy Albrecht, Joan Epstein, Temple Kinyon, and Sandra Dunn.

Finally, Johnson & Johnson and Goldman Sachs International have my appreciation for granting reprint rights. Thanks to their generosity, we can all benefit from Johnson & Johnson's credo and Goldman Sach's business principles. Both represent best practice and have stood the test of time.

CHAPTER 1

Sarbanes-Oxley Myth

Corporations are failing, employees are being laid off, pension funds are evaporating, and executives are heading to jail. In the wake of this new round of corporate scandals, the government again vainly attempts to prevent individuals from wrongdoing by passing more stringent legislation. While dollar-hungry managers suck the life out of our corporations, the government reaches for that representative wooden stake to kill the vampires taking refuge within these entities. The latest weapon is the Sarbanes-Oxley Act of 2002. Some of the more important changes incorporated within the act and related Securities and Exchange Commission (SEC) regulations include:

- Audit committees must now consist solely of independent directors and at least one financial expert.
- Chief executive officers (CEOs) and chief financial officers (CFOs) must certify that their financial statements fairly present the financial condition and results of their company.
- CEOs and CFOs must certify that they have an operational system of internal controls over financial reporting.
- A public company must disclose whether it has adopted a code of ethics for the principal executive officer and senior financial officers.
- Outside auditors must attest to and report on management's evaluation of the strength of its company's system of internal control.
- Public companies may no longer make loans to executive officers or directors.
- CEOs and CFOs may be required to give back compensation if financial statements are restated due to "material noncompliance" with reporting requirements.

- Officers, directors, and other insiders are prohibited from trading company stock during pension-fund blackout periods.
- The SEC has explicit power to establish the new Public Company Accounting Oversight Board.
- New professional responsibility rules for attorneys are required.
- New conflict-of-interest rules for financial analysts are required.
- New protections for whistle-blowers are created.

So will this new legislation slay the beast? Hardly. Just like the television soap opera *Dark Shadows*, the same story will run again in syndication. (For those of you too young to remember, *Dark Shadows* ran from 1966 to 1971. The main character of the program was Barnabas Collins, a hard-to-kill vampire operating in a human world in a manner similar to some of our unsavory corporate managers.) Where managers, employees, accountants, or attorneys intend to do wrong, no amount of legislation will stop them. The penalties may be more stringent and the chances of getting caught greater, but it is safe to say that neither Congress nor the SEC can legislate individuals into doing the right thing. History has shown that, regardless of the good intentions, such measures provide little deterrent.

Let's examine the managers, the employees, the accountants, and the lawyers to show why this is true. We will then be ready to discuss what we can do to meet the control-related goals of Sarbanes-Oxley and drive a stake through the heart of our vampires.

LEGISLATING EVIL OUT OF OUR CORPORATIONS

A good name, like good will, is got by many actions and lost by one.

—Lord Jeffery

There is no arguing that the stakes have been raised for board members, executives, and employees. The consequences of illegal and unethical business practices are now front and center in the nation's conscience. Government is taking a lead role by interrogating, prosecuting, and stiffening fines for those managers associated with a company scandal. Prosecutors are publicly parading to jail, with handcuffs prominently displayed, some of the wealthiest businesspeople in our country. Consider the following lengthy list of those caught in the current financial crisis: Dennis Kozlowski, former Tyco CEO; Mark Swartz, former Tyco CFO; Mark Belnick, former Tyco Chief Counsel; Frank E. Walsh, former independent Tyco Director; Jerry Boggess, former Tyco Fire & Security Services President; Paul Allaire, former Xerox CEO; G. Richard Thoman, former Xerox CEO; Barry D. Romeril, former Xerox CFO; Philip D. Fishbach, former Xerox Controller; Daniel S. Marchibroda, former Xerox Assistant Controller; Gregory B. Taylor, current Xerox Treasurer; Gary Winnick, Global Crossing Chairman; Jim Gorton, former Global Crossing Chief Counsel; Greg Casey, former Global Crossing Sales Executive; Jackie Armstrong, Global Crossing Counsel; Philip F. Anscutz, former Qwest Communications Chairman; Joseph P. Nacchio, former Qwest Communications CEO; Robin Szeliga, former Qwest Communications CFO; Grant P. Graham, former Qwest Global Business Unit CFO; Thomas W. Hall, former Qwest Global Business Unit Senior Vice President; John M. Walker, Qwest Global Business Unit Senior Vice President; Bryan K. Treadway, Qwest Global Business Unit Assistant Controller; Albert J. Dunlap, former Sunbeam CEO; Russell A. Kersh, former Sunbeam CFO; Bernard Ebbers, former WorldCom CEO; Scott Sullivan, former WorldCom CFO; David Myers, former WorldCom Controller; Buford Yates Jr., former WorldCom Accounting Director; Michael H. Salsbury, WorldCom General Counsel; Susan Mayer, WorldCom Treasurer; Betty L. Vinson, former WorldCom Accountant; Troy M. Normand, former WorldCom Accountant; John Rigas, Adelphia Communications Founder; Timothy Rigas, former Adelphia Communications CFO; James Brown, former Adelphia Vice President for Finance; Michael Mulcahey, former Adelphia Director for Internal Reporting; Kenneth Lay, former Enron Corporation Chairman; Jefferey Skilling, former Enron Corporation President; Andrew Fastow, former Enron CFO; Richard A. Causey, former Enron CAO; Michael J. Kopper, former Enron Executive; Kenneth Rice, former Enron Broadband Division Chief Executive; Ben F. Glisan Jr., former Enron Broadband Division Treasurer; Dan Boyle, former Enron Broadband Division Finance Executive; Kevin Hannon, former Enron Broadband Division Executive; Scott Yeager, former Enron Broadband Division Executive; Joe Hirko, former Enron Broadband Division Chief Executive; Kevin Howard, former Enron Broadband Division Executive; Rex Shelby, former Enron Broadband Division Executive; Michael Krautz, former Enron Broadband Division Executive; John Giesecke, former Homestore

COO; Joseph Shew, former Homestore CFO; Eric Keller, former AOL-Time Warner Executive; Sam Waksal, former Imclone Systems CEO; Richard M. Scrushy, HealthSouth Chairman; Michael Martin, HealthSouth CFO; Clark E. McLeod, former McLeod USA CEO; Stephen A Garofalo, Metromedia Fiber Networks Founder and Chairman; Jack Grubman, former Salomon Smith Barney Analyst; Schuyler Tilney, former Merrill Lynch Executive; Thomas Davis, former Merrill Lynch Executive; Phua Young, Merrill Lynch Analyst; David Duncan, Arthur Andersen Partner; Robert Asti, former Symbol Technologies Vice President; Enio Montini, Kmart Vice President; Joseph Hofmeister, Kmart Vice President; Frank Quattrone, Credit Suisse First Boston Investment Bank Executive; Charles W. McCall, former McKesson Chairman; Helen C. Sharkey, former Dynegy Risk Control & Deal Structure Executive; Gene S. Foster, former Dynegy Vice President of Taxation; Jaime Olis, former Dynegy Senior Director of Tax Planning; and Martha Stewart, Martha Stewart Living Omnimedia Chairman.

If it was not obvious prior to the swift demise of Enron, it is obvious now. The managers and employees on this list have one thing in common: their professional careers and personal lives have been negatively and severely affected by events at their companies and firms. They have been subpoenaed, investigated, interrogated, indicted, fired, or otherwise lost their jobs due to the accounting, financial reporting, and disclosure practices at their companies. In certain cases, these managers were directly involved in the destruction of their companies. Many even face jail time. The SEC and the Department of Justice are aggressively pursuing wayward managers. President George W. Bush established the Corporate Fraud Task Force on July 9, 2002, and by May of the following year, more than 250 corporate fraud convictions or guilty pleas were obtained; 25 of these were former chief executive officers. Criminal penalties for securities fraud now carry jail sentences of up to 25 years and fines of up to $2 million.

Some of the biggest losers, however, are the employees: 85,000 at Arthur Andersen, 4,000 at Enron, and the thousands laid off at Global Crossing, Qwest, Tyco, Adelphia, and other companies affected by these frauds. They are the innocents who pay the greatest price.

And while the list is stunning, it documents merely the most well-known cases of late. The SEC, Congress, and prosecutors are far from done. They are now turning their attention to the various boards of directors, whose members are charged with oversight, to their outside advisors, and to managers who were enriched by trading investment banking business for access to "hot" initial public offerings (IPOs).

The fallout from these financial scandals is massive. It involves some of the world's largest companies and accounting firms and touches many different industries. The landscape is changing, and managers at all levels, from the boardroom to the shop floor, need to take action to improve controls throughout their organizations and protect themselves in the process. According to governance expert Ira Millstein, "Today, every action or inaction is potentially cause for, at least, public discussion, and maybe even legal liability."[1] Managers may not be the cause of the problem or want to get involved, but they owe it to their families and employees to remain vigilant and do all they can to prevent and detect fraud. Only through quick action can a company save itself from a few bad managers. Greater transparency in how companies report their earnings is no longer optional, but a requirement.

Even companies with a longstanding tradition of being "shareholder-friendly" have failed to install the necessary checks and balances required to ensure that the financial position of the company is properly disclosed. Boards of directors and managers must make this happen. If ever there was a reason to take the initiative, the list of names given here should provide that wake-up call. Even if innocent, the experience of being investigated, indicted, or suddenly unemployed is not pleasant and can take a terrible toll on a person's health and on the well-being of his or her family. And that experience pales in comparison to losing one's job and being cheated out of one's pension, as were the employees of Enron.

Despite new laws, greater vigilance, and oversight, fraud still haunts us. The government has stepped in before to exorcise these demons. After the stock market crash of 1929, Congress passed the Securities Act of 1933 and the Securities Exchange Act of 1934 to address corporate abuse. The savings and loan crises of the 1980s led to even more regulation. Shareholder activists waged battles with corporations throughout the 1990s against so-called poison pills (corporate actions that prevent an unsolicited takeover) and secret executive compensation. These actions resulted in many boards and regulators requiring more transparency. Nevertheless, we still had an epidemic of frauds surface in 2002. It should be clear that while legislation can help strengthen the system, it cannot stop bad people from doing bad things. Just like the threat of life in prison will not deter a single-minded killer, strong penalties will not discourage a manager determined to play by his or her own rules. The evidence to support both of these facts is served to us with breakfast by way of our daily newspapers.

While I hope it will be different this time, history suggests that the importance of implementing and monitoring a robust control structure may be forgotten and subsequently doom many companies to fall victim again. Star managers will test boundaries just because they believe they can without penalty. Auditors will provide clean opinions on failing companies. Lawyers will set up legal entities that enable financial shenanigans. The government will respond with even more regulation. How senior management responds to these issues will determine the future of their organization. Ira Millstein speaks to our corporate governance responsibilities by urging that "Everyone helping to guide the corporate enterprise—directors, officers, accountants, bankers and lawyers alike—needs to 'get it'."[2] If we don't "get it", we will continue to undermine the very engine that drives the nation's wealth creation.

EMPLOYEES, FRAUD, AND LESSONS FORGOTTEN

It was late 1996, less than two years after Nick Leeson left his famous note at work and disappeared, leaving Barings Bank $1.2 billion poorer and headed for bankruptcy. ING, a giant financial services company, eventually bought Barings out of bankruptcy and attempted to turn the business around. Paul Gyra was the man in charge of addressing Barings' control issues worldwide. He hired me to address what he perceived to be a clear and present threat to the business. ING Barings continued to aggressively strengthen controls worldwide, and Paul was satisfied with progress made in Asia and Europe, but was still concerned with the Americas. Hence, he asked me to take on the challenge. Paul was correct to be concerned, not only because the control environment in the Americas required improvement, but because the culture of the industry made it difficult to identify and correct control deficiencies. In good times, financial services executives seemed willing to sacrifice controls to keep a star performer happy. They would turn a blind eye to the secrecy and control these stars exerted over their empires and avoid asking the hard questions that would have surfaced fraud. It seemed that lessons of the past were just swept under the carpet.

Examples of this behavior run deep. The SEC found in 1994 that Joseph Jett committed "record-keeping violations" and ordered him to repay Kidder

Peabody more than $8 million in bonuses paid to him. Lack of supervision and an unwillingness to challenge the huge margins earned by Jett contributed to, and even enabled, the "record-keeping violations." Kidder claimed more than $350 million in fake profits had been booked and the firm was eventually dismantled and sold.

Then along came Nick Leeson and Barings. Leeson was able to set up accounts to hide his losses from a declining Nikkei, resulting from the Kobe earthquake. Improper supervision and segregation of duties delayed detection of the losses. Management continued to fund these losses until Leeson went missing, but by then the damage was done. The resulting $1.2 billion loss brought down one of the largest and most fabled financial institutions in the world. (Barings, formed in 1762, purchased the Louisiana territories from France on behalf of the United States and funded the Napoleonic Wars. It was sold out of bankruptcy for 1 pound.) Leeson was found in Germany and returned to a Singapore prison.

On the heels of Leeson came Toshihide Iguchi of Daiwa Bank's New York branch, who executed in excess of $1.1 billion in unauthorized trades, including the sale of more than $375 million in *customer* securities. Imagine if the securities he sold were yours! The fraud was perpetrated over several years and discovery was complicated by management attempts to conceal the losses.

This was followed in 1996 by the acts of Sumitomo's Yasuo Hamanaka who, for over a decade, maintained two sets of books for his huge copper positions, concealing what eventually became $1.8 billion in losses. Also in 1996, it was discovered that NatWest's Kyriacos Papoulis was able to conceal well over $100 million in losses by overvaluing option positions held on the books. You know things are getting bad when this awesome amount seems like a pittance when compared to those losses experienced before it.

As recently as February 2002, John Rusak, a U.S.-based trader for Allfirst, a subsidiary of Allied Irish Bank, lost more than $750 million. He was able to keep losses unrecognized by booking phony options contracts to offset real losses. Even though the phony options would expire with a profit, no controls were in place to ensure that "in the money" or profitable options were exercised and money received. Instead, Rusak would simply replace the expired options with more phony trades. Allied publicly admitted the loss was directly related to a failure of internal controls and eventually entered into an agreement to sell Allfirst. Rusak was sentenced to over seven years in prison.

It is hard to explain how individuals, mostly acting alone, can cause such huge losses. In every instance, there was a strong, apparently successful personality, exerting complete control over key operations. There was also a lack of strong internal controls to prevent or alert senior management of the staggering losses that were eventually realized. Where there were clues, no one was willing to risk challenging these powerful icons. Many of these rogues had perfected the art of misdirecting or intimidating subordinates, peers, and even supervisors. Sumitomo's Hamanaka was so revered that anything he said could move the copper market. Externally, regulators were slow to challenge him; internally, auditors were powerless to force him to divulge financial information. Baring's Leeson would brag about his $2 million annual bonus and unlimited travel expenses. His authority over both management and trading operations, his physical presence, and his aggressiveness overpowered diminutive, respectful Asian traders. Kidder's Jett was physically intimidating and able to end any conversation abruptly just by asking, "Are you questioning me?"[3]

While these examples relate to companies with trading operations, arguably among the most risky business models utilized in legitimate industry, recent events at Enron, WorldCom, Global Crossing, and Adelphia Communications have proven that control breaks can occur at companies competing in a wide range of industries. One common thread among these recent failures is a company culture that rewards immediate results without regard to ethical considerations or long-term consequences. In the end, the biggest losers are the employees and those who invest in these organizations. The executives of these companies damage the public trust in the markets and the image of corporate managers everywhere. But executives are not the only ones to damage the public trust. Our view of the trusty accountant has also changed.

WHY YOU SHOULD NOT RELY ON AUDITORS

In the latest congressional Enron hearings, those senior managers who did testify complained that they did not know what was occurring on their watch and that the auditors never brought the material issues to their attention. Whether the auditors did or did not identify and report the irregularities at Enron, it is management that has final responsibility for the financial statements filed with the SEC. What they did not know, they should have prevented or discovered by way of strong controls.

Every independent auditor's report states clearly that the financial statements are the responsibility of the company's management. The auditors only provide an opinion on the financial statements based on their audits. This sounds like doublespeak, but the distinction is important. The auditors will normally have management represent their responsibility in a signed letter that explicitly states the company maintains a system of internal controls designed to provide reasonable assurance that accounting records are reliable for the preparation of financial statements and safeguarding assets.

External auditors are unlikely to identify a lapse in the control structure of a company. Their focus is to provide an opinion that the financial statements are fairly presented in accordance with Generally Accepted Accounting Principals (GAAP). If competent, it is likely that they will detect an irregularity only after it has a significant, negative effect on the reported results of the company. If not competent, they will not see to it that the financial statements fairly reflect the results and standing of the company, nor will they recognize that the entire enterprise may be at risk of collapse. However, internal auditors are charged with ensuring that preventive and detective controls are in place. But commonly, an audit team may review each auditable entity once a year or even less often. In the period between audits, the controls that were in place may have been changed or otherwise compromised. Once again, it is management that bears the risk of a control break. To put a career and a company at risk by solely relying on auditors to oversee a business is shortsighted at best.

David Allocco, a life-long operations and control expert at Goldman Sachs, as well as a personal friend and mentor, has a keen eye for helping managers spot their risks. Dave is fond of saying, "The problem with the current process is that while the internal auditors are chasing garbage trucks to determine if unshredded sensitive information is leaving the firm, a trader is sending a firm's trading positions to a competitor via e-mail when his [or her] supervisor isn't looking." This statement implies that yesterday's audit procedures are not effective in today's electronic world. Sensitive information can leave a firm in a number of ways, both physical (in the trash) and electronic (e-mail). Simply put, auditors have a hard time keeping up with the ingenuity and initiative of those who would break our rules and laws.

These are not new concepts. The General Accounting Office (GAO), in its investigation of the savings and loan (S&L) crises of the 1980s, found that the accounting profession had failed to keep abreast of the fundamental changes sweeping through the thrift industry. The profession continued to apply decades-old procedures to transactions new to the industry. The industry had shifted from making home loans to investing in real estate, land development, and junk bonds. The result was that many S&Ls went belly-up only weeks or months after the auditors provided clean audit opinions. When the bill came due, it cost taxpayers more than $200 billion.

Most recently, Arthur Andersen was effectively put out of business for its involvement in the accounting shell game at Enron. The fact that one of the world's largest corporations could just dissolve within months of receiving a clean opinion from one of the prestigious Big 5 accounting firms shook the nation. Through the Sarbanes-Oxley Act of 2002, Congress and the SEC have created a new regulatory oversight board for the accounting profession; it has been charged with the awesome responsibility of setting ethics and conflict-of-interest standards, disciplining accountants, and conducting annual reviews of the largest accounting firms. Called the Public Company Accounting Oversight Board, it has taken over many functions that were previously self-regulated. Prior to this legislation, the profession monitored itself through peer reviews and self-imposed standards with oversight from the Securities and Exchange Commission. It is important that the new board quickly exercise its new power, establish credibility with investors, and return integrity to the profession.

Unfortunately, the board is off to a poor start. The first person selected to head the board was forced to resign after it was learned that a company for which he was a director was under investigation. The revelation that Harvey Pitt knew of the investigation but did not disclose it contributed to his decision to resign his position as chairman of the SEC. The oversight board subsequently met without a chair, and as a first order of business, voted themselves a salary in excess of $400,000—each. Call me crazy, but it seems that the first order of business for a new body empowered to change the country's professional landscape should be something other than setting its members' own compensation, particularly at a level few laypeople would understand.

The SEC finally took a step in the right direction by appointing William J. McDonough, the respected former president of the Federal Reserve Bank of New York. Because of the prior missteps, however, I am keeping my expectations for this new board low in the hope that they exceed them by a wide margin. The board has already opened itself up to criticism and I rather fully expect that those resisting change will benefit. Only time will tell.

You Can't Trust the Lawyers Either

When one considers the various investment vehicles set up by Enron to shift assets and debts behind an opaque financial curtain, a question regarding their creation must be raised. Generally, a lawyer, or more likely, several of them, will diligently work to set up the legal vessels that enable the transactions. In the clear light of day, many of these transactions were so dubious it is hard to imagine a lawyer, or for that matter, an entire firm, not questioning them.

Just as egregious, there seems to be nothing that will disqualify a law firm from being retained to investigate accusations against management. The law firm investigating Sharon Watkin's memo (the Enron whistle-blower) was rife with conflicts of interest. The firm of Vinson & Elkins was a long-term advisor to the company and, predictably, its investigation was ineffective. Good investigators leave no stone unturned. This investigation left every stone undisturbed.

A law firm investigating the whistle-blower memo regarding Global Crossing's accounting had similar conflicts of interest. Some of the attorneys reportedly owned their client's stock. Are we surprised that this investigation also did not unearth any issues?

This is a good time to point out that while the accounting profession is regulated, lawyers continue to be relatively unpoliced. In fact, the American Bar Association (ABA) is still debating whether a lawyer's first duty is to a client or to prevent a crime. If the ABA is not sure, how can we expect our nation's attorneys to make the distinction? The answer is, we can't. Society can no more put its faith in the legal profession to do the right thing than to expect a criminal to self-report his or her crime. Until the ABA sees that the client is truly the shareholder of a company, rather than one or two company executives, and that they must do what is ethically right on his or her behalf, there will be no progress on this point.

Sarbanes-Oxley allows the SEC to establish professional standards of conduct for the nation's attorneys. These standards include "up the ladder" reporting obligations that would be triggered when an attorney "becomes aware of evidence of a material violation by the issuer or by any officer, director, employee or agent of the issuer." The lawyer would then have to report the matter to the chief legal counsel of the company. If the attorney does not receive an adequate response from the company's chief legal counsel and the CEO, the lawyer must report the violation to the board of directors. That is where the lawyer's duties currently end. These actions protect the lawyer from disciplinary action and civil liability. The SEC initially proposed language that required the attorney to make a "noisy withdrawal" if the board does not take appropriate action. A noisy withdrawal consists of resigning the engagement, slamming the door on the way out, and notifying the SEC. Unfortunately, the SEC yielded to intense lobbying from the legal community and withdrew this language from the final rule. The fact is that lawyers are the most potent lobbying force in the United States. This is why it is so hard for states to pass tort reform despite widespread support. The SEC has twice tried to regulate the profession, but both times the legal lobby prevailed. It appears increasingly likely that Sarbanes-Oxley could fall prey to this formidable special-interest group and have little real impact on the conduct of the nation's lawyers.

This point may be irrelevant, however, as SEC guidance on what is material and reportable is sufficiently vague as to question whether any attorney can ever be held accountable.

Supporting the Fraud Culture

We've seen a bit of a crisis of morals at all levels of society. We've see it in politics, the business world and the church. I think a very big thing is 20 or 30 years ago when a player did something wrong, he knew it was wrong. There's been a shift in values.[4]

—U.S. Congressman Tom Osborne,
former head football coach of the University of Nebraska

Social scientists describe culture as a way of life. It is one of those "soft" subjects that many companies and managers do not believe warrants significant daily attention. These managers unwittingly allow the potential of fraud to find a home and take root in their organization. They will launch their statement of values with great fanfare, never to refer to them again. Culture can be a powerful control tool, or ensure the destruction of a company.

A strong culture, positive or negative, will directly impact a control environment. Ignoring culture is like ignoring a cancer threat. Failure to take responsibility for the health of the corporate culture by way of periodic checkups and the constant exercise of values can lead to apathy and a diet deficient of reinforcing procedures. It allows a malignancy to take hold and grow undetected. While a manager may not be directly responsible for the cancer, inaction will allow it to spread.

Most companies today use buzzwords to describe how nice they are. Little time is spent developing a credible statement of shared values. Enron's set of corporate values lists communication, respect, integrity, and excellence. They sound like something to which we should all aspire. But a simple list of words does not mean much if it is not clear how to apply their meaning to our daily work lives. Even more important, it must be clear that the company leaders actually believe in their stated values. Not too many people would use the word "integrity" to describe the company's management. It is clear to all that Enron's managers either could not, or did not, care to enforce this value. They became the gold standard for poor corporate governance and culture.

A fuzzy or vacant set of values is not just neutral, but destructive. Employees can spot insincerity in the executive ranks all the way from the mailroom, and will make a company pay for it. In an excellent article in the *Harvard Business Review*, Patrick M. Lencioni discusses his 10 years working with companies to improve their corporate culture. "Most value statements are bland, toothless, or just plain dishonest. And far from being harmless, as most executives assume, they're often highly destructive."[5]

The culture of aggressive accounting at Enron made "gaming the system" an acceptable practice. According to former Enron executives, the company struck a sham energy deal with Merrill Lynch, to help it meet 1999 profit targets, that unleashed millions in bonus money and restricted stock to top executives. The $60 million in profits evaporated when the transaction was later canceled; however, the bonuses that accrued to managers were paid nevertheless.

Growth and pressure to meet Wall Street expectations can put tremendous pressure on a management team. If a strong culture of honesty and forthrightness is not cultivated and rewarded, a cancer of shady behavior can spread until it kills the company. Consider CUC International, which was acquired in 1997 by the company that would become Cendant. Cendant's due diligence failed to uncover more than $500 million of fake, pretax profits. Even more shocking is that it required employees and managers in more than 22 businesses to falsify records to this extent. The managers that booked the fictitious profits told investigators that they felt pressured by their bosses to meet Wall Street expectations. This goal took hold of the organization and triumphed over all other moral and ethical considerations.

It is hard to judge in financial terms what a strong, positive culture means to companies. Simply stated, in their promotion of shared values through business principles or a credo, companies that communicate and live by a strong culture of ethics will have a better control environment. Two companies that exemplify what it means to communicate and live by good corporate values are Johnson & Johnson and Goldman Sachs.

Johnson & Johnson is a company synonymous with compassionate health care. When people think of Tylenol, they think of safe and effective pain relief. This view remains despite the fact that, in 1982, seven people were poisoned when a murderer introduced cyanide into Tylenol bottles in the Chicago area. A number of years after that incident, I remember sitting in a classroom at the Harvard Business School listening to J&J CEO James Burke lecture. Predictably, a student asked him how he went about making tough decisions. To many of us, his answer was remarkable. He related that the decisions were relatively easy to make, as Johnson & Johnson had a culture and a credo that put people first. It may at first be difficult to imagine a sophisticated CEO looking to a credo to manage his business, but not when you realize that J&J takes its values seriously. When you open the J&J Web page, the credo is prominently displayed, and you can review it easily in 63 different countries in the local language. By analyzing the credo, I believe I understand the J&J culture and the decisions that emanate from it.

The statement begins by announcing the responsibility of the company: "The first responsibility is to the doctors, nurses, and patients, to mothers and fathers and to all others who use our products and services." Note that it does not start with management, employees, shareholders, profits, or corporate accounts that buy the product. Rather, the focus is on the people who use its products. If this is the first priority, that then frees a manager from having to consider short-term profits when faced with a moral dilemma. The type of question a manager will ask shifts from "How can we address this problem at the lowest cost?" to "What steps must we take to protect our consumers?" CEO Burke did not have to think twice about quickly removing Tylenol product from all shelves, regardless of cost. It was in the best interests of those who used its products; and, in the long run, it was also the best decision for the long-term reputation and financial health of the company.

At Goldman Sachs I experienced firsthand the power of culture. When I was interviewing for a position at this investment banking giant, I had many discussions with human resources staff and with hiring managers regarding the "culture" of the company. Goldman looks to its 14 business principles for corporate identity, and these managers wanted me to understand what was expected of me. In a relationship business, trust is everything. There is no room at Goldman for anything but honesty. A scenario similar to what happened at CUC would have difficulty taking hold at Goldman. The cancer that spread there would have been "surgically" removed before it had a chance to take root in their culture.

Goldman Sach's human resources department makes it clear that if you lie on your application, in even the smallest detail, you will be terminated. Every so often, a new hire would ignore this preemptive warning, but he or she would disappear after a few weeks of working there. Evidently, the wheels of justice within the HR department finally caught up with these applicants. Goldman's principles were not only applied to newcomers; star performers were also regularly let go by the firm during my tenure there for failing to abide by them. These rainmakers were generally considered to have put themselves above the firm or their clients. I was impressed by this at the time, and even more so later when I observed other firms that were loath to take such action. Compare this to Bausch & Lomb's handling of its CEO, Ronald L. Zarrella. The eye-care giant's CEO padded his resume by improperly claiming he had graduated from New York University's Stern School of Business. Rather than terminating the company's relationship with Zarrella, the board withheld $1.1 million in bonus. Seems like a steep price to be paid, for sure, but the larger question of integrity remains. How can shareholders trust their leader to do the right thing for them when he admits to misrepresenting himself?

Goldman Sachs is able to aggressively insist on honesty because of its team culture and its significant investment in developing its "bench talent," another ingrained cultural trait. There was always a qualified replacement ready if need be to keep the business running at any level. Furthermore, it was understood that the best way to get ahead was to be a team player and make your boss and the team look good. This cultural trait has served many of the firm's leaders well, as there is a worn path directly to Washington for firm graduates. In a town where hardball politics is the norm, honest, confidential, and deferential service is highly prized. Not surprisingly, former Goldman chairmen and CEOs have been very successful in Washington. John Whitehead served as the deputy secretary of state for the Reagan administration; Bob Rubin served as the chief economic advisor and, later, treasury secretary for President Clinton; Steve Friedman is now serving as the chief economic advisor to the Bush administration; Henry Paulson served in the Nixon White House; and Jon Corzine represents New Jersey in the Senate.

The culture is so strong that, recently, the current chairman, Henry Paulson, was forced to make a public apology to the firm's employees for implying that there are "15 or 20 percent of the people that really add 80 percent of the value." This upset many employees who were raised on the Goldman ethic that there is no star system, rather, that it is all about team-work. Troubled by this interpretation, Paulson issued a blanket apology stating, "I am profoundly embarrassed about my choice of words." Such a response is certainly not usual in American business.

Contacts still working at Goldman tell me that the firm has changed somewhat since reshaping the corporate structure from that of a partner-ship to a corporation. Though I'm certain it is not the same paternalistic place of my memory, there is evidence that the firm still values and acts on its business principles. These principles are presented in the firm's annual report, and are prominent on its Web site. While not immune, it seems that the firm has experienced fewer investigations and fines than those levied against its competitors relating to the latest corporate meltdown (although the firm has participated with many competitors in settlements involving industrywide practices). Chairman Paulson took a courageous public stand recently by condemning the aggressive corporate accounting that led to the high-profile bankruptcies of late. The cynics were quick to point out that it is pressure from Wall Street to hit or exceed profit estimates that drives aggressive behavior. However, Paulson's position is consistent with the firm's business principles and the public stance of Goldman's legendary leaders before him.

The degree to which the firm has changed will become apparent quickly. Of interest is the ongoing investigation into the relationship between the firm's investment bankers and research analysts. Regulators in Utah are conducting a review of unprecedented scope by searching more than 100,000 e-mails dating back several years for evidence that the firm breached the regulatory wall between its investment banking and research units. If evidence is found, the reward for Utah will be a fine levied similar to the $100 million Merrill Lynch had to pay the State of New York to settle a similar case. How well Goldman fares in this detailed investigation will tell outsiders a lot about the firm. The point will turn on whether there were breaches of firm policy by individuals or that the firm as a whole ignored regulatory requirements to manage these businesses separately. The outcome and how the firm responds will determine whether the culture is alive and well.

As a manager, it is important to communicate and monitor your "culture." Your staff will look to you to see how seriously to take a company's statement of shared values. Much like Johnson & Johnson's Burke, managers need to reinforce how they have relied on these values in making tough decisions. If your company does not have a statement of shared values, credo, or business principles, then you have the opportunity to create one. I did this for the audit department I built at ING Barings. I knew there were high expectations for the department and that there would be a lot of pressure on new hires as the team addressed the many control issues faced by the firm. I wanted there to be no doubt that I would always support my staff to do the right thing. There was no need to be intimidated by bad news in a star's business; conversely, the staff was required to treat their counterparts in an honest, professional manner. I prepared the first draft of the statement of shared values, refined them with my managers, and then presented them to the department. Whenever confronted with a public decision, I would often refer to how our team values applied.

The audit department definitely developed a culture and, in the process, a clear view of how its members contributed to the firm. No longer a dumping ground for incompetents or fodder for lashings of a star performer, our department gained the respect of the organization. Even the National Partner for Investment Banking at KPMG went on record with ING management stating that if we did not have the best audit team on the "Street," it was one of the top two. Not a small achievement in only two years. I place the credit for this success squarely on the team, for the way they perceived themselves (values) and what they aspired to (mission). Values played a crucial role.

If you need to create a statement of values, Johnson & Johnson's credo and Goldman Sach's business principles are provided in Appendix A for you to contemplate as a starting point. Another excellent resource for help in creating a statement of shared values can be found in the Criteria for Performance Excellence of the Malcolm Baldridge National Quality Award. The information there can guide a manager through the design and implementation of a value statement. The statement of shared values will be different for every organization, and each one needs to make it its own, infusing it into every aspect of the organization. J&J periodically revisits its credo to ensure it still matches the objectives of the organization. Like any great document, it "lives." It cannot be easily changed, but it has the ability to grow with proper nurturing.

To demonstrate that you take your value system seriously, you need to clearly articulate behavioral attributes that are rewarded and those actions that are off-limits. One barrier to openness can be the resistance to bad news. Those who express candid criticisms are often accused of not being a part of the team, and managers may withhold rewards from such employees. Employees at all levels learn *not* to speak up. They avoid being the one to alert management to real problems. The best and the brightest with any character will find a more rewarding place to work. The result will be an organization infested with sycophants and cowards who remain silent even as the company collapses around them. Employees must understand that they need to embrace positive corporate values if they are to be successful. The best way to do this is to reward open communication, even if the news is painful.

Naturally, a supervisor will repel the initiatives of subordinates to fix control issues if he or she is the one perpetuating the fraud. For those who wish to report troubling behavior, taking the problem to their supervisor may not be an option. Therefore, alternative methods of communication need to be provided for these employees. A corporate ethics hotline to *independent* outside legal counsel that reports solely to the board of directors can be particularly effective. Truly independent outside counsel can confidentially capture and relay issues back to the company's board.

Here, too, WorldCom provides an example of what can occur if no alternative method of communication is made available to employees. A congressional committee released copies of e-mail messages between the controller and a London-based vice president for international finance and control. It seems that the vice president for finance objected to the company's unilateral reduction of $33 million in expenses without explanation. Since this would increase publicly reported profits, he tried to bring in outside accountants from Arthur Andersen to support the position. The controller, David Meyers, ordered the vice president to not have any more meetings with the team from Andersen. He wrote, "I do not want to hear an excuse; just stop," and concluded with "Don't make me ask you again."[6]

If the vice president had had a credible alternative means of alerting the board of directors to this fraud, corrective action may have been taken much sooner. Had it been uncovered, the board would then have been presented with an opportunity to reward in some fashion the London vice president and set an example for others in the organization.

The Sarbanes-Oxley Act addresses the ethics of top executives by requiring that a public company "disclose whether they have adopted a code of ethics for the company's principal executive officer and senior financial officers, or if it has not, why it has not and to disclose on a current basis amendments to and waivers from the code of ethics relating to any of those officers." The code will be a "codification of standards that is reasonably necessary to deter wrongdoing and to promote:

1. honest and ethical conduct, including the ethical handling of actual or apparent conflicts of interest between personal and professional relationships;

2. avoidance of conflicts of interest, including disclosure to an appropriate person or persons identified in the code of any material transaction or that reasonably could be expected to give rise to such a conflict;

3. full, fair, accurate, timely, and understandable disclosure in reports and documents that a company files with, or submits to, the Commission and in other public communications made by the company;

4. compliance with applicable governmental laws, rules and regulations;

5. the prompt internal reporting of code violations to an appropriate person or persons identified in the code; and

6. accountability for adherence to the code."

Additionally, a public company must disclose in its annual report whether it has a code of ethics.

Frankly, it is sad that we are at a point at which the behaviors of our most senior executives have to be spelled out. Why would an experienced executive need to be told to be honest and ethical? The fact is that most don't. It is a very small group of executives who do not have the best interests of shareholders and the company at heart, and these executives will not be dissuaded from bad behavior by mere words. The words must be backed up by board action that directly ties the success of the executive to these words.

WHAT REALLY WORKS

So we know that a positive culture is vital to good governance and control and that the government cannot effectively legislate it. We also recognize that we can't fully trust our fellow executives and long-tenured employees, the accountants, or the lawyers to do the right thing. The wake-up call has been received, and our eyes are wide open. But where do we start? Each of us individually has the power to lead by example and set the proper tone within his or her area of influence. We can implement tools to alert us to potential problems and have the courage to act on the alarms. To do so, we need and require a control approach that will help us to identify and take action on any breaches of acceptable behavior. Furthermore, to be effective, this tool must be ingrained in our operations. A good control structure starts with a positive culture, will contain elements to help monitor the health of the enterprise, and alert management when a boundary of expected behavior is compromised. More important, it will also provide feedback regarding what is going right in the organization.

Internal control is not a separate discipline; rather, it is an important component of the overall management process guiding the enterprise. Management tools such as value chains, which help management understand their cost drivers; Balanced Scorecards, which help align activities to corporate objectives; Six Sigma procedures, which ensure product quality; benchmarking, which provides feedback regarding overall performance; and employee performance evaluations all contribute to the control framework, and vice versa.

Unlike other control manuals and processes, the Control Smart approach speaks to the health of the enterprise and its employees as a whole by infusing these management tools. Enlightened management dictates that controls do not focus on what employees *can't do*, but rather *what is expected* of them. Under this framework, managers and employees should remain free to perform their tasks with creativity and be encouraged to make improvements to processes within boundaries.

As good employees, managers, and directors, we recognize that it is no longer acceptable to allow a star manager to run roughshod over our organizations. We need to actively encourage and guide them. We can also do a better job of identifying those who would destroy our companies by means of communicating false information to the public. But even with increased vigilance, opaque financial reporting by a rogue CFO or star employees taking advantage of the system are not the only practices that can put a company, its managers, and its employees at risk. The crimes of tomorrow will be different from the ones today. To focus on a single risk is like overstuffing a suitcase. The more pressure applied to one area will either result in contents proportionately protruding from another area, or if successfully stuffed, may result in complete baggage failure in transit. Pushing on a single control point may only place pressure on another point of vulnerability in your company. It is better to evaluate the entire enterprise and select a vessel that can properly contain and protect all that is important. The Control Smart approach is that evaluation tool; it will help you establish boundaries appropriate for your operations.

While Congress has passed more legislation to dissuade damaging corporate practices, I am quite certain that we have not heard the last of such behavior. If solid internal controls are not in place, someone within an organization will find a way to take advantage of the oversight. It is up to owners, partners, and senior managers to ensure that their business is properly controlled and that no safe harbor exists for those intent on fraudulently utilizing its assets. Do not trust others to play by the rules; make certain that they do. You can be sure that employees will notice how seriously the company takes its cultural and procedural boundaries and how it responds to the visible failures. This is your wake-up call. Use this framework to learn from the mistakes of other managers. It is important that well-meaning managers do not find themselves in front of the House Committee on Oversight and Investigation trying to defend their actions. Protect yourself, your employees, and your company.

.

CHAPTER 2

Control Smart Approach

Over the course of 18 years, I have interviewed many smart, well-intentioned managers regarding the operational risks of their business. The mention of controls makes their eyes gloss over and attention spans dissipate like rain into the ocean. Owners and managers often complained to me that they did not have any training in controls. They would argue that it should be the role of the auditors to ensure that the control structure is in place and operating effectively. But managers who rely on internal or external auditors for assurance that the control structure is satisfactory are doing so at their peril. In general, auditors look at the process at a given point in time. They do not monitor it on a day-to-day basis. Only senior and line managers can effectively perform this task, and they are held accountable for doing so by the board of directors, investors, and, now, regulators.

So how does a manager ensure that his or her business is properly controlled, especially in the absence of tools to help? The answer can be elusive. The lack of research and development in this area is astounding; it appears to be the least sexy of any managerial discipline, so typically only accountants and auditors even attempt to ponder the world of controls. Understanding and implementing a proper control structure, however, is a basic managerial skill, not the sole province of accountants. While certain risks, such as credit and liquidity are best tasked to specialists (the CFO, treasurer, and credit committee), operational risks must be addressed by *all managers*.

Furthermore, past methodologies for addressing the control structure of an organization have focused on what employees *can't do*. Labor and processes were divided into detailed steps, with no variation tolerated and feedback not encouraged. Typically, these methodologies were developed to ensure that an employee could not inadvertently make a mistake or alter an outcome. For example, a factory worker in an auto assembly plant might be responsible for attaching a front fender to a car. He would be instructed how to place the fender on the car: which bolt to fasten first, second, and so on; and, when completed, he would be told to move on quickly to the next car. Never mind if he identified design or procedural changes that could make his job easier and speed up the manufacturing process. And why should he point out existing defects he noticed while doing his job? Management perception was that stopping the assembly line only cost the company money. If the line was stopped, he would have to stand around while the foreperson fumbled for a solution. It was not his job to recommend solutions to defects. It would only bring him unwanted attention and grief from his manager and coworkers.

Modern management theory encourages lineworkers to participate in the design of an automobile to make certain that the product can be produced with quality and efficiency. In many automobile factories, workers are now free to stop the assembly line when a problem surfaces. There is no stigma attached, as the company recognizes that the short-term costs will lead to long-term profits. Furthermore, the line assembly crew is expected to use their years of experience to help management find a solution. Such cooperation is highly valued. The result of this shift in thinking is ever greater productivity and efficiency, which helps bring higher-quality and lower-cost transportation to consumers.

In general, a highly divided labor process inhibits creativity, restricts activity, and raises barriers to operational improvement. Depending on corporate objectives, however, creativity may not be an encouraged attribute. Highly divided labor can be very efficient. Repetition can result in productivity improvement and cost advantages. In *The Wealth of Nations*, published in 1776, Adam Smith makes the case for division of labor. He cites the manufacture of straight pins to support his theories and argues that one person, not an expert in any process, would be strained to make one pin a day. But where each has specific knowledge of a particular task, great efficiencies can be realized. In his example, "one man draws out the wire, another straights it, a third cuts it, a fourth points it, a fifth grinds it at the top for receiving the head; to make the head requires two or three distinct operations; to put it on is a peculiar business, to whiten the pins is another; it is even a trade by itself to put them into the paper; and the important business of making pins is, in this manner, divided into about eighteen distinct operations...all performed by distinct hands...."[1] The argument Smith makes is that each employee's productivity will improve as he [or she] better learns the intricacies of the job. What the theory ignores is the mental and physical capacity of humans to continually perform such repetitive tasks. Fortunately, technology has provided a solution in the form of machines, which are now capable of performing routine tasks quickly and with ever higher quality, allowing their human masters to focus on more creative and value-added activities. Today's technology is capable of performing all the pin-making steps described by Smith, so that humans can turn their efforts to improving product quality, sourcing inputs, material handling, distribution efficiencies, and design improvements. Each process improvement increases productivity and drives the cost of a pin down, making them accessible to anyone who needs them.

There are also certain processes that require strict attention to rules for safety or quality reasons, such as the production of medications. From time to time, quality issues are reported that put human health at risk. One recent high-profile example focused on the sole supplier of anthrax vaccine to the U.S. military. The plant that produces the vaccine failed Food & Drug Administration (FDA) inspections in 1999 and 2000, which cited poor documentation and procedures. Problems with product quality caused the government to stop production for three years until the manufacturer could guarantee the quality of the output. With the threat of biological weapons on the rise, clearly the military could not rely on the vaccine while sending its soldiers into harm's way. Senator Tim Hutchinson, Republican from Arkansas, described these failures as "costing the American taxpayer millions and millions of dollars and jeopardizing the safety of our troops [to whom] we're not able to provide that anthrax vaccination."[2]

In most cases, however, rather than requiring employees to follow a highly regimented protocol, alternatives are available that can be implemented to quickly detect mistakes. As long as the employees know that safety and quality are important and monitored, it is likely that they will adopt behavior that is consistent with meeting these objectives. They will also be free to find the most efficient ways for performing their responsibilities within these boundaries.

Certain classical concepts or rules, such as proper segregation of duties, still apply under a good control framework. But if decision rights and procedures are properly defined and assigned, corporate objectives are communicated and understood, and cultural values are known and respected, then employees should not inadvertently bump into control boundaries on a regular basis, no matter how innovative their response to an objective.

Like our assembly worker, an employee can find more efficient ways to put on a fender without sacrificing quality, can suggest design improvements, and can participate in developing a solution to a manufacturing problem. All of these activities are for the benefit of the company. If, in the quality assurance process, it were identified that a change in how a fender was being attached resulted in lower quality, this feedback could be used to help the assembler modify behavior within acceptable boundaries.

By focusing on process and culture, managers can monitor the health of their control structure without draconian measures. Our assembly worker knows what is expected of him, and key performance indicators will alert management if his efforts need to be redirected toward a company objective. These are the implied tenets of the Control Smart approach.

SMART BASICS

By now we should all recognize the importance of a robust control structure. But since we cannot rely on the auditors to guarantee that controls are operating, how do we implement boundaries, identify threats, and develop a program that effectively enables us to monitor our business? Welcome to the Control Smart approach. Our pathway to a healthy control environment consists of an approach divided into five sections:

1. See the threats coming.
2. Know yourself.
3. Identify where you are vulnerable.
4. Protect yourself.
5. Monitor your health.

These sections, explained more fully in the following pages, will help you erase your vulnerabilities and erect a strong defense.

See the Threats Coming

How can you protect yourself if you can't see the danger? Before controls can be implemented, you must first figure out the risks you are trying to control. All businesses are exposed to potential hazards, but the extent of that exposure will vary directly with the unique characteristics of each enterprise. Even similar businesses in similar industries may have greatly different risk profiles as a result of their capital structure, customer base, operating methodologies, or even location. A reasonable person would think that two companies that operate gas pipelines of equal length, with a comparable amount of transported gas at similar quality and price would have the same risk profiles. But add to that information that one company has no debt while the other is encumbered by junk bonds, or that one is resident in the United States while the other is located in the South Pacific, and the risk profile of the two companies changes dramatically due to capital structure and location. In addition, managers will not be charged with mitigating all dangers to an organization; rather, they will be expected to address those threats to processes over which they exert influence.

This first section of the approach introduces you to common risk types, identifies those managers normally charged with monitoring them, and shows you methods to help you understand their impact on your business or department. Armed with this information, you can focus on and devise methods to mitigate the most critical threats.

Know Yourself

After you assess your risks, you will know the types of threats to watch for, and those that every manager is responsible to control. But managers not only have primary responsibilities; they also have ancillary processes over which they have decision-making capabilities. As an example, most managers must approve salary payments to new employees or submit purchase requisitions. Unfortunately, risk does not respect titles or functional boundaries. Poor controls in peripheral activities can also result in large losses. Most managers have heard of rogues creating fake employees to receive extra paychecks, or making unauthorized purchases for personal use. It is critical, therefore, that you document all processes for which you have decision-making rights so that you can subject it to the Smart Links assessment tool—discussed in the next section—to highlight gaps or threats to your business.

Identify Where You Are Vulnerable

Smart Links is the most simple yet effective control assessment tool ever developed. Voluminous audit checklists, programs, and workbooks are designed to take what an auditor knows and apply it to any situation. Since it is unlikely that he or she will ever know your business as well as you, the auditor develops lengthy checklists that apply to any number of processes and cover every conceivable risk factor. In contrast, Smart Links relies on your knowledge of the business. It consists of 13 steps designed to make you think about key components of your business process, and focuses on the operational risks borne by all managers. It is designed to help you to identify both the controls and the control gaps or threats to your organization.

Most managers find it useful to understand standard terms used by control experts. A preparatory step to help a manager develop a basic understanding of what is meant by "preventive or detective controls, control levers, or activities" is provided in this section as well, along with real-life examples of fraud, embezzlement, and massive financial losses, to bring these concepts to life.

This section of the approach next explores how to perform a control assessment utilizing the 13-step Smart Link assessment tool. It delves into how each of these steps helps you identify boundaries and improve your control structure. To provide context, each step is supported by examples ripped from the headlines of the national media. Enron, WorldCom, Qwest Communications, Global Crossing, and Adelphia are just a few of the well-known cases discussed. After applying Smart Links, you will know where you are most vulnerable and, hence, should concentrate your efforts.

Protect Yourself

Call them risks, threats, hazards, or dangers; the fact is that they are all irrelevant. By using the Smart Links "antibiotic," you will become resistant to infection. You will not be vulnerable because you have identified your control gaps and replaced them with strong procedures. This section helps you develop that perfect procedure or report to address any shortcomings you identified using the Smart Links tool. A case study, among other features, will help you understand how to identify and implement the proper defense.

Monitor Your Health

You are feeling strong. Confident that your defenses are tight, you are ready to turn your attention elsewhere. But just as your mind starts to change focus, you stop and ask yourself, "How will I know if the controls break down or stop working?"

Feedback and reinforcement are required to guarantee that the structure put in place continues to operate. For every Smart Links step, you now have a functioning control or set of controls. It is just a fact that controls sometimes fail. It may be the result of a new system, the absence of a key employee, or the failure of a supervisor to properly monitor a process—it might as well be kryptonite for all it matters. Once a control fails, you are exposed. So you need an early warning system. It is likely that key performance indicators or management statistics already exist that can identify an issue with any given control. But for others, you may need to create a metric or a report to provide that critical red flag.

This final section of the framework provides tools to help identify key performance indicators and the various delivery systems that can be employed to alert you to the presence of kryptonite or similar debilitating concerns.

In Summary

The Control Smart approach is summarized graphically in Exhibit 2.1. We will use this diagram throughout the book to help us keep track of our progress. This pathway will help every manager realize the goal of a strong

EXHIBIT 2.1   RISK AND CONTROL ASSESSMENT PROCESS

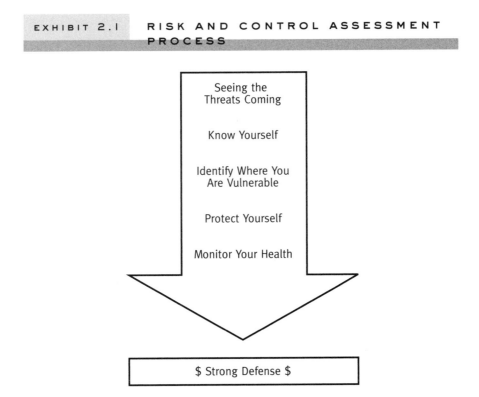

Seeing the
Threats Coming

Know Yourself

Identify Where You
Are Vulnerable

Protect Yourself

Monitor Your Health

$ Strong Defense $

control structure designed to prevent or detect the types of frauds that can bring down a company. While the topic of this book is major fraud and operational loss, careful consideration of each step in the process will help a manager obtain important feedback regarding the health of his or her operations, redirect employees and other resources towards corporate objectives, and identify operational efficiency opportunities as a by-product. Time, cost, and resources will be determinants of the final product. It is up to each manager to decide how far he or she wants to explore, test, and strengthen the operating environment. As with many things in life, the benefits correlate directly to the effort put into it.

Before we launch into the Control Smart approach, let's examine a case that highlights how the culture at Enron and its relationship with its accountants enabled one of the most famous frauds in history.

CASE STUDY

Andy Fastow's Shell Game

These partnerships...were used by Enron management to enter into transactions that it could not, or would not, do with unrelated commercial entities. Many of the most significant transactions apparently were designed to accomplish favorable financial statement results, not to achieve bona fide economic objectives or to transfer risk.

—Excerpt from the Report of Investigation by the Board of Directors of Enron Corporation (Powers Report)

Andy Fastow grew up in a tiny New Jersey suburb near New York City. In a bit of foreshadowing, Fastow was a huge *Star Wars* fan. He would later name some of the ill-fated Enron-related partnerships after *Star Wars* characters, such as Chewco and Jedi. By all accounts, Fastow was extremely ambitious well before his arrival at Enron. In high school, he was always seeking election to student government, and he became the first student representative to the New Jersey State Board of Education. Convinced of the business potential in China, he successfully lobbied administrators to add a Chinese studies major to the curriculum at Tufts University. He graduated with a major in Chinese studies and economics. Fastow also earned an MBA from Northwestern University's Kellogg School of Business.

Prior to his stint at Enron, Fastow learned the art of "securitization" at Continental-Illinois, a failed Chicago bank. Securitization is nothing more

Case Study (continued)

than raising money by pledging security against default, a process similar to obtaining a second mortgage on a house. You obtain money from a bank by pledging the equity in your home as collateral. Smart investment bankers (and some not-so-smart ones) have found all sorts of assets to securitize on behalf of clients. Pools of mortgages and whole loans owned by banks, accounts receivables, inventories, entire manufacturing plants, stock, lotto receivables—you name it, someone will securitize it.

Fastow joined Enron in 1990 and quickly bought into executive Jeffrey Skilling's plan to turn Enron into a trading giant. Trading giants need money to conduct their transactions, lots of it. So there was considerable pressure on Fastow to generate financing opportunities. It was widely known within Enron that Fastow was keen to gain the favor of Skilling. He positioned himself as a trusted lieutenant and quickly partnered with him to advance the Skilling agenda. At first, the securitizations were not particularly risky and were fairly vanilla. Fastow would raise money by pledging payments owed Enron from oil and gas producers. But as the company's financing needs grew, the quality of the assets Enron made available for securitizing declined.

In 1997, Fastow began creating Special Purpose Entities (SPEs) to hold assets and provide the appearance of creating legitimate financing transactions when, in fact, they were a sham. SPEs can be very effective financing and risk management vehicles if used properly. A parent company's debt level or other risk factors can hinder the capability of a strong business segment to obtain favorable interest rates to finance its operations. In such a situation, the parent can create an SPE and transfer the asset to it with the goal of receiving more favorable lending rates. As long as there is another independent third-party investor that has contributed at least 3 percent of the assets, the SPE does not have to be consolidated into the parent for financial reporting purposes. Furthermore, if the assets in the SPE are of high quality, banks will fall over themselves to lend to it, resulting in lower lending rates. The SPE will then use this money to pay the parent for the asset received. The bottom line is that the company obtains the money it requires, but pays less to obtain it than would otherwise be the case.

But Fastow did not have quality assets, so he transferred inferior assets and pledged Enron stock as a guarantee of payment to the banks. And who did Enron find to be that 3-percent investor in the SPEs? One Andy Fastow, through a partnership called LJM, among others. But why would he want to invest in poor-quality assets? Because the fees Enron paid LJM eliminated his risk in these vehicles. He effectively cashed out; so while he was an investor on paper, he really had no downside risk.

Case Study (continued)

Enron was then able to move poor performing assets off its books and even report the sales as revenues (inflating profits). Fastow received more than $30 million for his deal-making role, and the banks had the assets and stock as collateral (some were even wise enough to buy credit insurance in case Enron imploded) to offset their risk. Everyone appeared to win.

Fastow's creativity did not go unnoticed. In 1998, at age 37, he became CFO of one of the world's largest companies. In 1999, *CFO* magazine conferred an excellence award to him for his ingenuity.

So how was Fastow able to create and perpetuate this fraud without the knowledge of superiors, accountants, lawyers, and other Enron employees? It is hard to believe, contrary to their claims, that senior executives were unaware of Fastow's activities. They depended on them to keep the money machine working. Fastow did work to limit the number of employees who were exposed to his partnerships. Those who were admitted to the club he "took care of" with large monetary rewards. Those who were not onboard, he belittled and intimidated. As for the accountants and lawyers, who can believe that they could not connect the dots to realize that as an investor, Fastow had no real risk in the SPEs? Realization of this simple fact would have required the consolidation of the SPEs into Enron's financial statements, and the game would have been over. And it is not as if the accountants or senior management were never warned. Sherron Watkins, the now famous whistle-blower, specifically told both Arthur Anderson as well as senior Enron management of her concerns.

The *Star Wars* theme is an appropriate metaphor for Enron. The company became the Death Star, and Fastow Darth Vader, doing the bidding of the Dark Side. In their wake, they left in ruins the jobs and pensions of their employees. They destroyed billions of dollars of shareholder value and a once stable, respected company. Fastow is now facing indictment on 78 felony charges and decades of jail time if convicted. On October 2, 2002, he was led away from his home in handcuffs; his and his wife's passports were confiscated. And in his last securitization deal, he had his parents post their home as collateral for his bail.

CHAPTER 3

Threats and Dangers

The Control Smart approach represents a path to strong business processes. The milestones along this pathway are represented in Exhibit 3.1. We begin the Control Smart journey by learning how to see threats to our business.

How can you mitigate threats if you cannot see them coming? The obvious answer is that you can't. Managers must build a control tower and employ radar technology to help them see potential dangers before they arrive.

EXHIBIT 3.1   CONTROL SMART PATHWAY

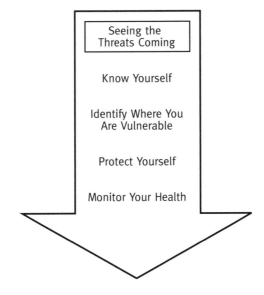

Seeing the
Threats Coming

Know Yourself

Identify Where You
Are Vulnerable

Protect Yourself

Monitor Your Health

The first section of the risk and control assessment process helps you evaluate the specific hazards of your business. Not all risks apply to all managers, but understanding what they are and how they affect the business will help managers understand their role in the overall control environment of the company. It is less important that every manager perfectly analyze every threat. More important is to understand that there is an owner for every risk and how that owner communicates essential changes in the danger assessment. This knowledge is particularly valuable if a risk type can impact or alter how a manager executes his or her operational plan.

How to Recognize a Pending Nightmare

There are many types of threats to a company, and new subcategories seem to be defined daily. While there are many risks that can affect your operations, our primary focus will be on the threats faced by all managers. The detection of harmful activities, including fraud, embezzlement, and massive financial losses due to a lack of operational controls are addressed in detail, because the management of these risks is the responsibility of every manager. And though the types of hazards an enterprise faces are important to forming a control structure, the in-depth exploration of all risk types is not relevant to most managers, and so is beyond the scope of this book. (The subjects of value at risk, risk-adjusted return on capital, hedging strategies, credit risk analysis, competitive strategy, and so on, are all valid subjects of entire tomes.) Specialists will handle most of these threats; nevertheless, it is important that all managers understand the impact they can have on their operations, as well as the methods employed to control them. Risks migrate and there are operational controls that interface with procedures implemented by specialists to mitigate market, credit, concentration, finance, liquidity and event risk. For instance, a liquidity crisis may impact a purchasing manager's ability to source raw materials. While the purchasing manager is not expected to manage the company's liquidity—that is generally the province of the CFO and his or her reports—the purchasing manager's ability to perform his or her job is directly impacted by this key factor. Thus, good managers will ensure that the controls supporting these risk interfaces are operating effectively. In this case, the purchasing manager would need to make certain to be informed of a pending cash crunch so that he or she could do everything possible to ensure the supply of raw materials continues unimpeded and with as little impact as feasible on the cash position of the company.

We will identify and explore the various types of risk an organization will face and who would normally take responsibility for managing those risks. It is important that the executives assigned as risk owners be aware of their mandate. They will need to have a methodology to monitor the results of their efforts, such as regular reporting of relevant metrics and benchmarks. For instance, a metric of financial exposure that combines accounts receivable at least six months past due, inventory aged greater than one year, rising payables, and debt maturities coming due would wave a red flag if the danger of a liquidity crisis were increasing. WorldCom had receivables on its books seven years past due. Clearly, the chance of collecting on these reported assets was practically zero. A metric such as that just described would help an executive or board member identify such a problem.

Risk Types

In order to see risks coming, a director, executive, or manager needs to obtain a clear understanding of the various threats, identify the designated owner, determine how he or she manages the risks and, to the extent the business is impacted, how the owner communicates changes in risk levels and tolerance. Generic threats applicable to most business operations include:

- *Market.* Adverse effects of consumer/customer sentiment or tastes. An example includes the preference of travelers to book their flights and hotels online. Market share for this delivery method is growing exponentially and already accounts for 13 percent and 7 percent of the market, respectively.

- *Credit.* Counterpart default, where value has been delivered but not yet fully received in return. An example of counterpart default might include recording artists receiving an advance for their next album that is never produced due to the breakup or bankruptcy of the band.

- *Financial and liquidity.* The amount of leverage used by a company is unsustainable, or access to credit and funding sources has been compromised. Enron is an interesting example. Its energy trading business needed liquidity to fund its positions. Once word of trouble hit the Street, no one wanted to chance having Enron as a counterpart as it might not be able to honor its trading commitments. Funding sources quickly dried up, revenue could not be produced because counterparts stopped trading with the company, and its expensive trading platform became a white elephant that it could not sell. Within a matter of weeks, Enron could no longer pay its bills.

- *Operational.* Breakdown in controls relating to initiation, pricing, delivering and booking a transaction, and making good delivery of product or service, including systems controls and errors. The examples here are numerous and varied. They include fraud, embezzlement, and unintentional losses due to a lack of functioning controls such as the manufacturing of a defective product that is widely distributed before the defect is discovered. We will study many cases of operational loss in the following pages.

- *Event.* A specific action or occurrence that affects the company's ability to do business, such as changes in the political, legal, or regulatory environment, a natural or man-made disaster, or other event that negatively impacts the reputation of the company. An example might include the recent terrorist attacks on New York and Washington, which had a nationwide impact on our citizens and our economy.

There are also two important subcategories of threat we need to address: *technology and concentration.* Many companies consider technology and concentration risks as primary threats to their business.

Technology dangers can take the form of system malfunctions, hacker incursions, or even new technology-driven disruptive forces that give a competitor an advantage. Concentration dangers take the form of overreliance on a single or limited number of customers, investments, or products. However, for our purposes, we will consider them subcategories. This is not to say that technology or concentrations are not important, or even critical, to an enterprise—only that they can be assessed in relation to the threats just detailed for the purpose of control assessment.

Technology Risk

Technology is pervasive throughout every organization; it is a productivity tool, an enabler. The risk that a given technology may not work, or be compromised, is an operational risk; hence obsolescence and availability must be assessed as a part of the company's business continuity planning.

It may be that for some businesses, technology differentiates a product. For instance, the new third-generation cell phones allow users to retrieve e-mail, browse the Internet, and buy products online, capabilities that did not exist just a couple of years ago. In this and similar cases, new or disruptive technologies raise the possibility that customers will choose a new product or delivery system over your current offering. If technology plays an important role in product design and differentiation or impacts the ability of the enterprise to compete as a low-cost producer, then technology should be considered in the development of the organization's competitive strategy and market placement.

Concentration Risk

Concentration risk can take several forms. Take Stan's restaurant, gift shop, and bar, for example. Located across the street from Yankee Stadium, Stan's does a great business when there are home games, and significantly less business during the off-season. It is safe to assume that at least 80 percent of the business is derived from fans before and after home games. If you classify Yankee fans as a type of customer, then Stan's has a concentrated risk to this market. The business also has significant capital concentrated in its establishments along this street. I do not know if the owner of Stan's has investments elsewhere, but if not, he or she has concentrated financial and liquidity risk. At least, management has diversified the product offerings to include memorabilia and clothing, in addition to food and drink. The value of these businesses must be a multiple of comparable restaurants, but what would be their value if George Steinbrenner decided to move the ball club to newly built stadium in Manhattan? The damage to Stan's from an event such as this would be compounded by the concentration risks it accepts.

Risk Migration

Most managers think of operational risk in terms of fraud, collusion, theft, or embezzlement, but it is more that that. Operational risk can be differentiated from other risks in that it exists in every step of the business process or value chain. For example, improper business practices could lead to materially incorrect information or defective products. It is important for a manager to understand all the risks an enterprise must manage, as they can morph into operational threats throughout the company.

Of course, each of the threats defined will take on a different significance for the type of market in which a business competes. The financial services broker/dealer business model, for example, is inherently risky, as individuals, acting on behalf of a broker/dealer, can commit large amounts of a firm's capital causing concentrated financial exposure. To compound the risk, the committed capital is usually heavily leveraged, resulting in even greater vulnerability to financial and liquidity shocks. Markets can cause wide price swings within a trading day, which exposes a trader to market risk in the normal course of business or to event hazards such as an earthquake or outbreak of war. Large amounts of money regularly move in and out of a brokerage operation making operational threats such as unauthorized transfers difficult to detect. Large amounts of money can also move between businesses due to market forces and new products. The sudden growth of a business can create additional operational dangers by straining its employees and those systems already in place. Finally, the cycle time for a trade, from initiation to settlement, is usually very short, normally a matter of days. Without proper preventive operational controls in place, an individual can commit enough of the firm's capital and financial resources to bring it down very quickly.

Lending institutions, too, take on significant risk, by leveraging their capital structure. Like traders, they also deal in large amounts of money, but unlike traders, lending committees can diffuse their power to commit capital, helping to mitigate credit exposure. The cycle time for their product tends to be much longer, thereby allowing more time for a problem in a portfolio to be identified. Using a mortgage product as a simplified example, a mortgage cycle typically lasts from 15 to 30 years, from the time the money is lent to the time it is fully repaid. During that period, a dramatic change in interest rates might cause liquidity problems for the institution, or an economic slowdown might increase default rates in the portfolio due to job losses. These threats usually occur over several quarters. Astute managers can mitigate these as they become apparent, preserving the viability of the institution.

Disruptive technologies can also end your business as easily as flicking a light switch. The old story of the buggy whip business becoming obsolete due to the widespread acceptance of the automobile still has a relevant lesson to teach today. Video-on-demand from cable companies is challenging the future of video rental retailers such as Blockbuster. Likewise, new, more powerful computers are providing a state-of-the-art delivery system for games, complete with astonishing graphics, challenging the survival of game arcade franchises such as Midway Arcades.

While each of the generic risks can be evaluated individually, lack of control over one risk can lead to increased risk in the other generic risk categories. Risk can even migrate downstream to other counterparts. For instance, constructors, utilities, basic materials, and mining companies routinely develop large projects such as dams, power plants, smelters, and mines. The amount of capital required for any given project may put the survival of a company on the line, causing financial and liquidity concerns. An operational mistake in the bidding process could lead to financial and liquidity damages that render a contractor unable to complete the project. Such a scenario could snowball, leaving clients, banks, investors, or taxpayers with an unfinished project that would likely cost much more to complete, thereby increasing the financial and liquidity risk to these counterparts. The Washington Public Power Supply System (WPPSS) bond defaults are a striking example of such a problem.

WPPSS issued bonds to help finance the construction of five nuclear power plants in the State of Washington, three of which were to be built at Hanford, Washington. Construction of the reactors continued through the 1970s. By the early 1980s, the reactors ran into enormous cost overruns, which, combined with downward revisions of future electricity demand and the loss of Americans' support for nuclear power, forced WPPSS to default on its bonds. It became fashionable to jokingly refer to these bonds as "Whoops!" bonds, but those who had purchased them to finance the unfinished reactors were not laughing at the real financial pain. One of my accounting professors, a conservative investor nearing retirement, had invested in these bonds, believing them to be safe. The lesson he learned he unselfishly passed on to his students, and I have never forgotten it: Only one of Hanford's reactors was actually finished, and it was significantly behind schedule and overbudget.

I SEE IT. SHOULD I WORRY?

You have spent a great deal of time building your control tower and now have your radar turned on. With new eyes you see bogies everywhere. Which are real and which should you be concerned about? To compare and evaluate risks to your organization, you must determine comparable parts—that is, divide your business operations into manageable bits that can be compared and contrasted. (You may prefer to evaluate your business by operating segment or generic product type.)

In Exhibit 3.2, we perform a risk analysis of a hypothetical conglomerate that provides services in various travel industries: airline, hotel management, and online travel, promotions, and ticketing. We will evaluate each segment against the others to determine which we consider the riskiest. For simplicity, we will assign high risk as a 3, medium risk a 2, and low risk a 1. In practice, you can use any numbering scheme to help you compare products or segments. The only criterion is that you be consistent among segments.

The analysis conducted in the exhibit makes a number of assumptions, but of all the businesses in which our hypothetical company competes, the airline industry is identified as the segment subject to the greatest threats. Why? Let's look at some of the components analyzed.

We determined that the airline industry has high financial, operational, and event risk profiles. Airlines, by their nature, require large capital investment to purchase or lease airplanes. These costs are fixed, and payments must be made regularly no matter what the business climate is. Even if the aircraft do not fly, there is still a large cash obligation to a bank or finance company. As a result, if revenue does not come in the door, the airline can find itself in financial distress very quickly. Airlines must also be masters at scheduling flights, booking itineraries, selling seats, maintaining aircraft, providing in-flight services, and monitoring passengers and flight crews. These processes are highly automated, and if a problem occurs anywhere in the system, it can have a sudden impact on the operation of the airline until the problem is detected or resolved. Maintenance procedures for an

EXHIBIT 3.2   RISK ANALYSIS MATRIX

Risk	Airline	Hotel Management	Online Travel
Market	2	2	2
Credit	1	1	1
Financial and Liquidity	3	1	2
Operational	3	2	3
Event	3	2	2
Average	**2.4**	**1.6**	**2.0**

airline are also critical. Poor maintenance procedures can lead directly to a loss of life. Finally, an event such as a terrorist attack, a hijacking, or the downing of an aircraft can threaten the reputation of an airline and, ultimately, its very survival.

Hotel management was deemed less risky. This is because the management and servicing of hotels (as opposed to owning them) requires little capital. The company's assets are its management contracts and the people who manage, clean, and maintain the hotels. Many of the costs are variable personnel costs. If business is lost, these costs can be immediately reduced.

The online travel reservations segment was also considered less vulnerable. There is a significant investment and reliance on systems that leads to high operational risk, but otherwise, the threats tend to be low. The reservations systems are portals that collect monies in advance from the general public, limiting credit exposure. The transaction cycle time tends to be a few weeks, and market forces are currently favoring online purchasing of travel services.

While we would like to immediately implement control processes across our hypothetical company, we recognize that if our resources are limited, we will focus on our most risky products and processes. Under our scenario, then, we would focus on the financial, operational, and event risks of our airline company, as these are the most dangerous bogies on our radar. We would need to employ a process that establishes a comfort zone, where we're confident that we've properly evaluated our financial health under various stress-testing scenarios and arranged for backup credit lines. We also need to evaluate our processing and system controls and put procedures in place to handle unpleasant airline event risks, such as terrorist attacks or a downed aircraft. It is unlikely, for example, that an airline would want to put a flight attendant in front of the media or in contact with victims' families to explain such an event. Not only would it be unfair to the attendant, who is trained in flight safety, not crisis management, it would probably compound the disaster that has already befallen the airline, employees, and affected families. Rather, detailed procedures regarding financial, liquidity, and event risks should be prepared (including the identification of a media spokesperson) and ownership assigned to specialists such as the CFO, treasurer, and communications departments, respectively. The operational risks, however, would be shared by many managers. Most likely there is a manager in charge of reservation systems, another in charge of flight scheduling, and at least one in charge of maintenance. There is also probably a manager in charge of security at each airport; likewise someone is responsible for sourcing and loading food, refueling and cleaning the aircraft, and getting baggage on and off. Of course, the captain of each aircraft assumes responsibility for its safe operation. At each stage, the individual parties must evaluate the risks inherent in their decision rights, and design cost-effective controls to ensure the safe and smooth operation of the airline.

In light of the financial reporting requirements of the Sarbanes-Oxley Act, we will also view the financial reporting process as a priority for our businesses. Rather than analyzing the company product line, this regulatory event requires that we also evaluate our company along functional lines. We discuss and analyze this risk further in Chapters 6 and 7.

The risk evaluation template provided in Exhibit 3.2 is purposely simple. Increasingly, however, companies are attempting to take their risk analysis one step further by quantifying potential losses and estimating the probability that these losses will occur. For example, a new German law requires risk management systems for some companies. In response, an American subsidiary of a German manufacturer is currently rolling out a program to identify, quantify, and assign probabilities to the threats inherent in its business. The German parent sent out a standardized template to each of their operations world-wide asking each manager to evaluate six areas:

1. Organization (e.g., documenting procedures)
2. External factors (e.g., environmental risks, natural catastrophes)
3. Distribution (e.g., product liability, customs processing)
4. Finance (e.g., bad debts, currency risks, and embezzlement)
5. Personnel (e.g., succession, privacy rules)
6. Information technology (e.g., data security, system failure)

The parent then provided a risk quantification table resembling Exhibit 3.3 for management to complete for each of the six areas. Once the template is completed, the potential operational losses, adjusted for probability, can be computed and reported to management as a key performance indicator, and reserves can be established.

While any attempt at quantifying potential losses is a step in the right direction, and can be an excellent addition to the risk assessment we performed earlier, the German approach is weak. The risk definitions are unclear, the owners are not known, and there appears to be no process in place to ensure that the program is applied consistently in all countries. For instance, what exactly defines an "external environmental risk factor"?

EXHIBIT 3.3   RISK QUANTIFICATION TEMPLATE

Risk Area	Damage Potential	Occurrence Probability
Organization	$	%
External Factors ·	$	%
Distribution	$	%
Finance	$	%
Personnel	$	%
Information Technology	$	%

This term is used as an example for "external factors," which is one of the risks to be evaluated, but the example provides little added clarity. Does cutting down all the trees on a property qualify? Sounds silly, but what if the trees are harvested and there is an environmental backlash from eco-terrorists? This response is unlikely, but not unheard of. If we want to avoid such a risk, who is responsible for safeguarding the trees? Is it a corporate specialist in charge of environmental issues or event insurance, or is it the local plant manager? The answers are not clear. The problem with operational losses and fraud is that they tend to occur where, when, and in a manner least expected. Furthermore, when the losses occur, they tend to spike and can be massive, endangering the life of the company. After the fallout, many companies launch a witch hunt to find the person who was asleep at the switch—the one who failed to identify the risk and report it. Much to everyone's chagrin, they generally discover that no single person was designated as an owner for the "operational loss" that occurred, so often the most junior manager most closely tied to the business is sacrificed whether or not he or she knew he or she was charged with monitoring the threat.

To be effective, any attempt to evaluate operational losses has to be performed as a component of a systematic approach similar to Control Smart to ensure that all risks are assigned owners and that all processes are properly documented, analyzed, and monitored. Without a framework, many processes or control gaps may be missed, leaving the related potential loss unrecognized. The most sophisticated risk analysis system available is ineffective if the information it uses is incomplete. Even more troubling, it may provide a false sense of control and financial security.

A final word about risk evaluation programs: They must be tied to corporate values and performed in a nonpunitive manner. While I have not reprinted the instructions that accompanied the German template, I can tell you that it effectively communicated that "extreme risk that may threaten the very existence of the enterprise will be intensively examined in the course of individual interviews or through the creation of Project Teams." As a manager, this does not sound like the type of process to which I would want to subject myself. There is also no discussion or tie-in to compensation or other rewards. The only reward mentioned is the intensive examination.

Perhaps a better approach would be to explain that resources would be made available to management to address any major control weaknesses identified. Additionally, it might be stated that the number of major control gaps identified and closed would be taken into consideration in the year-end compensation process, with the more gaps identified garnering the most reward. Under this scenario, there is a benefit to management to self-report gaps.

WHOSE JOB IS IT ANYWAY?

In any busy air-traffic control tower, there are a number of controllers working seamlessly to make certain that all aircraft are identified and managed and that problems are avoided. Each controller is responsible for a section of airspace and the safe handoff of aircraft to other controllers. Likewise, there are a number of managers in an organization who are responsible for mitigating specific risks. These managers must work together to ensure all risks are accounted for and monitored. As mentioned earlier, credit, financial, concentration, market, and event risks can generally be assigned to a specialist, department head, or committee to study, monitor, and manage. This person or committee becomes the "owner." It is relatively easy to understand the impact these threats have on a company and the steps required to address them. In contrast, operational risk is diffused across the entire enterprise, and for this reason can be difficult to identify, let alone assign to an owner. Therefore, network access, system errors, turnover of key personnel, purchasing controls, proper classification of revenues and expenses, and so on, must be supervised at the managerial level.

In a large corporation, the chief operations officer (COO), CFO, or assigned committees cannot effectively micromanage every executive in every business line—a COO at headquarters in Boise, Idaho, cannot, for example, determine whether system access rights for programmers in

India are appropriate. Yet poor access controls can lead to stunning losses. This is not to say that executive management should not establish organizational strategies and policies and evaluate each manager on how well he or she conforms to the established protocol. The point is that each manager must own and control threats to his or her people and processes. Exhibit 3.4 illustrates the various generic risks and the senior managers typically responsible for monitoring these threats.

So far we have not discussed the roles of CEOs or the boards of directors in this process. The pundits might point out that the CEO and board are responsible for oversight of all risks, and they would be right. The CEO is responsible for setting the overall tone of the control culture and assigning risk owners. A good CEO will formally assign market and product/customer concentration risks to business heads and/or strategy and planning groups, credit risk to credit committees, financial and liquidity risks to the CFO, legal event risk to the legal department, and disaster recovery planning (DRP) to a DRP specialist. The CEO will then monitor the outputs from each of these risk owners. He or she will review and actively participate in business plans and strategies produced, as well as evaluate their progress, and

EXHIBIT 3.4   GENERIC RISK OWNERS

manage the capital allocation process in line with these strategies. He or she will review reported credit exposure and expect to see periodic stress-testing of the company's financial structure and resources. He or she will expect frequent legal updates, complete with an analysis of the impact that pending legislation in the field will have on the company. He or she will also want to know the results of periodic testing of the firm's off-site recovery center, to ensure that the company is prepared to remain operational in case of a disruptive event. Finally, the CEO will link company managers' ability to control risk objectives to their performance review process.

But what about operational risk? Just as a doctor uses an EKG to monitor the heartbeat of a patient, every manager, including the CEO, needs a way to monitor the health of his or her business processes. This can be accomplished by establishing key indicators that alert management to a problem. Furthermore, it is the responsibility of every manager to establish a culture that will enable communication of increased threats. This entails creating an environment that rewards candor and honesty, even if the news brought forward is bad. The more eyes that search for a potential threat, the greater the likelihood that the menace will be spotted early. Without a strong control culture and an effective monitoring program, there is a much greater chance that the company will experience a severe loss.

CHAPTER 4

Know Yourself

It is human nature to use labels to describe ourselves to others. We may be economists, writers, environmentalists, Republicans, Democrats, Rotarians, husbands or wives, fathers or mothers, alumni, church members, pacifists, hawks, fans, brunettes, or, simply, Americans. These labels are an easy way to convey who or what we are, but the sheer number of tags to identify a single person can be extensive.

We are complex beings, and as such, no single label can describe who we are. So it is with the label "manager." As a manager, we may be in charge of a company, a plant, or a department; there are a number of components that comprise our manager label. We are also budget specialists, supervisors, signatories, agents, and administrators. In short, there are a number of other parts we perform as a requirement of our overall role as manager, each of which has a corresponding process by which we execute our responsibilities. We may have the ability to determine how certain of these duties are performed, while others may be dictated by corporate protocol. For those that we have the authority to mold and change, we have decision rights. Furthermore, if we have the ability to create or modify a process, we have a corresponding responsibility to ensure there are proper safeguards to make certain that the expected outcomes are realized.

Our next step, illustrated in Exhibit 4.1, is to "know yourself," by identifying all processes for which you have authority or responsibility.

Do You Have Decision Rights?

Managers generally define their businesses very narrowly. As an example, let's analyze the decision rights accorded to George, a sales manager for a

EXHIBIT 4.1 CONTROL SMART PATHWAY

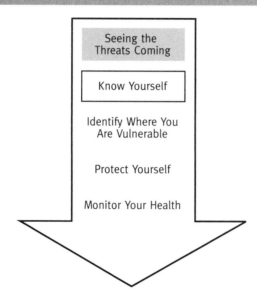

sports products distribution company. George may believe his job is to manage his sales force in such a way as to maximize revenue, which is true enough. But if he takes the time during the day to write down where he spends his time, nonrevenue activities and responsibilities will surface.

As George sits down to work in the morning, his first action is to take the daily sales report from his in-basket and review it. The report is generated automatically every morning by the sales system. He notes how each of his salespeople is doing compared to budget. Also in the in-box is a travel and entertainment submission from one of his best salespeople. George approves it and puts in the out-box. He then looks at his calendar for the day. He has his weekly production meeting at 9:00 A.M. where he sits with manufacturing to discuss product availability and delivery targets. George has been thinking about splitting a selling region in two and adding another salesperson. He notices that he will interview a potential new salesperson at 10:00 A.M. At noon he is having lunch with the CEO to discuss his idea for selling directly to schools and universities. Late this afternoon, he must have a difficult meeting with a salesperson whose biggest customer is in financial distress. George cannot increase company exposure to this customer and must instruct his salesperson to discontinue sales unless on a cash-on-delivery basis.

In this simple example, we have already identified several processes for which the sales manager has at least partial decision rights that need to be exercised with proper oversight controls. These include:

- Sales strategy
- Budgeting
- Hiring and termination
- Compensation
- Sales territories
- Travel and entertainment reimbursement
- Product offerings
- Sales systems
- Credit

We can think of each of these processes as discrete products and services with individual life cycles. Each consists of activities that include a beginning and an end, and each contains operational risk if structured poorly. This model assumes all processes conform to these basic activities. It makes no difference whether the customers are internal or external; the deliverables tangible products, services, or information; or payment is received in the form of currency, expense allocation, or services performed. Many managers know of the value chain featured in Michael Porter's book *Competitive Advantage: Creating and Sustaining Superior Performance*, as it is now taught in most MBA programs.[1] This model is great for understanding and evaluating the activities of a business as a whole and providing a framework for building competitive advantage. It breaks down each activity into manageable components that can be evaluated and whose cost drivers can be measured.

For instance, Porter's framework leads you through inbound logistics, operations, outbound logistics, marketing, and sales and service. Supporting these functions is the firm infrastructure, human resources management, technology development, and procurement. The difference between revenues and expenses is margin. The model can be used to develop a strategy based on cost, differentiation, or focus. By analyzing revenues and expenses along these lines, the cost drivers will surface. For instance, assume a manufacturer of residential water meters (used by local water companies to determine usage for billing purposes) has a cost structure as follows:

Area	Percent
Firm infrastructure	10
Human resources	2
Procurement	2
Inbound logistics	2
Operations	65
Outbound logistics	1
Marketing and sales	7
Service	1
Margin	10
TOTAL	100

It is clear that the largest cost driver, hence the greatest opportunity for savings, is in operations. If further analysis indicates that operations consists of 70 percent purchased inputs and 30 percent labor, and that there are large fixed capital costs for machinery, then it would appear that management could create significant leverage and increase margin by lowering the cost of its purchased inputs. All things being equal, every 1 percent decrease in purchasing costs will result in 1 percent increase in margin. Purchasing economies can be gained through building single-source relationships, joining buyer groups that acquire similar components, participating in online auctions, or even simply increasing production volume that might lead to volume discounts from suppliers.

I have used this model to evaluate and improve varying processes and related controls. It appears that the Treadway Commission also used it as a platform to create its generic business models for the COSO framework. If you have already created and evaluated your value chain, you may be able to leverage this work by subjecting those processes to the questions found in the Smart Links approach, which I will introduce later. A manager can simply answer the questions for the previously documented process.

The shortcoming of using the value chain for the evaluation of threats is that it was not designed for this purpose and lumps many infrastructure activities together. Smart Links instead treats each of these functions as discrete processes that should be individually analyzed. For example, rather than analyzing the costs of human resources as a component supporting the overall process of manufacturing a water meter, Smart Links looks at it as a standalone process that can, and should, be analyzed in isolation as well as in combination with other activities. Take the payroll function that is normally managed by human resources or finance: It has inputs (time cards, salary, and deductions), operations (creation of paychecks), outbound logistics (direct deposit, mailed checks), and services (changes in deductions and benefits, corrections of errors, management of the raise and bonus process); and the department gets paid by allocating its expenses to other departments based on headcount. So human resources is not only a supporting function, but a complete process that should be independently evaluated for efficiency and control purposes.

Now that we have identified each of the components, we can analyze the cost and identify a control for each activity using Smart Links. Alice, our manager in this example, will identify controls that ensure she meets the regulatory requirements of the Department of Labor and IRS. She will put in validity and completeness checks to make sure that all employees who get paid actually exist and that all are getting paid what they are owed. She will also implement a method to guarantee that there is enough cash in her payroll account to cover the total liability. These are only a few examples of payroll controls. By answering every question in Smart Links as it relates to payroll, Alice will be able to make certain that these activities are tightly controlled and monitored.

KEY ACTIVITIES MODEL

For many of the processes identified in the previous section, it will be easier for most of us to understand and evaluate our methods using a more simplistic approach than the value chain. The key components common to most activities include:

- Receiving and evaluating customer orders
- Sourcing and paying for inputs such as materials, labor, and information
- Creating a deliverable
- Storing product
- Distributing the output to customers
- Receiving payment for goods and services
- Evaluating performance with an eye toward improving operations

These activities are mapped in Exhibit 4.2. The key activities model is purposely generic, so that each action can be applied to internal or external customers, to manufactured goods, services, or even to information products such as management reports, pricing data, or transmission of regulatory forms to government agencies.

EXHIBIT 4.2   KEY ACTIVITIES MODEL

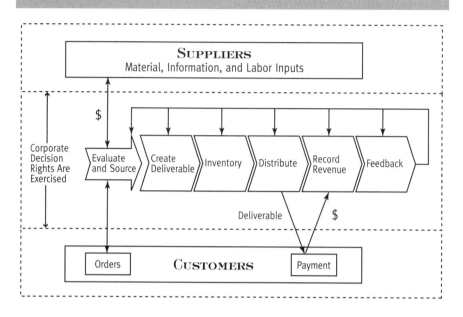

Evaluate the Customer Order

A business cycle usually begins with an inbound customer request or sales order. For certain industries, not all customer orders are welcome. In the securities industry, brokers/dealers are expected to perform due diligence on their customers to make certain that the customer's source of funds is legitimate. Banks and brokers/dealers can be used to launder money from illegal operations, so it is imperative that they know with whom they are conducting business and document that knowledge.

As an example, prosecutors contend that Consuelo Marquez, a private banker with Lehman Brothers, not only opened an account, but helped set up phony companies and move tens of millions of dollars to Swiss and offshore accounts for a drug kingpin. There are regulations requiring financial institutions to "know their customer." This normally takes the form of documenting a viable source of income for the money kept at the financial institution. So how does a Mexican state governor make millions of dollars? Not from his day job. It was fairly well known that this client had earned the nickname "El Chueco," the "Crooked One," due to his activities to protect a drug mafia's operations. His suspected links to drug trafficking were even previously reported in the *New York Times*. Lehman Brothers admits that it "may have been lax, but not criminal" in conducting its compliance operations with regard to this customer. Given the publicity that this criminal received, labeling itself as "lax" may have been an understatement. An annual compliance review or a robust approval process for opening new accounts should have easily flagged El Chueco.

For other businesses, such as construction, the customer order may actually begin with a request for a proposal. A company may not want to bid on a job that is particularly risky or if its resources are currently fully utilized. In each of these cases, the customer order must be fully evaluated before it is accepted.

If the request is a standard need, product pricing may already be known by both parties to the transaction. Pricing may be disclosed in a catalog or advertised on a Web page. Any customer with a valid credit card can log on to Amazon.com, for example, and buy a book or compact disc. The customer knows exactly how much it will cost because the price of each item is prominently displayed with information about the product. In this scenario, little due diligence is required at the evaluation stage; rather, the order is immediately accepted. In fact, the more the customer buys now, the better.

In a retail establishment such as a supermarket or department store, the customer is free to evaluate all product offerings available in current inventory, take custody, and move directly to payment. A shopper strolls the aisles searching for what he or she wants and comparing the value of available alternatives. The greater variety offered, the more likely that the consumer will spend more in the store rather than bothering to visit a competitor to find what he or she wants.

For an internal customer, price discovery is not always easy. It may be understood that departmental expenses will be allocated for providing a service or information. By example, the human resources department introduced earlier performs duties for the entire company; these may include background checks and testing of new hires for controlled substances, offering training classes, administering the performance evaluation process, managing payroll and benefits, and so on. Each of these deliverables costs money, and these expenses will normally be allocated to other departments and businesses based on their headcount. This does not mean that the services provided internally are any less important. Internal services can be an important factor in mitigating the risk of fraud or operational loss.

To illustrate more of the important payroll controls in our previous example, consider the additional risk associated with hiring an employee who will have access to biological agents. Presumably, you would want to know as much as possible about this person before allowing him or her into such a facility. Furthermore, you certainly would not want to allow a candidate with an arrest record to gain access to some of the country's most dangerous research data on biological agents. However, a background check at the Plum Island Animal Disease Center of the eastern tip of Long Island uncovered just such an incident. Although the internal control procedure of checking the arrest record of applicants was in place and did uncover the arrest record of the applicant, unfortunately, the record was discovered after the employee had already worked at the facility for over six weeks, needlessly increasing the threat to national security.

While convicts may deserve a second chance, there are jobs that are simply too risky to allow them to hold. You may be willing to trust a felon with your life, but you would not want to trust the lives of others by employing him or her at a facility such as Plum Island. As a broker, I may decide to trust a person who has an arrest record with my money, but certainly not the money of my client. My client expects me to protect his or her assets to the fullest extent possible. Sadly, many felons do repeat their actions, so it is important that human resources perform an important gatekeeper function by conducting background checks on all applicants.

Source and Pay for Inputs

Once the customer order is accepted, components for creating the deliverable need to be sourced, and vendors or laborers paid. Inputs can be traditional, such as raw materials and labor, or nontraditional, such as data. For instance, raw materials for a steel mill would include iron and coal, and skilled labor would be required to make a quality product safely. Steel mills are a notoriously difficult work environment, and unskilled or improperly trained labor could result in poor product quality or, worse, the loss of life.

With the explosive adoption of the Internet for business purposes, the sourcing of materials has undergone significant change. Global eXchange Services (formerly GE Global Exchange Services) provides "end to end, integrated business to business (B2B) solutions and services." [2] This means that Global's systems enable both a vendor and its customer to view an order, track its progress, and automate payment. The ability to improve visibility in the supply chain leads to a number of efficiencies. First, vendors and customers can work together to manage production and delivery to reduce required inventories. Mistakes are easier to discover because orders and shipments are visible to both parties. Finally, cash utilization is improved, as you can reduce overpayments by automatically matching contract terms to product received. The water meter manufacturer mentioned earlier would likely benefit from a relationship with Global eXchange Services, given its high material usage in its operations.

If your product is information, data is your raw material. To file the annual results of a public company with the Securities and Exchange Commission on Form 10-K, the financial information inputs must be sourced from the various physical and system sources within the organization. The information will then be compiled by the office of the CFO and subjected to an independent audit as required by law prior to distribution. As detailed at the beginning of this book, because of the recent high-profile frauds relating to financial reporting and disclosure, Congress passed the Sarbanes-Oxley Act. The act not only requires CEOs to attest to the accuracy of their financial statements, but also increases possible fines and jail time to $5 million and 20 years, respectively. But regulations are not controls. By themselves, they cannot prevent or detect a fraud. Rather, they exist to provide guidance and compel appropriate behavior.

As a testament to the inability of rules and regulations to prevent illegal action, the CEO of 800America.com was recently charged with two counts of securities fraud. According to the complaint, David Elie Rabi cooked the books of a public company despite attesting to their accuracy under the new certification rules. He raised approximately $2 million selling stock in the company, then allegedly stole $300,000. No one should be surprised. According to the SEC, Rabi has been in and out of prison many times over the past 50 years and was previously a wanted man in Italy, Canada, and Switzerland. The SEC also says that he had help. Another convict who assumed the identity of a dead woman to hide her criminal record became an officer of the company. Collusion is particularly hard to uncover, and so it was in this case. Even though several employees were deeply suspicious of the pair, it took a year and an SEC investigation to uncover their backgrounds and the fraud.

The receipt of raw materials, labor, or information is, however, only one side of a sourcing transaction. The vendor or employee expects value in return for goods or services provided. Most payments are made in cash, though they can also take the form of allocated expenses or other goods and services in trade. For instance, the earlier example of the HR department illustrates the concept of accepting payment for services by way of allocating expenses to those departments receiving the benefit. The payment for a department to transmit financial information to the office of the CFO may take the form of compiled profit and loss statements in return that help the manager supervise his or her business.

Create Deliverable

The process most unique to every business cycle is the creation of the deliverable. Companies differentiate themselves based not only on what they make, but also how they make it. For instance, Compaq and Dell both make computers, but the way they make computers could not be more different. Compaq builds standard systems and sells them through a number of retail channels. Dell builds to specific customer orders and only sells through the Internet or over the phone. How the deliverable is created can be a tremendous source of competitive advantage, as evidenced by Dell's phenomenal growth and profitability. As mentioned earlier, the output of a company, department, or individual may be a manufactured or assembled product, a service produced, or compiled information. Regardless of what is created, the creation of the deliverable has its own inherent risks. No one wants to buy a computer that is difficult to use or does not work as intended. A good control structure will provide timely feedback to help management adjust to quality threats. Poorly controlled businesses can, and have continued to churn out, defective product well past the point at which such a problem should have been discovered.

A good example is the recent recall of Weed Wizard trimmer heads, which use chain in their manufacture instead of the more well-proven string. According to the U.S. Consumer Product Safety Commission (CSPC), the company manufactured the heads from 1987 through April 2000. The CPSC alleges that the company knew it had a defective product when, in August 1997, the failure of a chain resulted in one of its links being lodged in the brain of three-year-old Alabama girl, causing her death. The CPSC further claims that the company was aware of 19 other incidents, which they failed to report to the commission. As a result, the

CPSC fined the company $885,000 and initiated a recall of the product. Management either failed to capture or ignored signs of problems, whose resolution could have led to production improvements and the saving of at least one life.

Inventory

Many businesses manufacture standardized products that can be inventoried until needed. For example, a microchip manufacturer may produce millions of chips that can be stored in anticipation of future demand. But there are certain risks involved with inventory. For one, constantly improving chip yields and performance can result in the impairment of existing inventory. Simply put, the newest chips manufactured are faster and cheaper than their predecessors. In such a case, inventory values may be overstated. Safeguarding assets is another risk. As long as a product is in inventory, the company bears the risk of loss. An act of God, such as a flood or theft, can result in large losses.

A Tennessee sofa maker uses its proximity to customers to eliminate finished inventory and provide competitive advantage. Many sofa manufacturers are located abroad, so dealers stock merchandise in their showrooms to meet demand. Even with transportation and storage, foreign product can cost a fraction of a similar domestic product. It would seem, then, that the demise of the U.S. sofa industry is imminent. However, if a customer has a requirement for a specific fabric or color, that special order can take up to four months to fill from a foreign manufacturer. Since many customers want their sofas and chairs to match their décor, there is an opportunity for local producers. England Inc., based in New Tazewell, Tennessee, fills this niche. It is able to turn out and deliver custom product in as little as three weeks. The company produces more than 11,000 custom sofas and chairs a week. Is this strategy effective? Sales are growing at over 8 percent a year, in an industry where sales generally fell over 9 percent. At the other end of the inventory story, England has reduced the number of fabric vendors it uses from over 40 to 4. It presses the remaining manufacturers to deliver frequent, small quantities of fabric quickly so that the company does not carry excessive raw material or get stuck with obsolete goods. England has addressed the foreign threat and appears to be a survivor.

Distribute

Delivery, by itself, can lead to competitive advantage. The various ways goods and services can be brought to market is as diverse as the products themselves. Recall the different distribution systems utilized by Compaq and Dell: Compaq distributes standard merchandise through various retail channels; Dell builds to order and ships output directly to the user.

Some companies utilize various methods to place their products. Starbucks, the premium coffee company, not only sells its coffee through coffee shops. Other delivery systems include branded coffee and ice cream sold in grocery stores, premium dried product provided with a coffeemaker in certain hotel rooms, and prepared beverages on airlines and in restaurants. All of these methods put the Starbucks trademark front and center, and its product in the hands of consumers.

Regardless of the delivery system, each method of distribution carries different threats that smart managers will study and mitigate. Their response could be as simple as purchasing insurance on a load of merchandise, or as complicated as requiring armed-guard transportation with multiple checks of every shipment, as is practiced by security carriers such as Brinks.

Record Revenue

The primary reason most businesses are organized is to create wealth; we expect to be paid for our efforts. Similar to our vendor payments, receipts can take many forms, including currency, allocation of expenses, or goods and services received in trade.

Goods and services received in trade create additional issues. It is often difficult to identify the value of, or contingencies tied to, services received as payment. For example, a recent shareholder lawsuit against Homestore.com accuses AOL Time Warner of plans to fraudulently inflate revenue at both companies. The complaint alleges that the value of ads sold to Homestore.com was excessive and that the two parties participated in "round tripping," or artificially increasing revenue. In effect, the two companies agreed to trade advertising, and both booked revenue. To complicate matters, some of the compensation AOL received for ad placements was in the form of stock. Eventually, the company restated its reported revenue by $190 million.

The risk that we may not get paid by external customers also needs to be managed. Credit, collateral, and financial reserve requirements will somewhat mitigate these threats. But even with such policies, accurate, timely information is needed to properly supervise and react to increased exposure.

Feedback

How did we do? Are we profitable? Is there a better way? At the end of every process, we should be able to evaluate our performance and improve our ability to manufacture and deliver a higher-quality product cheaper. We evaluate ourselves based on key performance indicators. Such feedback will aid our evaluation of the timeliness, efficiency, and effectiveness of our efforts, including an assessment of profitability and other financial objectives.

We can easily imagine the popular Dell character, Steven, excitedly telling his friend, "Dude, you're getting a Dell!" But what is Steven's friend really concerned about? He is excited about getting a Dell because he knows he will get it quickly, delivered to his door, already loaded with software, and in working condition at a reasonable cost. To make sure this reaction is occurring regularly, management should monitor critical metrics such as the amount of time required to build a computer, component defect percentage, customer satisfaction rating, and competitor pricing. This feedback will help guarantee that the dude's next computer is also a Dell.

It is likely that each of the key activities discussed here apply to your business. The specific procedures performed can only be supplied by you. It is time to think through each of your processes, identify the actions that relate to each activity, and, finally, document the results. Memorializing your results will provide the foundation you need to subject the process to the Smart Links analysis.

TELL YOUR STORY

You are now committed to writing your story. You want to communicate in clear fashion so that your audience will understand what you do and how you do it. To do that, let's focus on just one of the processes identified earlier for George, the sales manager for the sports distribution company. Budgeting is something most managers are familiar with, so we'll use this process to illustrate how to identify key activities and chronicle our operations.

Creating a budget is not the primary product or service being produced by the sales department, but it is nonetheless a process for which George has decision rights. It is his responsibility to control and monitor every step from the request for information by the finance department to the evaluation of his department's performance against the budget. Exhibit 4.3 illustrates how this process is executed. Every year, the finance department will issue a budget template containing instructions and guidelines representing an internal customer order for information. George will source information from his salesman and complete the template deliverable and review it with his supervisor, who will distribute it to finance.

EXHIBIT 4.3   BUDGETING PROCESS

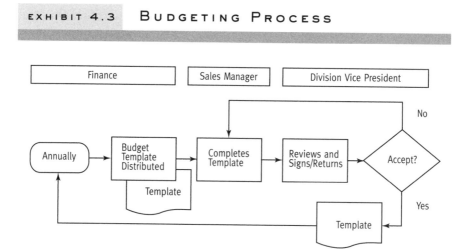

By preparing this simple flowchart, we have a graphic understanding of the process and the controls in place. Later I will take you through the Smart Links assessment tool to help you identify controls in any process, but there are several safeguards I will identify now for the budget process presented here. Finance manages the process so that there is a single source for budget information. By reducing the chance that someone can manipulate budget information, this control reasonably ensures its validity. The supervisor reviews the budget to see that it meets the organization's guidelines and his or her goals for the sales manager. Finance will look for the supervisor's signature as evidence of this review and authorization. The department manager has now documented this process. But budgets do not mean much if there is not a method to monitor actual performance against these objectives. It is important to point out that further process and controls will likely enter the picture as the sales manager determines the best way to evaluate departmental performance against the budget. The additional process may be one already identified and documented, or one that came to light as a result of the manager's evaluation. In this case, having prepared the budget, feedback is now necessary, in the form of budget versus actual performance reporting. That procedure is illustrated in Exhibit 4.4.

EXHIBIT 4.4 MANAGERIAL REPORTING PROCESS

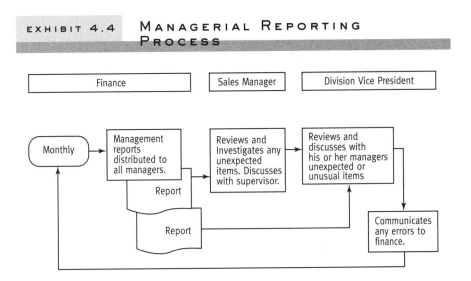

Every month, the finance department sends out reports to all managers and their supervisors (this can be thought of as "payment" for the budget deliverable). These management reports provide the monthly and year-to-date budget-to-actual results. They may also compute the overall margin percentage, the margin by product, and, possibly, the aging of receivables. Both the manager and supervisor review the reports and follow up on items that look unusual or results that were unexpected. For instance, assume that sales were exceeding budget, but that collections on those sales were lagging, resulting in an increase in receivables. Management could investigate and make a determination whether bad debts were likely to increase, thus requiring immediate attention, or this month's numbers were likely an aberration that should be monitored. This may sound like basic management, but review of this data (think key performance indicators) is an important control. If supervisors had properly considered what kinds of margins were possible in the government bond market, such a review would have initiated questions regarding Joseph Jett's phony trading prof-its discussed earlier. If a supervisor had properly considered the aging and value of contracts entered into by Allfirst's John Rusak, such a review would have initiated questions regarding the lack of realized profits (and the continued accretion of unrealized profits for Allfirst). So often, basic management tasks equal good control procedures.

We may be getting a little bit ahead of ourselves, but it is important to understand that all managers have decision rights over a number of processes, and that those processes have a number of generic activities. We can use the key activities model introduced earlier to guarantee that we have thought through each of the processes we identified. We are then in a position to document these processes. But how do we identify the con-trols we have in place? More important, which controls are we missing?

In the next chapter, I will define what I mean by the term "control" and the various types available for us to call on when needed.

CHAPTER 5

Identify Where You Are Vulnerable

According to Ben Franklin, "an ounce of prevention is worth a pound of cure." But the question remains, where do we apply that ounce of prevention? Thus far, we have identified our risks, assigned risk owners, and identified and documented the processes over which we have decision rights. Our pathway in Exhibit 5.1 tells us that we have yet to determine where we are vulnerable. That is where we want to apply old Ben's adage. To properly prepare for using the Smart Links assessment tool, it will be helpful to first develop a basic understanding of what we mean by the term "control."

EXHIBIT 5.1 CONTROL SMART PATHWAY

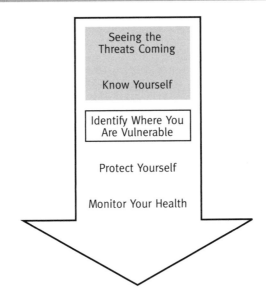

Seeing the Threats Coming

Know Yourself

Identify Where You Are Vulnerable

Protect Yourself

Monitor Your Health

Controls are the reinforcing steel we will use to protect our operations. Just as there are different types and grades of steel, there are different types and degrees of control. Not all steel is appropriate for every application just as certain controls are not appropriate in every instance.

WHAT ARE CONTROLS?

Our mission to identify present and missing controls will be greatly enhanced if we understand what is meant by internal control or objectives and whether a control is *preventive* or *detective*. Most of us think of the term "control" as generically referring to an action that prevents a loss. That is how I have used the term to this point in the book. There are, however, a number of different definitions of internal control tossed around in the world of academia. The SEC, in an effort to lessen confusion, settled on the following:

> A process designed by, or under the supervision of, the registrant's principal executive and principal financial officers, or persons performing similar functions, and effected by the registrant's board of directors, management and other personnel, to provide reasonable assurance regarding the reliability of financial reporting and the preparation of financial statements for external purposes in accordance with generally accepted accounting principles and includes those policies and procedures that:
>
> (1) pertain to the maintenance of records that in reasonable detail accurately and fairly reflect the transactions and dispositions of the assets of the registrant;
>
> (2) provide reasonable assurance that transactions are recorded as necessary to permit preparation of financial statements in accordance with generally accepted accounting principles, and that receipts and expenditures for the registrant are being made only in accordance with authorizations of management and directors of the registrant; and
>
> (3) provide reasonable assurance regarding prevention or timely detection of unauthorized acquisition, use or disposition of the registrant's assets that could have a material effect on the financial statements.

Clear as mud? What this really says is that a good internal control system ensures that the financial statements are accurate and compliant with accepted standards, that good records are kept, and that the assets of the entity are employed as intended by the company. The SEC focused on internal control as it relates to financial reporting; but for our purposes, we will look at internal control more broadly under the theory that any type of control break, whether financial, operational, or regulatory, can lead to significant financial loss if not detected in a timely manner. In other words, an unknown breach of a regulatory requirement might not be covered in the financial reporting control system, but related fines might eventually be realized that could materially impact a company, not to mention the career of the manager in charge. Likewise, operational issues might not immediately impact the financial statements, but could be material to future financial performance. A good example might be the next generation of disk drives. If a company has issues ramping up the new generation of platter, its market could leave it behind over a period of weeks. Additionally, fraudulent activities are not restricted only to financial reporting. Therefore, we will cut a broader path that will include financial, operational, and regulatory issues, and evaluate preventive and detective controls that will alert us to potential problems.

What are preventive and detective controls? Simply, preventive controls are designed to avoid a control break, and detective controls are designed to identify a break after it has occurred. In my practice, I have always focused on preventive controls as the priority. In financial services, if an unauthorized trade for several million dollars has settled, it can be too late to fully reverse the damage. A detective control that identifies the break after settlement will only tell you the size of the break and the challenges you face to limit the damage. It is more prudent to put in trading limits that can be electronically enforced to prevent an unauthorized trade from occurring.

That said, detective controls are also important. If a preventive control is missing, has failed, or has been circumvented via collusion, then the detective control will highlight the break so that management can take appropriate action before further damage is done. For this reason, I always insist on at *least* two *control points* for every objective over which I have decision rights. Control points are positions on the business process or value chain where the results of a procedure will prevent or detect a control break. I require at least two control points simply to allow the structure to have a chance to work in the event that the first control fails or is purposely circumvented.

A former supervisor and mentor, John Cirrito, was one of the most naturally instinctive managers I have ever worked for; he had an innate sense of good control. He always required "three separate sets of eyes" for every process where the risk of loss could threaten the continued health of the business. Although not identified as such, these sets of eyes represented control points consisting of preventive and detective controls. With three control points, John knew that collusion would be more difficult and that it was highly likely that an operational control break would be prevented or discovered. An example of a process requiring the three sets-of-eyes principle might include wire room procedures. Good process requires the wire room to receive a written request properly authorized by a supervisor (first set of eyes). The wire room clerk then sets up the payment in the system. The wire room manager compares the input to the supporting documentation and approves the payment for batch processing (second set of eyes). Finally, the department head reviews all instructions and supporting documentation queued and, if satisfied, releases the payment instructions to the appropriate banking institutions (third set of eyes). John's "three separate sets of eyes" rule made it easy for me to install a strong control culture throughout the organization.

As highlighted earlier, much of the damage done to companies occurs over many months and even years. Good detective controls would have identified these problems much sooner. As an illustration of how more than one control point is needed to detect fraud and save a career, consider the case of Salomon Brothers' Paul Mozer. On February 21, 1991, Mr. Mozer, a managing director in charge of Salomon Inc.'s government securities trading desk submitted a bid at the 35 percent limit of the total amount of bonds offered by the Treasury, apparently within government and firm limits. He also submitted two unauthorized firm bids in customers' names, each at the 35 percent limit, thus flouting Treasury rules. Salomon effectively bid for 105 percent of the offering and successfully purchased 57 percent of the offering, well in excess of the 35 percent purchase limit rule. He later moved the unauthorized positions from customer accounts onto the firm's balance sheet at the original auction price. This is where the concept of having two or more control points for each control activity would have paid off. If the firm ran a daily exception report in the compliance department of total government positions held by the firm in excess of 35 percent, the auction manipulation probably would have been detected. The fraud would have still occurred, as the preventive control was purposely circumvented, but the detective control would have identified the fraud much sooner. Senior management learned of the incident in April, when Mr. Mozer reported his conduct, but they did not report the incident to authorities until August. It is not clear why executive management did not immediately inform the authorities, but the delayed response of Salomon's management ended up costing the firm $290 million in fines and causing the resignation of the chairman, vice chairman, and president.

PULL LEVERS—OFTEN

There are a number of levers that can be employed to enable management to establish preventive and detective controls. These include:

- Performance reviews
- Information processing
- Physical controls
- Segregation of duties

These levers can be used in isolation or in combination to provide a line of defense. The more levers you pull, the stronger your protective armor. The more often you pull the levers, the more timely your response to threats.

Performance Reviews

Performance reviews can be used to provide rewards for good behavior as well as to correct undesirable activity. In combination with a well-designed compensation program, performance reviews can be quite effective.

The compensation program at GE is often held up as a stellar model in the management field. The objectives of the organization were folded into the performance review process and senior management spent a considerable amount of their time traveling and conducting face-to-face "Session C" human resources reviews. Good reviews that met not only P&L goals, but nonfinancial goals such as implementing Internet tools into the business model, would result in raises, bonuses, and options as well. If, when measured against company objectives, a manager performed poorly, it meant that he or she had to change fast or leave.

The performance review program at GE is often cited as one of the keys to its continued profitability and success. Unfortunately, poorly designed compensation programs can produce the opposite of what is desired if employees try to "game the system." Joe Jett was paid millions in bonuses without creating wealth for his firm. It appears that the performance evaluation techniques that worked so well at GE had not been adequately implemented at its Kidder Peabody subsidiary. Jett was not compensated on his ability to get along with others or teamwork capabilities. As such, he was able to intimidate anyone who questioned his explanations. No one wanted to ask him a question for fear of looking stupid. Input from finance, legal, credit, and other departments, as well as the results of internal, external, and regulatory audits in the compensation process can add a layer of comfort that objectives are being honestly met.

Information Processing

In today's world, you cannot manage and control your business without the crucial control lever of information processing, as those who would manipulate to take your business from you will employ computers to meet their unethical objectives.

Let's look at one striking example: Without ever entering the United States, Vladimir Levin, a Russian computer hacker, sent a wake-up call to the financial services industry by hacking into Citibank's information systems, causing millions of dollars in unauthorized transfers from customer accounts. For months, Citicorp executives watched helplessly as the hacker transferred money from customer accounts. They were able to arrest pawns sent to collect the fraudulent funds in countries all over the world, and over time they became better at isolating the mastermind located in St. Petersburg, Russia. During a trip to England in 1995, the 28-year-old Levin was arrested and finally extradited to serve justice in the United States.

Levin's actions predictably led to Citibank's development of new electronic security measures and other money center banks to evaluate its defenses. While no bank would want to detail how it protects customer assets, good defensive countermeasures using electronic firewalls, access restrictions, intrusion detection, access markers, audit trails, and the like are required to protect such an enterprise. Effective tools will not only alert managers when an outsider attempts to enter their systems, but will also tell them when and where internal employees obtained access.

Physical Controls

We all know someone who has been the victim of a robbery or fire. The methods we employ at home, such as locks and deadbolts on the doors, electronic security monitors on the windows, strongboxes for valuables, fire extinguishers, smoke detectors, and so on, are some of the same physical controls we would want at our place of work to protect our people and safeguard the assets of our enterprise. Among the more visible and longstanding physical controls in use include installing electronic locks on a data center or preventing the general public from entering sensitive areas like a warehouse or trading floor.

Segregation of Duties

Segregation of duties is a common and basic control lever often deployed in organizations that have enough human resources to divide tasks into discrete bits so that no single person can effect a transaction without the help of others. This is done by separating the *custody*, *recording*, and *approval* functions for any process. Functional segregation theory can be visually mapped as presented in Exhibit 5.2.

Some of the largest frauds in history were made possible due to poor segregation of duties. I have already explained how Barings' rogue trader Nick Leeson was able to set up an account to hide his losses because he was responsible for both the front office (*authorization*) and operations (*recording*) functions at the firm's Singapore branch. Likewise, Yasuo

EXHIBIT 5.2   FUNCTIONAL SEGREGATION

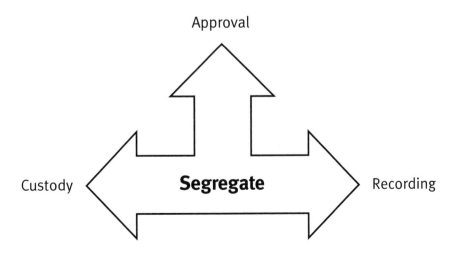

Hamanaka, a copper trader for Sumitomo Corporation, not only entered trades (*authorization*), but also was able to keep two sets of books (*recording*) to disguise nonexistent accounts. His complete control over authorization and recording enabled him to conceal the fraud for over a decade. Both of these frauds resulted in losses in excess of a billion dollars.

While a business with only one owner and a single employee can utilize segregation of duties successfully, a business would not necessarily have a poor control environment if activities were not segregated. Alternative controls can be put in place. This is common in small companies where it is difficult to properly segregate job functions due to the limited number of employees. In these cases, other control levers can be pulled (performance reviews, information processing, physical controls). However, if an enterprise has sufficient scale, segregation is often the easiest and most effective method to strengthen controls. Costs to implement segregation controls are usually low, as the assets (people) are already in place. In addition, there are many different ways to segregate a single process, providing flexibility.

Take the operating activities of George, the sales manager with the budget process introduced in Chapter 4. Normally, salespeople would not physically deliver (*custody*) or take payment (*custody*) for the product. Nor would they *approve* customer credit or the release of goods for shipping. They would *record* the order into the sales system, so that they would get credit for the sale, and call the customer, to make certain that delivery was made and that the customer was happy.

But what if salespeople had a truck full of goods that traveled with them on a defined and regular route? This is a common delivery method for stocking small stores and shops with such goods as salty snacks. Clearly, the custody function resides with salespeople, and they will record the amount of goods they sell (stock). They might even accept cash payment for what they leave. So how would a manager control this? Perhaps cash is to be received by a clerk at the end of every day and independently reconciled to the truck inventory before the salespeople can request more goods.

As an alternative, perhaps the salespeople pay for the goods on their own accounts. Then they can dump them in the river for all the company cares. Many businesses that deliver product to their salespeople's homes are structured in this way. This limits the financial risk of loss to the organization to a tolerable level. For example, Avon Products, the cosmetics company, sells its merchandise to independent contractors or franchisees that in turn sell to the consumer. The salespeople buy products on their own accounts and are responsible for collecting payment from the consumer.

As you can see, there are many ways to segregate duties. Some businesses, however, do not have the operational mass to properly segregate all duties. In the absence of segregation, supervision by way of information processing and performance reviews, or access limitations by way of physical controls, could be substituted to limit risk of loss to tolerable levels. One of my clients, an established hedge fund with a long, successful track record, remained a small shop despite its success and its management of billions of dollars in assets. It had only three IT personnel to provide desktop support, programming, and data center administration. Clearly, segregating the IT duties without sacrificing a qualified backup for each position would be a challenge. A corrective plan was conceived in which access to systems was split among the three and limited to the extent possible. Backup activities were to be enabled only when needed. Daily access and program change management reporting was provided to the managing principal in charge of IT. These reports would alert the manager if inappropriate access or program changes were made. The key to this process was that the manager was cognizant of which types of access or production program changes raised a red flag of increased operational risk. While generally it is not a good idea to design controls around a single person's capabilities, this client understood this risk and made a rational cost/benefit analysis. Important components of the process used to develop the firm's control solution included the evaluation of resources, the risk of loss, oversight capabilities, and the cost of effective preventive and detective controls necessary to bring risk to a tolerable level. The end result was a properly segregated and controlled operation with duties that could be carried by a small staff.

What managers want to avoid is the type of control break that could be material to or even bankrupt a company in a short period of time. There is a series of vital questions you, as a manager, can ask to assess risk of loss due to poor segregation:

- Can a single person control the recording, custody, and approval functions of any process for which the manager has decision rights? If so, preventive controls are lacking.
- How would you know if someone decided to steal from the company? A positive answer to this question identifies a detective control.

- If a control break were to occur, what is the maximum damage that could be done? The response to a total possible loss of $1,000 will be viewed differently from one resulting in a catastrophic failure.

- Is this damage within the tolerable range of loss for the company? This question will help you determine your risk appetite.

- If a possible loss exceeds the tolerable range, how much would the company be willing to spend to control this risk?

By answering these simple questions, you can identify segregation issues, determine risk tolerance, and develop a budget for corrective action.

ACTIVITIES THAT IMPROVE YOUR BUSINESS

We have addressed the two types of internal controls (preventive and detective), and the levers we can pull (performance reviews, information processing, physical controls, and segregation of duties). The next step is to define our control objectives. So, before we move on to Smart Links, let's review the type of objectives we want to realize and their related activities. (I will refer to these goals in our Smart Links assessment, so you may wish to mark this page to refresh your memory as we work through the assessment process.) The objectives we will utilize have been defined by the AICPA. These are:

- Validity
- Completeness
- Authorization
- Valuation
- Classification
- Presentation and disclosure
- Timing and cutoff
- Regulatory

Validity

Validity activities answer the question: "How would I know if someone tried to book a fake transaction?" These activities are designed to reasonably ensure that recorded transactions include only those that have actually occurred. An example of a validity control would be the matching of items on a sales order to a shipping manifest by a person independent of the shipping function. This preventive measure would reasonably ensure that only goods shipped would be recorded as sales. Subsequent aging of receivables would detect if there were a problem. All shipments would eventually have to be paid for the transaction to be valid. For services, where there is no physical item to verify whether the purchase has been received, one Midwest company requires separate people to approve service requisitions and related invoices. A third person ensures compliance with this policy (another example of the "three sets of eyes" concept) before making payment.

Perhaps the story of Barry Minkow best illustrates the absence of validity controls. In the 1980s, Minkow created a fledging carpet cleaning business, ZZZZ Best, which became a darling of Wall Street and, eventually, the subject of a complex fraud. In order to support growth projections for a public offering, Minkow created a fictitious insurance restoration business that existed on paper only.

ZZZZ Best reported staggering profit growth from $400,000 in 1983 to an estimated $40 million for 1987. In 1986, the company hired Ernst & Whinney (E&W) to give some credibility to its balance sheet for its Wall Street consumers. It would be expected that any auditor would invoke normal control procedures to validate insurance restoration revenue. Such procedures would include confirmation of restoration projects and payments from insurance companies. This would entail preparing letters to the carriers asking them to confirm the amount that they paid the company for a specific restoration. Knowing this, Minkow convinced E&W to voluntarily sign a "confidentiality letter" precluding it from contacting "contractors, insurance companies, the building owner or other individuals (other than suppliers whose names have been provided to this firm by the company) involved in the restoration project."

Any attempt to limit the audit scope should have sent off warning flares and prevented E&W from conducting its audit. In fact, after E&W resigned, Coopers & Lybrand refused to propose on the engagement due to ZZZZ Best's refusal to allow it to review restoration contracts. Justice finally caught up to Barry Minkow. He was eventually sentenced to 25 years in prison and fined $26 million. This was cold comfort for investors. They lost everything.

Completeness

Completeness activities are intended to reasonably ensure that valid transactions are not omitted entirely from the accounting records. Examples of these kinds of controls include the reconciliation of a cash account to a bank statement or a trade comparison process. If more cash is in a bank account than expected, then this detective measure alerts us that either the books and records are not up to date or that a transaction has been omitted. If, during the clearance process, a trade surfaces from a counterpart that is not known, then this detective control signals that a trade has either been recorded incorrectly or the transaction has been omitted entirely.

An incident at Sumitomo that I introduced earlier provides a good example of a company lacking completeness controls. Yasuo Hamanaka may not have been a household name in the United States, but he was well known to commodities traders around the world. Referred to as Mr. Five Percent due to the fact that his team controlled at least that amount of the huge copper market, Hamanaka was given unusually broad power by his employer, the Sumitomo Corporation. Like many other Japanese businessmen, Sumitomo practiced the trust-based management style rather than implementing a system of controls. This autonomy allowed Hamanaka to keep two sets of books, one with profits, and one with unauthorized "off the book" trading, which contained stunning losses. Amazingly, Hamanaka was able to trade "off the book" for over a decade before an investigation uncovered an unauthorized trade that led to Hamanaka's downfall. How these trades were funded, compared, and settled without detection for over 10 years speaks to a lack of completeness controls over the balance sheet. It is clear that there were significant clues internally and externally that were just missed. Internally, his division reported cash reserves much greater than what it, in fact, had. Surely a reconciliation of these reserves should have highlighted this problem. Internal auditors were twice sent to investigate Hamanaka's dealings, but were unable to obtain key information, and both times abandoned their investigation. Externally, an influential trader told the London Metal Exchange five years earlier that Hamanaka had made fictitious trades, but no regulatory action was taken. The lack of action, internally or externally, resulted in losses of more $1.8 billion for the trading giant. The head of the company's metals-trading internal control division admitted that the scandal and related spectacular losses might have been avoided had the company shared (segregated) responsibilities among copper traders and hired additional employees to verify trades. Not a death blow, but a very expensive lesson for Sumitomo.

Authorization

As implied by the word, authorization activities are intended to reasonably ensure that transactions are approved before they are executed and recorded. An example of authorization controls would be the inability to book an order into a sales system to a customer that had exceeded its credit limit or to a new customer that had not been properly screened. These preventive controls provide reasonable assurance that all transactions are appropriate to the goals of the organization prior to execution. Other examples might be authorization limits for purchases, as well as for wire or check requests. In fact, every organization should take careful note of its payment systems, as these processes are a favorite target of those engaging in fraud and embezzlement.

Authorization controls are often the lever circumvented by those committing fraud. For example, James Stewart, a former crude oil trader for Plains All American, was accused of making unauthorized speculative oil trades between 1998 and 1999, resulting in losses of $162 million. He has been indicted on charges of wire fraud. The indictment charges that Mr. Stewart allegedly forged the signature of Plains All American's president on documents that purported to give Mr. Stewart authorization to make trades. The letters were sent to trading counterparts. The indictment also charges that Mr. Stewart manipulated the record-keeping system by inaccurately entering the prices of trades. Mr. Stewart's trades required Plains to sell large amounts of oil at below-market prices without purchasing oil in offsetting trades. By entering into uncovered short positions, Mr. Stewart expected oil prices to fall. When oil prices began to rise, he renewed his existing contracts by rolling his unrealized losses forward, according to the U.S. attorney. By implementing this strategy, he avoided confirming his losses.

Once again, this is an example where more than one control point would have exposed a fraud. While no organization should rely on the procedures of outside parties, Plains' counterparts did provide an external control by requiring Mr. Stewart to send evidence of authorization to roll his positions. Mr. Stewart allegedly circumvented this by forging a signature and hid his actions from his superiors. Regardless, several control points could have been implemented, any one of which would have immediately exposed the alleged fraud. Automated exception reports warning of trading limit breaches would have immediately alerted management of unauthorized exposure. A daily review by Mr. Stewart's superior of trading activity and positions would have exposed both the forgery and the unhedged positions. Independent confirmation of trades by the back office would have brought to light the inaccurate trading prices entered. Independent pricing of positions by back-office personnel would have identified the magnitude of the accumulated unrealized losses. Finally, a daily value at risk calculation would have helped management understand its financial exposure to the oil markets. It would appear that none of these controls were in place given the length of time the alleged fraud was perpetuated. In addition to the $162 million loss, the price of Plains' stock fell by half due to its disclosure. Additionally, the company paid $30 million to settle related shareholder lawsuits. All of these losses could have been prevented by spending modest amounts to improve the control structure.

Valuation

Valuation activities are designed to reasonably ensure that dollar amounts are correctly determined. An example of a valuation control would be the regular pricing of a securities portfolio to ensure that gains and losses are properly recorded. Another example would include periodic counts and identification of obsolete inventory to ensure inventories are recorded at their correct value. These detective controls will alert managers to material decreases in the value of these assets.

One of the most famous examples of a valuation fraud is attributed to Kyriacos Papouis and Neil Dodgson of NatWest Capital Markets. In order to hide over £90 million of losses, Mr. Papouis, with the help of his boss, Mr. Dodgson, overvalued the option positions held on their book. More simply put, Mr. Papouis assigned his positions a price that was higher than anything he could achieve in the open market. When his boss became aware of the irregularity, he went to lengths to conceal the fraud to protect his protégé. While collusion is particularly difficult to detect, common securities controls, which normally include the independent pricing of option positions by the back office, should have surfaced this fraud. No matter what type of asset is on the balance sheet of a company, one of the strongest detective control procedures a manager can put in place is the regular *independent* valuation of assets.

Classification

Classification activities make certain that business activities are recorded in accounts designed to illuminate, rather than hide, their nature. These procedures are intended to reasonably ensure that transactions are recorded in the right accounts, charged and credited to the right customers, and so on. Examples of classification controls would include a supervisor review and approval of a journal entry prepared by a staff accountant. Another example would include the review and approval of a detailed sales and commission statement by a salesperson and his or her supervisor. The approval of a journal entry would be a preventive measure designed to guarantee proper categorization prior to the recording of the transaction. The review of the sales and commission statement would be a detective measure that would alert management if there were material recording errors among customer accounts.

WorldCom has shocked the financial community many times over the past year and has become the poster child for bad accounting. The CFO resigned when it was disclosed that WorldCom classified billions of dollars of expenses as capital items. By misclassifying these expenses, WorldCom attempted to defer recognition of these costs into future periods. So, it really does matter where costs are booked. According to reports, the CFO intended to take a nonrecurring charge in the next quarter to remove the expenses from the balance sheet. A review by an internal auditor, however, brought the deception to the surface. It led to the resignation of not only the CFO, but also the controller.

Presentation and Disclosure

Presentation and disclosure activities ensure that financial information and other disclosures provided to regulators and the public fairly convey the health of the company. These activities are designed to reasonably ensure that the accounting process for a transaction is performed completely and is in conformity with Generally Accepted Accounting Principles (GAAP) as determined by the accounting profession.

An example of a presentation and disclosure control would be the review of old receivable balances against reserves and expenses for unpaid customer debts. Generally, companies have knowledge of how many customers will find themselves unable to pay their debts. Based on this, they will set up reserves and record an expense as a percentage of the overall receivable balance, even though they do not know specifically which accounts will default on their obligation. As a balance ages, it becomes more unlikely to be paid, so at this point companies will "write off," or remove, the balance by reducing the reserve. This preventive control provides reasonable assurance that receivables, allowance for doubtful accounts and bad debts, are fairly stated in accordance with GAAP. It also makes certain that expenses are recorded in the proper period prior to release of the financial statements.

Presentation and disclosure is now a hot-button issue with regulators, Wall Street analysts, the press, executives, and directors. Concern over the reliability of financial statements has led the SEC to require CEOs of the largest companies to attest to the accuracy of their financial filings. Recent public restatements are numerous, and include Enron, WorldCom, Global Crossing, Qwest, and Adelphia Communications, to name a few. Poor accounting practices have been going on for so long in many of these companies that they are having difficulty determining their true financial position. In some cases, the answer is that they are bankrupt.

Presentation and disclosure risk is discussed in detail in Chapters 6 and 7, where we will explore which steps senior managers and directors can take to protect themselves and their shareholders from this threat.

Timing and Cutoff

Timing activities are designed to reasonably ensure a transaction is accounted for in the proper time period. An example of a timing control would be the automated separation of sales for each accounting period. During my tenure in public accounting, I had a client who determined that one of his sales managers had prematurely booked sales at the end of the year to improve his performance. He did this by including revenue earned in the beginning of the new year in the results of the prior year. This preventive control protects the financial statements from this type of manipulation by a manager trying to game the system. Another example would be the existence of a trained backup for every position. If an employee is sick, injured, or otherwise unavailable, the transactions can still be recorded in a timely manner. This is also a preventive measure designed to address a problem before it occurs.

Timing controls can also be implemented when it is important to determine where and when a product was made. Examples include food and drugs where a bad batch can have serious health consequences. Contaminated batches must be fully investigated, all affected product destroyed, and production issues corrected. To ensure these steps can occur, a company may assign lot codes that provide the date and shift on which the product was made. This audit trail will speed the investigation and correction of the problem.

Regulatory

Regulatory control activities are designed to reasonably ensure that a transaction complies with the applicable laws and regulations of the SEC and other regulatory bodies. An example of a regulatory control would be the necessity to gain approval from a legal or compliance department before a customer or counterpart could be set up in a broker/dealer's sales or trading system. One would expect that either of these departments could reasonably ensure that a customer had met regulatory requirements. Another example would be an automatic alert when a firm's bidding on government bonds approached regulatory limits. Both of these controls are preventive and protect the firm by alerting management before a regulatory breach has occurred.

Breaches of laws and regulations can be expensive for a company, but how a firm reacts can be even more important. For example, consider the reaction of management at Daiwa Bank, where Toshihide Iguchi executed in excess of $1.1 billion in unauthorized trades, including the sale of more than $375 million in customer securities. After management learned of the crimes, it tried to conceal evidence of the fraud rather than report them to regulators. The firm made false entries into its books and records, removed records of the crimes to the apartment of the New York branch manager, and filed a false report to the Federal Reserve. When these activities were discovered, the firm was ejected and prevented from doing business in the United States.

In my experience, a policy of openness with regulators, be they FDA, OSHA, FTC, or the SEC, is the best way to address a business problem. This is not always easy, and certainly not second nature. Basically, there is not much upside to a regulatory review, but the downside can be the complete cessation of business. Additionally, regulators often come across as defensive or uneducated regarding your business. It should be clear to any intelligent manager that an outsider can never know his or her business as well as he or she does. Also, many government jobs are training grounds for the industries they regulate. In that regard, they do not pay as well as the private sector, hence experience high turnover. That does not make them unintelligent, and it would be a mistake to treat them as such. Those regulators who do not move into the private sector have long memories.

Firms that have a policy of openness and that regularly report even minor flaws without delay build goodwill and trust with regulators. For example, a senior manager at a broker/dealer opened the newspaper one day and found that the reported Street short position in a security was less than the short position of his desk alone. Naturally, he recognized something was wrong. The firm found a problem with its short position reporting process and immediately reported it to the NASD, with an explanation of how the firm was going to correct the problem. Given the reputation the firm had with the regulatory community, the regulators saw it for what it was: a mistake, not an attempt at market manipulation. They accepted the fix and the firm continued to conduct its business uninterrupted.

As you subject your business processes to a control assessment, it will be helpful to review these control objectives. They will help you identify methods for dealing with gaps and weaknesses. As an added tool, a list of controls sorted by generic activity, lever, and Smart Links step is presented in Appendix D. We explore Smart Links further in Chapter 6.

CHAPTER 6

Smart Links

We have all heard the saying that we are only as strong as our weakest link. This could not be truer than when describing a control structure. Just as a chain that is reinforced with higher-quality and thicker steel is stronger than one that uses inferior materials, a structure with more robust and numerous controls will better defend a company than a thin one. No single link is more important than the next. Twelve of the 13 steps may have deep defenses, but the single weak link can be the one that leads to a terminal ending. With a grounding in control levers and objectives, we are now ready to introduce Smart Links.

Smart Links is an essential, user-friendly flowchart designed to help managers think about business processes, controls, and key performance indicators (KPIs). This template (see Exhibit 6.1) treats each process as if it were a discrete business producing a "product" or "deliverable." The starting point for the exercise is to take all of the activities for which a manager has decision rights and identify the products or deliverables to be produced. Keeping that product or deliverable in mind, a manager simply needs to start answering the questions under the Analysis section of the flowchart for every step or link. If an answer is no to any question, a control is missing and needs to be identified and implemented. Possible types of control objectives for a manager to consider will be provided in the Common Actions section of the flowchart. (Refer to Appendix D to identify common controls for that particular activity.) If a manager answers yes to any question, the proper control is in place. For every step, the manager will later identify a key performance indicator that will help him or her monitor the activity, which will be documented on a KPI matrix or report. Management can use this checklist as a daily, weekly, or monthly reference tool to ensure that all key performance indicators have been received and reviewed.

EXHIBIT 6.1   SMART LINKS

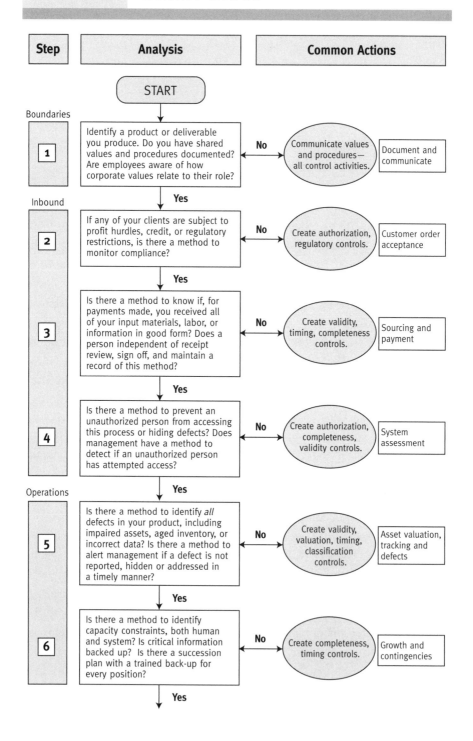

EXHIBIT 6.1 (CONTINUED)

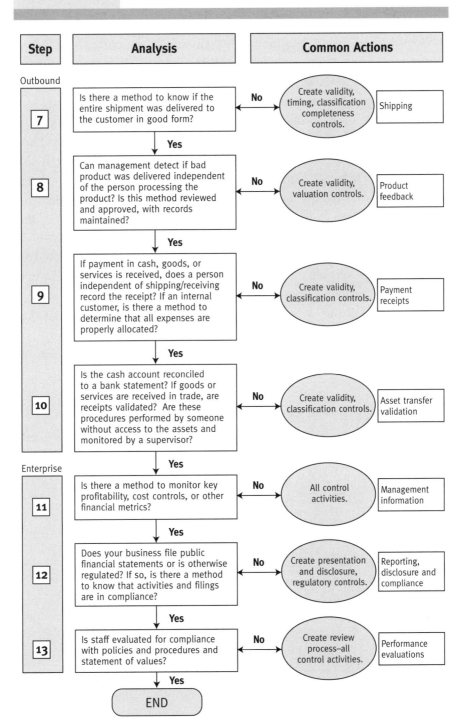

STEP 1: ESTABLISH BEHAVIORAL BOUNDARIES

The anchor link is one of the most important. Employees and managers at all levels must have a common understanding of the company mission, vision, and shared values, and how they relate to their specific tasks. Employees want to know what is expected of them. Shared corporate values and job-specific procedures provide this feedback.

To obtain a common understanding, mission, vision, values, and procedures must be connected in a coherent and understandable way. They should tell a story; a good one with a happy ending that will energize the organization. The first chapter begins with the mission. It communicates the organization's reason for being. Vision provides the imagery, the picture of the desired end state and should help employees visualize the strategic direction that will help them achieve the dream. Values establish boundaries around methods and behavior deemed acceptable to obtain the vision and objective. Finally, procedures describe, at a level each employee can relate to, how his or her efforts contribute to the organization's mission. All this is tied together with performance evaluations that ensure activities are directed toward company objectives. The role mission, vision, values, procedures, and performance evaluations play in providing clear behavioral boundaries and feedback is presented in Exhibit 6.2.

EXHIBIT 6.2   ESTABLISHING BEHAVIORAL BOUNDARIES

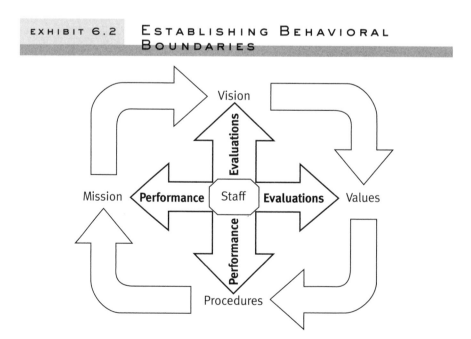

The story can be written at any level within the organization. While it is most commonly told at a company level, not all organizations have bothered to write these chapters. Such an omission will provide a manager the opportunity to create one. Even if the company has its own mission, vision, and values statement, a manager can still write his or her own book.

A good example comes to us from the investment bank of Keefe, Buryette and Woods (KBW). It has developed a reputation for excellence in the niche of financial services company research. Whenever an institution wants to invest in the insurance, commercial banking, investment banking, or asset management sectors, often its first step is to consult the research published by KBW. However, the firm recently suffered a tremendous setback when they lost a large number of their employees in the attack on the World Trade Center. The company has provided for the families of those lost, and continues to take care of those who survived the trauma of this experience. It has also, through Herculean effort, largely rebuilt the franchise.

A large part of this rebuilding effort was to reconstruct and improve the technology infrastructure of the enterprise. The firm recruited Linda Orlando to head this endeavor. In Linda, they obtained not a prototypical techie, rather a seasoned and smart manager. Linda recognized that she had inherited not only an uncertain systems platform, but also a fragile and incomplete team. She needed to address both if she was going to be successful.

Linda knew the firm needed her to stabilize and protect its systems, but she also recognized that the hard work of writing her management story was important. Consequently, she not only began tackling the critical stability issues, she also made time to prepare a mission, vision, and values statement to cement the IT foundation. She wanted her story to not only reflect the culture of the firm, but also to convey an understanding that the firm needed a strong technology function to be successful. Success would be realized when her department was viewed as a strategic partner rather than just a back-office function. Each team member needed to appreciate that the firm was counting on him or her to contribute what he or she could to their common success. Her first draft was as follows:

Mission

Global Technology Operations (GTO) provides world-class service and management tools to our customers via the integration of people, technology, and business systems.

Vision

We understand that in order for GTO to be recognized as successful, our customers must come first. We enable our clients to perform their jobs better, improving the overall performance of the firm. We are viewed as a strategic business partner, providing reliable, efficient, flexible, and scalable IT enterprise solutions. We are committed to our team philosophy of professional teamwork and communication.

Shared Values

We understand that for the firm to be successful, our customers must be successful. We partner with our customers to ensure that they have every opportunity to succeed.

Our goal is to provide quality service to our customers. We take pride in the professional quality of our work and strive for excellence in all we do.

We stress teamwork above individual achievement. While personal creativity and innovation are encouraged, we believe that the best results are reached as a cohesive team.

It is understood that the firm relies on our ability to control and safeguard confidential information maintained by our team. Every precaution should be taken to ensure access to sensitive information is properly controlled.

We strive to implement best practice wherever practical. Without continual improvement, both our infrastructure and skills will atrophy, retarding the firm's ability to compete.

Integrity, honesty, and ethical behavior are at the core of our department. We continually strive to develop a culture of being forth-right, truthful, and respectful of our peers and customers.

We recognize that we should recruit the best person for every position. Without the best people, we limit the success of the firm.

Linda has made a strong start. Not only is it clear why the department exists ("to provide world-class service and management tools to our customers"), but also spelled out in the statement is the department's strategy ("to become successful by placing the customer first") and what the department will look like when it gets there ("viewed as a strategic business partner, providing reliable, efficient, flexible, and scalable IT enterprise solutions").

She then defines acceptable behavior and boundaries by way of strong, unambiguous shared values. She begins the statement with the importance of customers, followed by the service they receive from her team. It is obvious that if an IT employee puts him- or herself ahead of a client, he or she will have stepped out of bounds. Such behavior not only dishonors the spirit of their shared values, but also places the mission and strategy of the department in jeopardy. It is equally apparent that the team is considered more valuable than any single individual, and that to mistreat any team member would not be acceptable behavior.

Importantly, the department also has a role in protecting confidential information. It is evident that failure to do so would damage the department and the firm. Linda also desires to instill a culture of continuous improvement, something that has been lacking in the past. This value will not be easy to implement, but she has given notice of her intent by mentioning a commitment to best practices. Plans are already underway to provide training that will introduce teamwork and customer service, as well as technical best practices to back up these values.

Honesty and integrity are not only valued, but expected. Linda chose language to convey that these traits are "core" to the department. She also wants to ensure that only qualified people are hired. This may sound like something so obvious that it does not need to be mentioned, but the department is shifting its focus from simply filling a role with an acceptable candidate to identifying someone with "runway," or the ability to grow with the firm. It is critical that this is frequently conveyed to the firm and that the positive impact is understood. A different hiring pattern is about to emerge that will draw the attention of the firm, and Linda will need to continually remind decision makers of the change and remarket her vision to her public.

Linda now has a document that she can use to set and evaluate employee goals and performance. Her mission, vision, and values will be effective only if employees embrace them. Reinforcing these values in group meetings and through targeted training is critical to success. But the most effective method for infusing these values is by including measurable employee objectives that are aligned with shared values in the evaluation process. In this way she will be able to differentiate between those who add to the firm's mission and those who detract. She can then take appropriate action based on the results.

Linda recognizes that she is missing the final chapter of her story. None of her systems or processes are documented. She has specifically requested and obtained funding to help her tackle this task and is in the process of creating a new change control process to keep systems and related documentation current and safe. Given her fast start, sense of urgency, and ability to sell her vision, I am putting my money on a successful turnaround.

Managers tend to define their businesses narrowly, meaning each of the key activities, whether inbound (sourcing materials, labor, and other inputs), operations (creating deliverables, inventory), outbound (distributing to the customer), marketing and sales (evaluating and pricing), customer service (evaluating performance), or support (monitoring receipts and payments) should be identified and documented for every process over which they have authority. Constant discussion and feedback regarding corporate shared values, performance, and process improvement will reinforce behavioral boundaries with employees.

While the hard science of internal control rests on process and procedure, the strongest environments will have shared values ingrained in their corporate culture. Managers are encouraged to spend time with their employees to make sure that processes are properly documented and values understood, by establishing projects or workshops to accomplish this task.

Failure to effectively complete this initial step can result in fuzzy boundaries that are not well understood by all employees and that weaken the quality of your control analysis. Remember, a poorly defined or empty set of values is not just neutral, but destructive. Properly completed, you are ready to evaluate these processes against the other steps of Smart Links, which will result in a strong control environment.

STEP 2: CHOOSE YOUR CUSTOMERS

Depending on your business, every customer may be welcomed and even encouraged to initiate contact with your company. This is true of nearly all retail-oriented operations. However, some businesses are highly regulated and only customers that meet certain criteria are allowed by law to become a customer of the enterprise. Clients and customers in the financial, healthcare, and defense industries are common examples. Knowledge of customer requirements must be resident prior to, or at the point of, purchase, to prevent a breach of law. For example, a retail firearms dealer must ensure his or her employees are intimately aware of state laws regarding background checks, gun registration, and age restrictions regarding the sale of firearms.

Controls must be in place at the point of purchase to ensure all requirements are met. A legal breach could result in lawsuits, fines, and closure of the business—not to mention the damage a firearm can do in the wrong hands. A preventive regulatory control in this case might be the approval of a manager to complete the sale. A detective control might include the daily reconciliation of transactions to approvals. The manager or his or her designee could compare the number of guns sold to authorizations. Any differences would alert the manager that procedure was not followed.

As another example of regulatory exposure to customers, Citigroup settled a case with the Federal Trade Commission by paying a fine of $200 million. It was alleged that Associates First Capital Corporation, a Dallas-based subprime lender, engaged in deceptive marketing practices. It was also asserted that it induced clients to consolidate their debts into home loans with high interest rates, costs, and fees, and persuaded borrowers to buy insurance on loans. Citigroup bought Associates in November 2000, and since then has moved to sever relationships with more than 5,000 brokers. It has also implemented new foreclosure procedures. If a pending foreclosure is the result of a loan with unfair terms, the company now negotiates an alternative with the buyer. The firm also eliminated the controversial insurance product. Citigroup maintains that now there are procedures in place to protect against the purchase of unnecessary insurance. If Associates had originally put procedures in place to ensure that customers were sold appropriate loan products as required by law, it could have prevented the $200 million fine that Citigroup was obligated to pay after purchasing the company.

Another customer preventive control pertains to bidding practices. Large projects can lead to large losses if the proper controls are not in place. Margin requirements and contract language can be key to a profitable conclusion of a project. The Washington Group (formerly Morrison & Knudson) provides a good example of this type of risk. It purchased Raytheon Engineers and Constructors only to learn later that many of the company's projects were in financial jeopardy. The results would indicate that the Washington Group did not have adequate due diligence and procurement controls in place. Equally, it appears that Raytheon lacked strong bidding controls. Thorough due diligence procedures regularly include an exhaustive evaluation of each significant product purchased. Such an evaluation would have uncovered the poor bidding practices and cost overruns. Washington Group brought a $444 million arbitration claim against Raytheon, but the disclosure put the company into immediate financial distress. Though it initiated lawsuits against Raytheon to try to recover the losses, the Washington Group was eventually forced to declare bankruptcy and it abandoned its litigation.

STEP 3: DID YOU GET WHAT YOU PAID FOR?

Sourcing and payment procedures are a favorite target of individuals intent on embezzlement and theft. By definition, those involved in the procurement and payment to vendors or company programs will come into lawful contact with company assets. Good controls will ensure that employees properly dispense with their duties regarding these assets without appropriating them for their own use.

An example of embezzlement comes to us from Harvard University's world-renowned Hasty Pudding Theatricals, which is the nation's oldest undergraduate dramatic organization. Former alumni include President Theodore Roosevelt, among others. Each year Hasty Pudding Theatricals presents awards to the country's top entertainers. It is alleged that one member, Suzanne Pomey, transferred money to her own account and that she gave another member a club credit card. That member, Randy Gomes, was accused of using the credit card to pay for drugs. According to prosecutors, a co-producer noticed that the group's bank balance was $50,000 less than it should have been. She then noticed a month later that an additional $16,000 had been withdrawn, even though withdrawals required her approval. While the approval control and review of bank statements are good detective controls that eventually worked, it is clear that the review of the bank statements and investigative actions could have occurred in a more timely fashion. Issuing a credit card where the holder is not responsible for making payment also negates any approval controls that would protect the organization's liquid assets. Individuals should be personally liable for corporate cards and submit claims through a well-controlled expense reimbursement process. The requirement of ever higher levels of authority to approve larger payments by check is also a good preventive control.

While the previous example was allegedly perpetrated by students, the most damaging crimes are committed by older, educated, and trusted male employees. According to the Association of Certified Fraud Examiners (ACFE), losses from fraud caused by managers and executives are 16 times greater than those caused by rank-and-file employees. Losses caused by people 60 and older are 28 times those caused by people 25 and under. Losses caused by those with postgraduate degrees are five times greater than those caused by high school graduates. Finally, losses caused by men are four times greater than those by women. There are many different types of fraud and embezzlement; the most common criminal activity involves either the appropriation or misuse of cash or the checking account of a business.

Even companies with superior payment controls in one branch of their business may have poor payment controls in another. As an example, a former vice president of ABN Amro, Stephen Fitzgerald, was recently accused of stealing almost $360,000. ABN Amro is known to have strong payment controls in its New York office. Mr. Fitzgerald, however, worked in ABN Amro's Chicago office. He is being charged with fraud for liquidating mutual fund accounts with unclaimed monies and transferring these monies to his personal bank accounts and even writing himself a check for more than $100,000.

Given the huge operational risk of payment systems, financial services firms such as ABN Amro are thought to have implemented the strongest controls. Yet it appears that a single person was able to compromise not one of ABN's payment systems, but two: the wire transfer system and the physical check system. Smart managers have a belt-and-suspenders attitude regarding payment systems: Not only should the functions of requesting, authorizing, preparing, and releasing a wire or a check be performed by separate people, but extra controls should be instituted as backup measures. These include requiring additional signatures for large wires and checks, added approvals for check and wires to new vendors or customers, and an end-of-day review of all large payments by a senior manager of the area requesting the payment (in this case, the head of the mutual fund operations who might recognize the payee). In addition, strong physical (secure wire room and checks) and system access controls (proper authorization levels, regularly changed passwords, strong firewalls, etc.) should be implemented.

More control-conscious organizations will go even further, with periodic computer-matching of vendor addresses and phone numbers to employee addresses and phone numbers (as a means of scouting for fictitious vendors), searches for multiple employees with direct deposit to a single account (to check for fictitious employees), or computerized pattern analysis of claims or purchases just below known authorization thresholds (to detect theft or abuse of shareholder assets).

There is also a lesson here regarding learning organizations: Best practices in one part of an organization should be communicated and implemented elsewhere. The knowledge of good payment controls was resident inside ABN Amro, probably in a number of its offices worldwide, but it only took one badly controlled payment process to hurt an entire organization.

Another common form of fraud is the forging of commercial documents. At one of my previous employers, one enterprising crook managed to create replicas of our checks and cash them. The forgeries were quite good and not easy to spot. The check number was the most telling identifier, as it was well out of sequence when compared to other checks that had recently cleared. Organizations experiencing this problem can implement a positive pay procedure with their financial institution. Under this process, the company will send an electronic record of the checks written on a specific account to its bank. Any checks presented that do not match the record will be rejected, thus preventing the fraud.

Cash, while the most common asset, is not the only one that can be embezzled. While working at a professional services firm, I learned that an employee had been caught stealing new laptop computers. The employee worked in technology support and was responsible for ordering and receiving equipment. As new computer shipments were received, and before they were put on the firm's asset register or assigned to an employee, she put them into a self-addressed box and had the firm's mailroom ship them to her home. This delivery method was both practical and creative. By using the mailroom, she did not need to move a heavy box out of the office and she circumvented the need for prior authorization for taking equipment out of the building. The mailroom circumvented these controls for her. Fortunately for the firm, a mailroom clerk decided to repackage the box, as he was concerned that it did not adequately handle the weight of the contents. When opened, the embezzlement was discovered.

This example illustrates how important it is to properly segregate custody, approval, and recording functions. This employee had order and payment authorization, custody duties, and responsibility for issuing and tracking the computers as they were provided to staff. By having someone independent of technology receive and enter equipment into the asset register, and another periodically review computers issued to the register, a detective control would have been successfully in place.

Greed's Siren Song: Dennis Kozlowski

Dennis Kozlowski started out as a respected and talented executive. He developed a reputation for quickly turning around poorly performing operations and seamlessly integrating them into highly profitable businesses. His operating prowess vaulted him into the top spot at Tyco International. But once there, his training as a former auditor provided him the skills necessary to circumvent controls and loot his company. The booty haul was legendary. He stands accused of 38 felony counts of stealing $170 million directly, and $430 million indirectly through illicit stock sales.

Kozlowski grew up in the rough neighborhoods of Newark, New Jersey. His father, who was an investigator for what would become New Jersey Transit, was known as a not overly friendly, tough guy. Kozlowski was more affable than his father. He was a well-liked member of a fraternity at Seton Hall, where he graduated as a B student in accounting. He entered the business world as an auditor, where he continued to work until his move to Tyco in 1975. There he met, and no doubt was greatly influenced by, Joseph Gaziano, the chairman and CEO of Tyco. Gaziano was a known for flaunting his corporate perks, which included a jet, a helicopter, and three luxury apartments.

Kozlowski flourished under Gaziano, and his eventual successor, John Fort. He successfully grew Tyco's stagnant fire-suppression systems business by purchasing competitors, eliminating unneeded operations, and integrating them with Tyco's operations. Kozlowski's success gained him the favor of the board, which enabled an eventual boardroom coup that elevated Kozlowski to the top spot.

During his first couple of years as CEO, he continued to perform strongly. In 1994, he bought Kendall International Group, a specialty manufacturer of medical devices. It was not a particularly strong business, but Kozlowski turned Kendall around and used it as a foundation to build up a medical devices business that became second only to Johnson & Johnson. The acquisition of Kendall also dramatically improved Tyco's bottom line.

The seeds of excess seemed to be planted in 1995, when Kozlowski convinced the board to let him move the corporate headquarters from New Hampshire to plush accommodations overlooking New York City's Central Park. He also convinced them to set up a relocation program to move staff from New Hampshire to New York. Under the guise of relocation, he instructed human resources to set up a second executive relocation program, which allegedly was not disclosed to the board. It was this relocation

Case Study (continued)

program and others like it that prosecutors later insisted Kozlowski came to use as his personal checking account.

Kozlowski furthered his hold on the board and related perks in 1997 when he bought the security firm ADT. The officers and directors of ADT were no strangers to generous compensation packages. The chairman kept his headquarters in Bermuda and used his yacht as a floating executive suite. Kozlowski appointed two of ADT's directors to the four-man compensation committee, which quickly adopted ADT's more generous compensation schemes. Under the plan, Kozlowski's total compensation rocketed from $8.8 million in 1997 to $170 million in 1999.

Still it was not enough. During this period, Kozlowski allegedly utilized his relocation accounts and an employee corporate loan program (a program designed to help employees pay taxes due on stock granted under a Tyco stock ownership plan) to buy homes, artwork, jewelry, and a 1930's vintage yacht. He is also accused of using the accounts to reward favored executives, provide huge charitable gifts in his name, and throw extravagant parties.

One such party was a fortieth birthday celebration Kozlowski threw for his wife on the Mediterranean island of Sardinia. He allegedly spent more than $2 million on the event, which included an ice sculpture of Michelangelo's *David*, which was noteworthy for the fact that vodka poured from his penis.

It did not stop there, either. According to the indictment filed by New York State, Kozlowski was running a sophisticated criminal enterprise—so sophisticated, in fact, that prosecutors named it "Top Executives Criminal Enterprise," which they used to describe Kozlowski's management team throughout the indictment. Some of the other excesses the State accused Kozlowski of included:

- Deciding what bonuses would be paid to whom, and when, without regard to restrictions that the board placed on executive compensation.
- Hiding unauthorized bonuses in transactions booked as "nonrecurring charges."
- Using the company treasury to pay his personal bills.
- Publicly supporting Tyco stock while privately selling it.
- Using corporate money to purchase directors' residences at greatly inflated prices.
- Selling corporate residences to him at far less than fair value.
- Influencing the removal and replacement of a stock analyst deemed unfriendly to Tyco's stock.

Case Study (continued)

The SEC piled on the offenses by including in its complaint that Kozlowski:

- Used $7 million of Tyco's funds to purchase a Park Avenue apartment for his first wife, from whom he had been separated.
- Forgave tens of millions of dollars in loans to executives and directors, including himself.
- Accelerated the vesting of Tyco stock for himself and others.
- Used corporate money to buy his New Hampshire house for three times its apparent fair market value.

At some point, the excess just becomes silly.

Why a person legitimately making $170 million in a single year would put it all on the line by embezzling from his company is one for the psychoanalysts. After all, how many multimillion-dollar homes can one reasonably use? Dennis owned houses in the posh districts of Greenwich, Connecticut; Boca Raton, Florida; Nantucket, Massachusetts; New York City; and Beaver Creek, Colorado. His next home may be the decidedly unposh Riker's Island. Unlike the federal government, the State of New York does not maintain a high-end prison system for executives. At 56 years old, any time spent in prison will be hard time for Dennis.

STEP 4: WHO'S READING YOUR E-MAIL?

The threat of unauthorized system access and the damage an intruder can do to a business is increasing daily. The more business relies on technology, the greater the danger, but the risks seem to be worth it. Automated systems have improved the productivity of businesses by performing repetitive and mundane tasks quickly and accurately. Technology can enhance corporate performance, leading to a culture of continuous improvement that can result in competitive advantage. But continuous improvement requires a formal periodic checkup of the systems to determine their health. Many companies utilize the Malcolm Baldrige National Quality Award criteria to evaluate their systems. The award is given annually to U.S. companies in recognition of their quality achievement. This rigorous process improves the quality of any system review. Many companies using the model report that the process increases productivity, reduces waste, lowers costs, improves margins, and, most importantly, creates satisfied customers.

While well-designed systems will provide performance feedback and stimulate positive change, the integrity of the data and the system must be sound. Data cannot be corrupted or systems compromised, which could lead to an operational loss and customer dissatisfaction. Statistics often cite that 80 percent of attacks on computer systems originate from within the company. Strong access controls can provide the necessary integrity. An evaluation of any system must encompass not only customer focus (the output the system is designed to deliver), but also the soundness of the system. While most attacks come from within a company, implementing system controls as a tool used solely for punishment can be as dangerous as the system vulnerabilities themselves. Nearly all employees will act honestly and appropriately, and may accidentally bump up against control boundaries now and then. Overreacting to a single inadvertent boundary contact may send a message to employees that initiative and creativity are not welcomed and may limit operational improvements. Just because an employee attempts access to a restricted level in a system does not mean it was for an illicit purpose. But it is important that employees know what is acceptable, and gentle redirection of their efforts is important to maintaining a strong control culture.

Those intent on disrupting or taking advantage of your systems will surface through their own repeated pattern of probing and testing system boundaries. An alert manager will recognize serial offenses and, when identified, take strong corrective action to redirect the behavior of the employee toward company objectives, or else remove the employee to protect the company culture. Publicly redirecting employee behavior is in itself a powerful message to an organization. It communicates that the company is aware of boundary probes and takes them seriously.

The process of delineating, assigning, and supervising access levels must be included in a system assessment. For most applications, determining access is not a technology function, rather a business function. This is because access controls are not designed to prevent legitimate business from happening; instead, their function is to ensure the integrity of a company's systems. Those who have a legitimate business purpose for accessing a system module or application should be welcomed and encouraged to use all of the system's attributes to achieve the best possible results. The business manager is best positioned to determine who should have access, and the depth of that access.

At the investment banking firm ING Barings, technology and business owners are assigned to each business system. Together they plan and prioritize system and improvement upgrades. The technology owner makes certain that programmer access is properly controlled, and the business manager takes responsibility for assigning admission to system users. Admittance requests are approved by the appropriate system owner and forwarded to Information Risk Management, which independently evaluates the requests for any conflicting rights.

The needs of the business are, however, sometimes in conflict with good internal control. To illustrate, let's listen in on a phone call between Jane, a risk manager, and Irene, the manager of the wire room, regarding new access rights to Irene's employee:

Jane: Hi Irene, it's Jane.

Irene: Hi, what's up?

Jane: I received your request to assign John, whom I believe is your wire room supervisor, the right to release wire payment instructions.

Irene: That's right.

Jane: Well, I notice that he already has wire creation capability, so he could create and release a wire without anyone else involved in the process. As you know, we like to see at least two sets of eyes—and ideally three—review a payment request before it is executed.

Irene: I understand, but I need to delegate my supervisory responsibility to John. I just do not have time to do it any longer, given the new wire room installation project.

Jane: That's fine, but we should remove the wire creation capability.

Irene: But then there will be no backup for the clerk. We will have to hire a new clerk just to provide backup. That just does not make any sense.

Jane: I agree that does not make sense. Why don't we remove John's ability to create a wire? And if the clerk is absent, I can temporarily reinstate his capability. You could then perform the supervisory function in a backup capacity to John.

Irene: I guess that works. Alright, restrict the wire creation module.

Jane: Done. I'll see you at the operation's manager meeting this afternoon.

As we learned earlier, the creation of the transfer should be segregated from the approval and release of the wire payment. Normally, a clerk would prepare the wire instructions and a supervisor would release it for processing. When these processes are not segregated, a good risk manager will challenge the assignments. In our example, Jane not only challenged access rights, but also helped design a solution. Additional responsibilities of an information risk manager include monitoring unauthorized access attempts and reporting them to the appropriate system owner. They also coordinate a quarterly review of access levels with system owners to guarantee that access levels are current.

Technology management will generally address the operational risk of internal programmers and outside technology consultants through a rigorous change control program. Change control procedures make certain that all software upgrades or changes to code are properly tested in a environment that is separate from, but identical to, the live production environment. The code is only moved into production after both the technology *and* business owners sign off that they are satisfied as to the level of testing and readiness of the change.

Legacy systems, those systems put into service several years ago, can raise unique control issues. A former client of mine, a financial institution located in midtown Manhattan, has a proprietary client tracking system written and maintained by a single programmer. The system maintains customer information such as addresses and phone numbers. It preserves a log of client contacts, regardless of which salesperson makes the contact, so the firm does not trip over itself trying to oversell. It also tracks buy and sell recommendations, and has functionality to help salespeople mail research to the client list. Both the architecture and the programming language are archaic, but the system works and the salespeople like it. They do not want to take time to learn another system no matter what bells and whistles it may have. They also like the fact that they can request changes to the program and have them implemented immediately by the programmer.

Despite user satisfaction with the system, management is taking on massive risk, which they are only now beginning to understand. The archaic infrastructure of this system is already visible, as it is straining to meet current demand. Additional growth without addressing the platform could render it useless. It is also likely that the vendor providing the programming tools used to maintain the system will soon decline further support of this product due to its age. Furthermore, there is no change control process in place; rather, all changes are made directly to live production. Mistakes made in production could bring down the system. Finally, there is no documentation for this system or related processes. If an angry programmer went in and deleted the program, it would be permanently lost.

No programmer should have unfettered access to production unless an emergency situation exists. Furthermore, any changes to a computer program should be performed and tested on a standalone test server before implementation. In such an environment, code can be checked for security flaws before it is installed. Once tested, implementation can be safely approved by appropriate technology management.

Sometimes, systems require emergency service in production, and in these rare instances, a password lockbox procedure can be effective. Under such a system, the programmer can approach the data system manager, who keeps one half of a password to attain access to the system; the programmer possesses the other half. At the request of the senior technology management, the data center supervisor can release the password so that the programmer can access the system at detailed levels. Senior technology management can then audit the work performed in production and ensure the integrity of the systems. The data center manager changes the password after each use and places it back in the lockbox.

The importance of change control is illustrated by the alleged rigging of a bet placed at the 2002 Breeders' Cup, one of the nation's great horse racing events. In a con reminiscent of the classic movie *The Sting*, with Paul Newman and Robert Redford, a modern-day Newman character, a "rogue software engineer," exploited a weakness in a wagering program to change bets subsequent to the race. Working with his former college fraternity brothers, the team would bet pick six tickets, which required that the holder pick the winning horse in six straight races. As a matter of procedure, betting information was not immediately processed; rather, it was compiled until after the fifth race and then transmitted to a processing center. The software engineer allegedly changed the bets of his college fraternity brothers to ensure they had the winners of the first five races. The ticket holders then picked every horse in the field for the final race to guarantee a payoff. The payoff on this day was in excess of $3 million, which initially drew the attention of authorities; then the unusual nature of the bet ensured an investigation. If not for the large payoff, one wonders whether the fraud would have been detected by existing controls or, for that matter, investigated at all. We do have some insight into this question as it was discovered that two previous bets were placed that went undiscovered. The first bet paid $1,152, and the second $104, 560. Neither was so large or unique as to raise suspicion. Only the large and illogical bet called attention to the alleged fraud. A well-designed change control testing program will identify "rogue code" and prevent potential losses such as this before a bet is placed. Under such a program, no changes can be made to an active system without testing on a separate test server. And, then, the migration of new code into production is closely supervised. If changes are made to production on an emergency basis, the review of code changes should be signed off by a supervisor knowledgeable about the code of the system.

While most system attacks originate from within a company, the trend is changing. The Computer Security Institute and the Federal Bureau of Investigation's Annual Computer Crime and Security Survey found that 70 percent of companies cited their Internet connections as a frequent point of attack in 2001. Protecting an organization's systems from outside incursions is primarily the responsibility of the chief technology officer. The information technology department is best positioned to know the methods hackers use to infiltrate a company's network and how to protect the firm from outside threats.

At a minimum, all managers should evaluate the systems used to produce their product or deliverable, identified in Smart Link Step 1, and discuss with their technology partner what they can do to protect their systems from inside and outside threats. A major priority for all managers is to evaluate access rights for each system to guarantee proper segregation of duties, such as the wire transfer process we studied earlier, as well as business purpose (is there a need for this employee to have this level of access?). As we learned earlier, the information risk manager can be good resource to help with this analysis. If your company does not have a risk manager, system auditors and technology consultants can also be useful resources for analyzing admission capabilities. Closing system accessibility gaps can occur quickly and significantly improve the integrity of the process.

STEP 5: WHAT'S IT REALLY WORTH?

Undetected product defects can generate large operational losses. Solid quality-assurance procedures will continually test your products to make certain that they meet customer standards. Implementing Six Sigma procedures in a process can help identify and eliminate product defects. The Six Sigma framework uses data and statistical analysis to measure performance. It refers to the targeted results, which is 3.4 defects per 1 million opportunities. Regardless of the process employed, testing procedures should be frequent enough to ensure that bad product can be identified prior to shipment to the customer. Infrequent or tardy testing can result in lost productivity, product liability, and damage to a company's reputation.

In June and July 2002, Con Agra announced the recall of more than 19 million pounds of beef products contaminated with the E coli bacterium. The beef was produced in the Greeley, Colorado, plant from April 12, 2002, through July 11, 2002. For 34 production days over a three-month period, the plant produced defective product without detection. The Centers for Disease Control (CDC) documented multiple cases of illness connected to the recalled beef. While the Department of Agriculture regularly inspects plants for safety, a proper testing program for E coli would have identified the contamination sooner and prevented one of the largest recalls in history. Preventive measures also would have protected a number of people from getting sick. Plant management should have insisted on receiving frequent and timely testing reports. Effective reporting would have communicated the quality of the product produced. If applied correctly, testing procedures could have prevented the additional production of millions of pounds of contaminated beef. Quality assurance procedures are not always easy or inexpensive to introduce, but compared to the damage done to the reputation of a company, the litigation, and the costs of a recall, testing is cheap. If they are effectively implemented, they can lead to immediate improvement in productivity and cost savings.

Quality assurance procedures are not only applicable to goods; service and information deliverables should also go through this process to guarantee that the service or information provided to a client meets expectations. Such procedures might include a supervisory review of a report to be delivered to a client, or the corroboration of information contained in the work product to a second source. Independent inspections and consumer satisfaction surveys are among other quality-control tools that can be utilized to evaluate the effectiveness of a service after it has been performed.

Periodic revaluation and counting of inventory and other assets will detect whether any are missing, as well as whether there has been impairment of values that should be disclosed to executive management, the board of directors, and investors. How often they should be appraised is a matter of judgment, but as a general rule, the more liquid or marketable the asset, the more often it should be revalued and counted, as illustrated in Exhibit 6.3. Prices for liquid assets, such as foreign currency and securities, can rise and fall in value very quickly; therefore, they should be priced more frequently than real estate or other illiquid possessions.

EXHIBIT 6.3 ASSET VALUATION AND VALIDATION FREQUENCY TO LIQUIDITY RELATIONSHIP

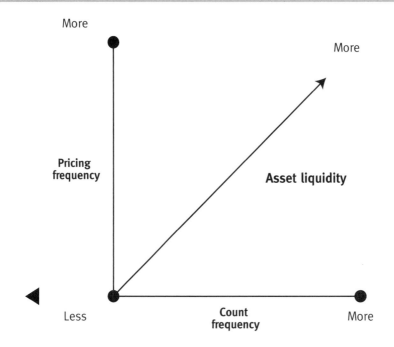

The valuation of holdings can cut both ways. If a company does not write down impaired assets, stock values may be artificially high based on those values. If a company does write them down, only to sell them later for full price, margin and profits will be artificially boosted. Obviously, there is plenty of room for manipulation.

Gateway, Inc., the computer manufacturer known for shipping its product in printed boxes resembling the hide of a cow, recently settled a lawsuit for more than $10 million. The complaint alleged that Gateway failed to write down impaired assets in a timely manner. When the company eventually revealed its plans to take a $200 million charge, the stock was devastated. Within minutes, billions of dollars in market capitalization were lost.

Another technology giant, Cisco Systems, recently reported taking a $2.5 billion charge against the value of its inventory. To put this in perspective, it is nearly equal to the cost of goods sold for an entire quarter. Some Wall Street analysts question whether Cisco's assets were really impaired, that perhaps the company was simply positioning itself to boost margins at a later date.

If I were a director of Cisco, I would be interested to know how the impairment was identified and which process was used to value the inventory. To ensure that asset values are properly recorded, the valuation of the assets should be performed by someone independent of the custody and approval functions. An outside valuation firm would be the most desirable; conversely, a rough calculation by the CFO would be the least desirable. Certain questions need to be answered, including: How much of the impaired inventory was sold in the last month? What is the trend and does it support the impaired value? Good performance indicators such as these would ensure that reported valuations seem reasonable. Finally, the decision to value the inventory should happen at regular intervals, and the decision to take a large write-off should relate to the fall in the prices of the assets since the last valuation.

Financial institutions often have trouble with pricing their inventory. The same principles that apply to technology and other segments of the economy also apply here. Poor segregation has led to traders and managers manipulating the valuation of their investments and securities to prevent losses that might impact their compensation. Earlier, I related many cases where traders managed to overstate assets and related profits. These included NatWest's Papoulis ($100 million), Sumitomo's Hamanaka ($1.8 billion.), Kidder's Joe Jett ($350 million), Plains All American's James Stewart ($162 million), Barings Nick Leeson ($1.2 billion), and Allfirst's John Rusak ($750 million).

While I was employed there, the international investment banking giant Goldman Sachs implemented a monthly valuation process to price its corporate bond portfolios. These procedures ensured that no single individual could set an artificial price. A program would receive pricing data from several sources and match them to the firm's securities. Where at least two prices were materially close, one of the sources would be used. For instance, if Reuters reported a price of a bond at 104 7/8, and Bloomberg quoted the same bond at 104 3/4, then the market values might be deemed close enough and the most conservative value would be used. If the prices were materially different, or there was only one or no price quoted, then the market would be deemed too illiquid to produce solid price discovery. In such a case, a pricing committee consisting of senior management would determine a price. This process brought more objectivity into the valuation process and a large measure of control.

The frequency at which assets should be counted is also a matter of judgment. It is harder to conduct a major fraud moving hard assets, but it can and has been done. In fact, the once venerable Arthur Andersen, recently undone by fraud and corporate scandal, initially made its name by paying attention to details and uncovering theft of hard assets. A story recently retold in the *Chicago Tribune*, describes how, in 1969, a young Andersen auditor was sent to certify the inventory of a million bricks. He counted the pallets over and over again, but kept coming up 100,000 bricks short. The angry factory owner refused to believe the young auditor and told him to count the bricks once again. Again, the count was 900,000. The factory owner finally investigated and determined that the plant manager had been taking bricks out of the back gate after hours. Performed competently, independent verification is an extremely effective method of validating assets.

In order to establish the basis for counting and validating hard assets, a good tracking system must be in place and operating effectively. If there is no effective basis, then you can count all you want, but there is nothing to validate the count against. In the case of the brickyard, the factory owner knew that there should have been 1 million bricks. This information set the baseline for the auditor's count.

To illustrate further, the General Accounting Office (GAO), the auditing arm of Congress, recently reported that the Pentagon's system for tracking protective biochemical gear is flawed. Nearly 1.5 million sets of trousers, jackets, gloves, and boots specially designed to protect against biohazards have been issued and cannot be completely accounted for. As the United States faces an increasing number of hostile countries suspected of harboring weapons of mass destruction, it might be a good idea to determine which items can be accounted for, which soldiers have the gear, and where they are located. In this case, it is not just a matter of money; lives are on the line.

There are a number of factors to consider when determining a count schedule for assets. These include liquidity, whether the asset is fungible, scarcity, size, mobility, value, and regulatory requirements. Product inventory should be taken at least once a year. Auditors will likely call for a real estate investment trust (REIT) to value its real estate holdings annually. Regulations demand quarterly security counts for brokers/dealers. Given the mobility of trucks, earth-moving equipment, trailers, and the like, these items should be counted after every construction project.

While unlikely to be material to all but the smallest public companies, the issuance of corporate assets to employees should also be periodically validated. At specific intervals, each employee should attest that he or she does have a laptop, pager, cell phone, and so on, in order to corroborate that the records are accurate and that the assets have not been misappropriated.

STEP 6: GROWTH BUSTERS!

Many of the companies making headlines today have experienced years of incredible growth. Enron, Tyco, and WorldCom all entered into new businesses or acquired entire companies to help fuel their expansion. Growth, by itself, is a key indicator of success, and it had turned these companies into "Wall Street darlings." But business expansion can also cover up a number of sins. Serious control issues can surface if a company is ill-prepared to manage escalation of the business and its implications. A company must solicit feedback from its managers and employees regarding its ability to handle planned growth. Key indicators regarding a company's preparedness include capacity utilization and throughput thresholds (the physical limits of machines and other capital assets employed); employee training, overtime capacity and morale; and the ability to acquire resources needed to meet increased demand. Expansion places stress on an organization's culture, processes, and resources. If the company finds itself unable to meet customer commitments, its reputation will be damaged, and operational losses could result.

Not all businesses will grow, however; it may be the strategy of an organization to simply maintain operations in order to funnel resources to other areas with brighter prospects. Once the strategy is known, a good planning process will gather cross-functional teams to prepare detailed plans to execute the strategy. If growth is a strategic aim, each process supporting the business must be evaluated to determine whether it can still meet corporate objectives at a higher operating level. The current manufacturing capacity of the plant and the availability of trained labor and components are some of the issues to consider. What will be the impact of growth on customer delivery times, product quality, employee morale, cost structure, other important internal projects or initiatives, and the suppliers? These types of questions need to be asked and answered. Once any adjustments are made, feedback regarding how well the organization is responding will be required so that improvements can be made. This will take the form of key performance indicators that are most relevant to each individual business. For example, the number of employees satisfactorily completing a training program may be a key metric if management believes that not having enough well-trained employees could be the company's greatest vulnerability. Or product defect percentage may be a key metric if management perceives that higher volume could put a strain on existing manufacturing processes. At higher volumes, machines wear faster, need more maintenance and calibration, and can result in higher defect levels and lower productivity per unit of product. Regardless of the indicator, a planned and measured strategy can lead to sustainable growth. As with a car, a "pedal to the metal" growth strategy can blow the engine or end in a speed-induced disaster. Good managers identify such problems before they occur or as they are occurring so that the organization can adjust and survive to compete another day.

Take Lincoln Electric, long one of the premier manufacturers of arc-welding products in the world. Lincoln got that way by being a pioneer in combining a bonus system with piecework. In a piecework compensation system, employees are paid based on the number of units they produce rather than the number of hours they work. At the end of the year, bonuses earned were given to each employee "based on four criteria: quantity of work, quality of work, dependability, and cooperation."[1] This system made Lincoln an efficient and fierce competitor whose employees earned among the highest remuneration in the world. In the late 1980s, Lincoln went on an extensive globalization program. Over a five-year period, the company expanded into Japan, Venezuela, Brazil, Germany, Norway, the United Kingdom, the Netherlands, Spain, and Mexico. In certain countries, such as Germany, the company bought existing businesses, and in others, such as Japan, it built new plants.

Prior to this expansion, Lincoln had little experience manufacturing and competing in foreign countries, and the pace of the international development effort left little room for determining what was working and what was not. By 1992, the company was in serious trouble. Its U.S. operations were still performing well, but the foreign operations were performing so poorly, they threatened the survival of the company. The primary problem was that the "European culture was hostile to the piecework and bonus system."[2] Lincoln also did not have many managers with international experience to help them identify and manage their problems overseas, so the CEO found it necessary to move to Europe to oversee management of the crisis. To get out of the mess, management implemented a strategy that called for the U.S. company profits to offset the foreign losses. A substantial amount of Lincoln's capital was invested in employee training and the company was not about to dismiss its U.S. employees, so management leveled with them and called on them to help increase production and sales in the United States in order to increase cash flow. It can take "two to three years for an employee to learn to properly run some of the equipment,"[3] so veterans were called on to postpone vacations and work on weekends to make the new production targets. The company curtailed operations in the United Kingdom, Spain, France, Norway, and the Netherlands. It closed down the entire German operation, as it was clear that the employees there were not willing to work harder to turn the operation around. Lincoln also shut down its Japanese operations as it became clear that its action of going it alone had been an insult to the local culture. The company could not continue to compete in the country without a partner. The strategy worked; by 1994, even the remaining European operations were earning a profit.

There are many lessons to be learned from Lincoln's story, but I found that the most intriguing one was that, for a well-managed company, the original plan for growth was not well-thought-out at all. The company did not recognize that the compensation structure that made it great would not work elsewhere. It also did not recognize that it did not have the management talent to compete in so many different markets. Lincoln discovered too late that it needed a partner to compete in Japan. The turnaround, however, was well-planned, and based on Lincoln's strength: its U.S. operations. Managers knew what the U.S. company was capable of, and with some management of manufacturing and labor constraints, met their higher targets and saved the company. The Lincoln story represents both the best and worst in planning for growth.

The strategy and planning of an enterprise must also consider the need for business continuity. Earlier I noted that operational risk was arguably the only risk that all managers must be concerned with. Many business leaders would also argue that event risk associated with a disaster should also be a concern of every manager; in fact, some would classify it as an operational risk. Even with the presence of an appointed owner for disaster recovery planning (DRP), there is little question that every manager should prepare his or her own detailed plan. Each manager should understand, challenge, and make his or her own preparations for unique situations not covered by the DRP process.

Preparing an organization to respond appropriately to a disaster is a significant undertaking and the subject of many books; hence, it is beyond the scope of this text. However, a number of relevant steps will be covered here: those a manager can take to ensure that his or her company's operations will be properly supported after a disaster strikes. It is likely a DRP coordinator will agree with senior management in advance on the type of investment the firm will have in off-site recovery facilities and backup systems. Each manager needs to understand these capabilities and how they will affect them. The way an enterprise responds to a blackout may be different from how it deals with a transit strike, or the loss of a data center or even the closing of a building. Questions to ask a DRP coordinator might include:

- Who is responsible for declaring an emergency?
- Who will be our contact point, and how will I or my staff be notified?
- Is there a policy with regard to media contact and, if so, who is authorized to speak on behalf of the firm?
- Does the firm have arrangements with local hotels in case of an event?
- If transit is disrupted, has the firm created a transportation plan?
- Is there an off-site disaster recovery (DR) facility? How do we get there?
- Under what circumstances will the DR facilities be activated?
- How long will it take for the DR facility to become fully operational (warm site versus hot site)?
- What system capabilities will we have at the DR facility?
- Have the business systems been tested?
- How much information might have to be reconstructed?
- How many of my staff will be able to work at the DR facility?

Based on the responses received, a manager may need to make adjustments to the recovery plan. Assuming that the company has a DRP coordinator and a developed plan, what else should a manager consider to plan for this type of event risk? Some considerations include:

- Determine the key personnel needed to maintain the business. If there is not room for them at a DR site, then consideration must be given to ensure they can access systems from home.

- Have a plan in place in the event of a transit strike. Carpooling or private bus transportation might be a means to address this risk. Ensure that those responsible for carpooling know who they are responsible for and where they are going before the strike occurs.

- For key personnel, ensure access to hotel rooms to keep them close to the office or DR site.

- Prepare a "calling tree." Keep a call list at home in case access to the office is lost.

- Store off-site hard copies of documents (such as legal contracts) that may be needed during an emergency.

- Back up critical data daily, particularly if the data could be lost in the void between the last data center backup and the disaster.

- Keep a first-aid kit easily attainable. Be advised who on the staff is trained in CPR.

- Ensure the team is practiced in evacuation procedures. Instill a policy of taking no chances with personal safety. Enforce fire drill participation. Ensure everyone knows their role.

Many managers may not believe that this type of preparation is worth their time and effort, regarding the chances of an event affecting them as slim. To dispel this belief, I point out that, in my career, I have lost access to my building and everything I had in it (One World Trade in 1993), lost access to a data center for several hours (which is the lifeblood of a trading operation), had an electrical short in a building that shut down power for a day, and had to once plan for a transit strike. If you think you will never be the victim of such an event, then surely you will experience one. The question is, how well prepared will you be to respond in a time of crisis?

My loss of access to the World Trade Center is related to an event most people have already heard about. I was working for Deloitte & Touche (D&T) on the one-hundredth floor of the WTC in 1993 when that terrorist attack occurred. Smoke and dust from the explosion not only made the space uninhabitable for a period of time, but the computers and all the floppy disks had to be cleaned before the computers could be used again. Fortunately, the firm did back up its systems in another location, so only a little over a day's worth of data was lost in the "void." And although D&T did not have an off-site recovery facility for staff use, it did have other office space in town. Most of the staff reassembled in the firm's midtown building, sharing desks, offices, computers—you name it. Not the most eloquent or comfortable recovery, but it was cost-effective and it did work. Audits and other engagements were completed, and the related financial statements were filed on time. Remarkably, most clients felt no service delivery effects at all—a worthy goal of any disaster recovery plan.

Without a successful recovery, it is not hard to imagine the damage Deloitte & Touche's reputation would have suffered. Each audit team would have had to start over, putting an additional burden on its clients and delaying the issuance of financial statements on which the investment community relies. The consulting business, which recommends proper system redundancy, may have been dealt a fatal blow. Customers could rightly point out that the firm did not practice what it preached. Instead, the firm had a success story it could use to help sell more services. Clear evidence that disaster recovery planning pays.

Several years later, while I was working at ING Barings, the data center shut itself down. We quickly determined that the preaction fire-suppression system malfunctioned and flooded the sprinkler pipes with water in preparation for putting out a detected fire. This action automatically triggered the emergency shutdown of the computer systems to protect them from exposure to water. Fortunately, since there was no fire, the water never released. However, the firm's traders had to conduct business without systems until the data center could reboot all of the computers and bring them online. Due to the complexity of the systems, a reboot can take several hours—long enough to be painful, but not long enough to arrange for bringing a "warm" backup facility online. The trading floor immediately went to manual trading blotters and cell phones to conduct business until the systems became available.

Prime Brokerage was a separate unit at ING Barings, which primarily supported hedge funds. Services included putting ING technology on clients' desktops to help them manage their business. Service outages could be catastrophic since the clients relied on these systems to manage their market exposure. The firm invested in a "hot recovery site" for this business, where operations could easily be switched over intraday. (The primary difference between a hot site and a warm site is recovery time and cost. A warm site can take a few days to make completely operational. A hot site runs parallel with the primary operations of the business and can be switched over in a matter of minutes. The cost between the two options can run into hundreds of thousands, even millions, of dollars, depending on the complexity of the business.) The senior management of the Prime Brokerage business wisely decided that it was in the best interest of its customers to invest in hot-site capability. Its clients did experience an outage when the data center went down, but of much shorter duration than it otherwise would have been. Systems were quickly switched over to the hot site and service was restored.

ING Barings had assessed its risk and apportioned capital to those businesses it deemed most critical. On a day such as this, management was rewarded for their foresight. According to trading management, there was no material financial impact from the outage, and the firm adequately protected the Prime Brokerage franchise. In short, everything worked as it was supposed to that day, except for the faulty fire-suppression alarm that started the event. Subsequently, the management team reassembled the engineers and contractors who designed and constructed the fire-suppression system and performed a rigorous reevaluation, repair, and testing program.

Not long after ABN Amro bought ING Barings' U.S. broker/dealer operations, the building containing the trading floor experienced an electrical short in a vent fan, which shut down power to the entire building. I was part of a transition team responsible for ensuring the smooth transfer of ABN's operations to its newly purchased operating platform. The first few weeks of business were critical to ABN Amro, as it needed to make a statement in the marketplace that it was now bigger and stronger than ever. A systems outage could be a serious business setback. However, most employees did not even notice the outage; the backup batteries and generators automatically kicked in, allowing all systems to continue to operate until the building was able to bring power back online. I remember the COO saying that the backup system paid for itself that day.

A final example relates to the transit strike that was called by the employees of the Mass Transit Authority of New York City and that threatened to shut down public transportation in all five metropolitan boroughs. For most event risk, you do not know what will trigger it or when; you have to plan for *all* contingencies. This event was different from most in that we were given notice that it was likely to happen in a little over a week. In my last position at ING Barings, I had decision rights over the transportation services provided by the firm. My travel team was responsible for procurement of car services and employee travel. As soon as the general manager of that team heard about the upcoming strike, she took on the task of business continuity planning for this event. In a little over a week, she was able to investigate possible service levels, have costs approved by senior management, contract with a private bus company, and communicate the plan to the approximately 2,000 people working in the New York office. In effect, she set up a fully functional bus company, complete with routes and timetables. If a strike occurred, the firm had transportation to move key employees to the office and back at a cost that was minor compared to the revenues that could be generated. If the strike did not take place, the downside to the firm would be the loss of a $30,000 deposit. The strike never materialized, but not one manager complained about losing the deposit. It was recognized by all that the cost/reward ratio was well worth the commitment.

The moral of these stories is that events happen regularly. Anticipate them in advance and have your action-steps in place. Don't get caught planning your response while an event is unfolding. There is no excuse to compromise the safety of your people and stakeholder assets by ignoring event risk.

STEP 7: HAS YOUR SHIP SAILED?

Step 5 addressed the importance of performing a quality assurance check of the product during the manufacturing process. This step addresses the implementation of controls at the point of shipment. Good process design will not only ensure that shipments to customers are complete and accurate, but that they are going to "real" customers, whose profiles are in line with company and regulatory policy.

One Fortune 100 consumer products company, which asked not to be identified, provides insight into how strong regulatory and operational controls are implemented. It is one of the largest producers of feminine hygiene goods in the world. Some of these products are regulated by the Food and Drug Administration (FDA) to ensure consumer safety. Poor materials handling can result in contamination that could lead to toxic shock syndrome, a serious and deadly condition. The company has adopted a belts-and-suspenders approach to product quality, and has implemented safety and release controls throughout the manufacturing process, not just at the point of shipment. This process begins when it receives raw material into its plant.

The company requires that its vendors not only identify shipments by lot number, but also the date of production to ensure inventory is not aged. When received, the materials are tested for bioburden (microorganisms) that could contaminate the end product. The results of the testing take five days, at which time the material can be released for production. Cotton is one raw material that undergoes this process. When released for processing, the cotton is turned into an intermediate material, which is tested again for bioburden; when released, it is turned into the end product. Before shipment, the items are then tested again and held in quarantine until the final test results come back five days later. A lot cannot be approved for release unless it is taken off "hold" and each has been assigned a date that allows a loader to easily identify it. Only one person in the plant has approval to release a lot on hold; and the inventory system will provide an alert if one has been misidentified as shippable. If the results are favorable, the products are then released. As a final check, a loader will manually match the shipment to a bill of lading or listing of contents to make sure it contains the correct lots. The result is that management has put in a series of testing and shipment controls that ensures that orders are properly filled and that eliminates the possibility of contaminated product reaching its consumers.

The strong process at this company reflects its culture of putting worker safety and product quality first. A manager at one of the company's plants told me that every meeting starts with worker and product safety metrics. Other issues always come later. She also told me that, periodically, there has been pressure to move product out of quarantine and into distribution centers prior to test results coming back. In theory, the product could still be intercepted prior to reaching consumers. But, once the goods leave the plant, their management loses a measure of control and it becomes more difficult to ensure that defective product does not accidentally make it to market. The company has always determined that it does not want to take any risk with consumer health, hence has resisted such a move, no matter how much money it might save. The employees at the company understand management's commitment to safety and take pride in working for an organization that walks the talk when it comes to quality.

STEP 8: KEEP EVERYONE HAPPY

Feedback can take many forms, from customer-initiated complaints or product returns to solicited surveys. Feedback can also come from other sources, such as the government, professional associations, industry associations, consumer or other special-interest advocacy groups, lawsuits, and so on. The problem with many organizations is that they perceive these important kinds of communication only as threats; or worse, they see them as a nuisance and ignore them.

Take Bridgestone Corporation as an example. The company recently conducted a massive recall of the Firestone ATX tire. According to a filed complaint, it was alleged that Bridgestone had knowledge of thousands of product failures directly related to tires manufactured at an Illinois plant. The lawsuit alleged that more than 2,200 rollover accidents, 500 serious injuries, and 150 fatalities had occurred by 2000 and were reported to the company. These incidents took place over a number of years, yet the tires continued to be produced. In addition to the costs of the recall and related litigation, the damage to the reputation of the Firestone brand cannot be understated.

A feedback process that contains best-practice attributes helps a company to compile, analyze, and respond to outside communication, regardless of the source. This practice not only provides information to aid a continuous improvement program, but also can alert an organization to operational issues or fraud. To be effective, the feedback has to be received by an entity independent of the one delivering the product, such as a main customer support center. By centralizing the collection of complaints, the issues can be categorized and sent to the appropriate manager for investigation. More important, the complaint can be tracked by senior management to ensure it is properly investigated and resolved.

In a former role, I managed a group of departments that included oversight responsibility for a general services department that performed procurement and mailroom functions. Calls were received frequently from vendors who hoped to sell us their services or to convince us to increase the firm's current spending on their products or services. Some were looking to offer perks to management in order to gain favor. Though a nuisance, all calls were eventually returned. One particular vendor of courier services called several times during a particular day trying to reach me. I did finally return the call and, rather than the expected sales pitch, I heard a story of how our mailroom supervisor was trying to shake down the vendor. The resulting investigation revealed that the employee had a severely ill family member, was in financial distress, and was allegedly soliciting a kickback to help ease the financial crunch. Our security department, with the aid of the vendor, was able to tape a conversation implicating the mailroom supervisor. He subsequently admitted guilt; and, as painful as it was for management, given his situation, he was terminated. The point is, even nuisance calls can provide important feedback and should not be ignored.

Returned merchandise can also provide important feedback. If there is a problem with the product, the returned merchandise can be analyzed, reasons for the defect investigated, and adjustments made to the design and creation of the product. For instance, perhaps the Send key on a cell phone tends to stick and the manufacturer experiences a spike in customer returns. The company might investigate and find that a certain batch of keys provided by a vendor was not within the specified size tolerance; or perhaps it was not properly inserted during the manufacturing process. Regardless of the cause, by acting on the information, the company can identify and correct the problem before it becomes more widespread. If the customer rejected the product due to performance relative to alternatives, this information can be assimilated into product research and design. Perhaps a competitor offers third-generation (3G) cell phone service. The company might note a falloff in new sales and renewals, but not enough to justify an acceleration of its own 3G product offering. Further investigation might also reveal that cost is a major impediment to the acceptance of 3G service. This information can be useful to managing the company's cash flow and competitive strategy. The organization may decide not to rush the service to market, which could increase costs, but to focus on finding the most efficient way to deliver it at a date not too far in the future. Finally, if a product is returned in good condition, segregated procedures should ensure that it is received and returned to inventory. A clerk separate from the receiving function should record the item as inventory, which will be periodically compared to an actual count.

So, contact with outside stakeholders is another means of gathering valuable feedback, which can lead to better operations, happier customers, and greater profits. Furthermore, ignoring stakeholder information can no longer be considered harmless; rather, it can lead to massive operational losses. If Bridgestone had listened to customer complaints, it might have identified product defects sooner. Every manager and every enterprise should evaluate how stakeholders interact with their business and determine how information is captured.

STEP 9: CASH IS THE SAME AS MONEY

The cash receipts process is particularly vulnerable to manipulation and fraud. Depending on the type of business, it can also be one of the easiest to control. As the widespread use of credit cards, debit cards, and the establishment of bank lockboxes takes hold, it becomes increasingly likely that all customer payments will be received directly into corporate accounts at financial institutions. Since such payments are never received by a company employee, the custody function has been effectively segregated from recording and authorization functions.

Alternative and backup procedures can be implemented, but if payment is received directly into the company, whoever opens the mail will have access to the receipts and will effectively control the recording process. It will be up to them to log the checks and make sure they are prepared for deposit. For instance, if checks are received directly into the company, one preventive control would be to have two people present at the time the mail is opened. One can open the mail, stamp checks "For Deposit Only" together with the name of the company, and then communicate to the other employee the customer name, invoice number, and payment amount so that it can be recorded by the employee for processing in company systems. The person who opens the mail can then prepare the deposit. Someone completely separate from this process should be responsible for reconciling the account. This will provide a detective control if a payment is not deposited.

These procedures are most certainly *not* appropriate for retail businesses where transactions are primarily consummated with cash. For these organizations, strong reconciliation controls must be implemented. A clerk not associated with sales should compare cash register balances to sales and, eventually, to bank statements. The risk still exists that an employee will omit a transaction entirely from the register. Alternative controls, such as offering customers half off if they do not get a receipt, surveillance cameras, or regular merchandise counts, can mitigate this risk. The movement of money also increases the risk of loss for retail establishments. Regular deposits should be prepared and made by someone other than the reconciliation clerk. An employee can also be bonded or insured, which lowers the potential impact a theft can have on a small- or medium-sized business. I was made aware of an instance where a successful restaurant was forced into bankruptcy when the manager stole several weeks' worth of receipts from a safe to which the owner had given him access. Had the owner bonded the manager or verified that deposits were made daily, it is likely that he would have remained in business.

STEP 10: WHERE DID IT GO? HOW DO YOU KNOW?

The reconciliation of bank accounts, company assets, and customer accounts is a control linchpin. In my experience, many operational control breaks are first identified at this stage. The control is, however, effective only if it's done by a capable individual independent from the rest of the process. For instance, a comparison of bank and company records should be performed by someone who cannot authorize a payment from the account, does not post purchases or sales, and does not have access to wire systems, check stock, or a debit card for the account in question. Complete independence ensures the integrity of the process. Differences can be passed on to others for investigation, but the items should be tracked, the time the item remains open monitored, and the solution signed off by the person who identified them. Correcting entries should also be approved by a finance supervisor who does not have recording capability.

Customer statements can also be a critical validation tool if the company controls customer assets. Once again, financial services firms, whether they are in the brokerage, banking, or investment management business, have a fiduciary responsibility for assets entrusted to them. Frequent customer transaction confirmations and monthly statements will ensure that independent but interested parties had the opportunity to identify problems with an individual's account. But this process can only work if the statements are prepared (recording function) and mailed out by someone other than the manager who controls the assets (custody function).

As an example, Frank Gruttadauria, an employee of S.G. Cowen, and later Lehman Brothers, was convicted of securities fraud, mail fraud, and identity theft for bilking his clients out of more than $50 million. According to the charges, for over a decade, Mr. Gruttadauria sent out false statements and shifted money among accounts to cover up the $50 million in losses. Had the statements been prepared independent of sales and trading, as is standard procedure at many brokerage firms, the losses and movements of funds would have been properly reported to customers, and the fraud could not have been perpetrated for so long.

STEP 11: TAKE YOUR TEMPERATURE OFTEN

Frequent feedback is a component of any closed system, and is a determinant of natural selection and survival. Without learning, an organism has no opportunity to adjust to ever-changing threats to its survival. For many generations, the Bighorn sheep in the wilderness areas of Idaho had not received visual information that Man was a threat; for years, hunting was not allowed and the Bighorn felt comfortable enough to walk within a couple of feet of any visitor. This was exciting to those participating in rafting trips in the wilderness areas along the Salmon River. Tourists would marvel at how close they could get to the sheep, and would leave food for them. Thus, Bighorns were not only unafraid of people, but regarded them as a food source. However, for the past several years, due to the increased herd population, the State of Idaho has allowed a limited hunt. Henceforth, to ensure their survival, it will be critical for the Bighorn sheep to begin to see Man as a threat. As they process the feedback that humans can be hunters, thus dangerous, they will respond in more appropriate—that is, cautious—ways.

Likewise, feedback is important for the continual enhancement and survival of an enterprise. Information is a tool that enables managers to monitor key processes, identify problems, analyze trends, and measure process improvement. Great companies understand that they can only manage what can be measured. The reporting of these key metrics can take different forms, and may be a series of reports rather than a single tool.

Regardless of the source, feedback from key indicators should meet corporate objectives. Too much information can create "noise" and cloud the picture. Apparel retailers that are able to quickly identify and react to customer buying trends can create a competitive advantage. Wal-Mart Stores, for one, has identified buying trends as a key indicator. The company responds to changes in consumer behavior in real time. The retailer uses an active data warehousing system to immediately adjust inventory to buyer habits.

Learning systems can also provide information to a company's vendors. Manufacturers are increasingly turning to sole suppliers that monitor component usage and automatically replenish inventories. Now, even products "learn." I have a neighbor who races sailboats. His boat was recently equipped with an on-board computer that is capable of calculating the most efficient method of sailing between two points based on wind strength, direction, and ocean currents. The boat is even capable of steering itself and avoiding known threats. As impressive as this is, I noticed during the outing that the autopilot often overadjusted, jerking the boat side to side when changing direction. I learned that the computer was still getting to "know the boat" and that its handling would smooth out over time. Sure enough, the next time I sailed on the boat, the autopilot made adjustments smoothly and accurately. One can envision a day when such a computer could eliminate mistakes, repair itself, and adjust easily to new threats.

The most comprehensive management information tool in use today is the Balanced Scorecard, which, as explained in the book of the same name by Robert Kaplan and David Norton, retains the traditional financial measures of past performance and complements them with drivers of future performance such as Wal-Mart's buying trends. This concept of historical versus future performance drivers is an important distinction. Most financial information only tells you where you've been, not where you are going. Take an independent refiner as an example. You may look at its financial statements for the past year and determine that this is an awful business. Oil prices are high and competition for refined products intense, squeezing margins and resulting in losses. But if you also know that the industry is running at 98 percent stated capacity, that no new refineries can be profitably built due to environmental requirements, and that demand is expected to increase markedly over the next few years, your view of this business changes. A manager might want to embark on a strategy that calls for investment in existing assets that could increase refined output to meet the anticipated high-margin demand, despite current losses.

The Balanced Scorecard institutionalizes key information needed to navigate your business. It links financial, customer, internal process, learning, and growth objectives to the corporate strategy. Resources are allocated and progress monitored to make sure that the enterprise is headed in the direction intended. Whether you formalize your processes with a Balanced Scorecard or utilize other methods that tie your organizational strategy to performance, good management information will report not only the current health of your organization, but also its capability to make strides toward corporate objectives. Indicators such as capacity utilization, employee satisfaction and retention, and market share can provide needed insight into the capability of the organization to grow. Being prepared for growth is an important control in itself. Many companies run into operational problems associated with expansion that can impact their customers and the reputation of the companies themselves. Clearly, if an enterprise is running near capacity, has high employee turnover, and the auditors have concerns about the strength of process boundaries, the objective of the enterprise should not be growth. More appropriate objectives might be to add capacity, investigate why employees are leaving and address their issues, and work to improve process controls. Once these objectives are met, then expansion can be a worthwhile and attainable goal.

Soliciting, assimilating, and acting on feedback is an art. As such, it can be misunderstood or rejected if it does not fit the manager's view of the operating environment. If a manager's antennae are not tuned to identify red flags, no amount of management information will help improve the operations of a company. Take the discovery in February 2001 of a reactor vessel in a nuclear power plant that was so severely corroded that it was in danger of bursting. The operators and safety inspectors of the Toledo, Ohio, reactor registered shock, but in fact there had been clues to the plant's condition dating back to 1988. A former Nuclear Regulatory Commission inspector had been hired by the company to write a report on maintenance procedures at the plant. In his analysis, he identified management's poor relations with the craft workers as a barrier to their full understanding of the condition of the plant. Rather than assimilating this information and taking corrective action, management ordered the inspector to change his report. The inspector, quite appropriately, quit instead.

As a result, nothing was done for years, until the near-disastrous condition was identified. The discovery was made after corrosion had spread to a ventilation duct observable in plain sight. The Nuclear Regulatory Commission is now examining the management structure and culture at the plant. Management has responded with communication workshops and facilitators to improve the company culture. Unfortunately, it took a chemical eating through 70 pounds of steel and bringing the plant to the brink of a catastrophic loss to bring about this change, thus putting a community and industry at risk for over a decade.

The management information step is designed to make managers think about what they need to monitor and to identify, analyze, and measure problems, trends, organizational strength, and capability. The health of the control structure is a piece of the puzzle. For every control identified in each step, a manager should search for corresponding indicators that describe its health. A feedback loop should be created where none currently exists. For instance, a manager may ask a back-office clerk to independently price trader positions in order to make certain that there is no potential to hide losses. How would he or she understand how well this control was working? Since only the most liquid markets will experience perfect price discovery, there is likely to be some differences between the trader's price and the independent verification. A manager could ask for a report that summarizes the number of positions, gross pricing differences, and the estimated value of illiquid or unpriced inventory. A spike in any of these might alert a manager to a problem either with the control methodology or with an employee's activities. The frequency of the feedback is subjective and will depend on how the indicator is produced and used. Customer complaints and percentage of product defects may be produced daily or weekly; capacity utilization, monthly; and attempted security breaches on an exception basis as they occur.

Managers earn their keep by using their judgment to make key decisions regarding which metrics are important and how often they need to see them. Healthy organizations get to choose how to take their temperature, just as healthy people can choose to use oral or otic measures. Medical professionals may force an unpleasant third method on the sick. Likewise, unhealthy companies have this decision made for them by regulators, creditors, and other unfriendly forces. The manner by which they take the temperature of the organization may be more than a little uncomfortable.

STEP 12: SPEAKING OUT LOUD TO A CROWD

As a complement to Step 11, which introduced the concept of feedback to management, this step considers the issues of the organization providing information to investors, regulators, and other outside parties. Investors expect feedback in return for their purchase of company stock. Regulators are charged by the public with ensuring that companies adhere to the rules, laws, and mores of our nation. They expect management to give proper information to help them gauge compliance. Much attention has been focused on these issues of late due to poor financial reporting and disclosure practices at some of the world's largest companies.

Recent experience has revealed the kind of damage that can occur to a company's reputation due to a lapse in presentation and disclosure controls. This kind of risk is usually borne by the CFO of an organization, therefore, most managers will not have decision rights regarding it. That said, though, this step may not apply to those managers who do not oversee any processes for which information is captured for financial reporting. Due to the current focus on this subject, however, *all managers* should be cognizant of the "red flags" of financial reporting. If you do have decision rights that will have an impact on the financial statements, you must implement controls to ensure you are complying with company policy. This would normally include an independent review of information being provided to ensure it fully complies with the firm's finance guidelines, regulatory requirements, and generally accepted accounting principles. In short, the information you pass on must be accurate and compliant with the company's accounting policies. Step 12: Speaking Out Loud to a Crowd will help you determine whether your company's accounting policies are conservative or aggressive. In Chapter 7, we will also focus on some additional tools for assessing financial reporting processes controls.

If you are a CEO or a member of the Audit Committee of the Board of Directors, this section of Control Smart is perhaps the most timely and important to you. The oversight function of CEOs and boards of directors makes it imperative to take immediate steps to ensure that financial statements filed with the SEC, other regulators, or banks, or otherwise disseminated to the public are materially accurate and that the accounting principles behind them are sound. Simply relying on the CFO is no longer sufficient. Auditors can provide some comfort, but the number of recent material presentation and disclosure errors overlooked by auditors would lead a rational CEO or audit committee to take additional precautions. Simply doing a one-off review to certify financials with the SEC is not enough. Controls need to be implemented at the CEO and board level to ensure that proper accounting practices, financial reporting, and disclosure continue beyond the current crisis. The National Association of Corporate Directors (NACD) Blue Ribbon Commission on Risk Oversight has said that active risk management should be a primary concern of both management and directors: "Directors should help management develop policies addressing risk, bringing new perspectives and ideas to the debate over what specific risks the company faces, and what the company should do about them."[4] Accordingly, the most effective control tool can be a board culture of open and uninhibited challenge of an organization's financial policies.

Certainly, the number of potential presentation errors and disclosure omissions are numerous, but there are patterns that CEOs and audit committee members can look for to help them identify where they must further dig into the organization's accounting policies. H. David Sherman and S. David Young in their article "Tread Lightly through These Accounting Minefields," published in the *Harvard Business Review*,[5] and Charles W. Mulford and Eugene Comiskey in their book, *The Financial Numbers Game: Detecting Creative Accounting Practices*,[6] have identified many of these red flags for us:

- Aggressive revenue recognition policies
- Frequent nonrecurring charges or reversal of charges
- Frequent changes in accounting policies regarding bad debt reserves, depreciation, and amortization expenses or comprehensive income
- Related party transactions
- Complex products or strategies few company managers understand

To these red flags, I add three more:

- Unsupported topside entries affecting income
- Underfunded defined benefit plans
- Management compensation that is seriously out of line with company performance

The flags may not be readily apparent and may take some digging to unearth, but it is incumbent upon directors to ask tough questions to uncover poor and improper practices. Asking tough questions is not an act of disloyalty; rather, doing so can lead to a healthy dialogue based on trust and candor. Complicating the effort, however, is that the interaction between a board and executive management is generally a formal affair with guarded communications. Yale School of Management Associate Dean for Executive Programs, Jeffery Sonnenfeld, in his article titled "What Makes Great Boards Great," makes the case that too much effort is spent on "tightening procedural rules for boards."[7] He argues that highly effective boards foster a culture of respect, trust, and candor, "challenge one another and engage directly with senior management."[8] Executives will often go to great lengths to ensure they do not say anything controversial at board meetings that might invite meddling. Indeed, corporate governance expert Ira Millstein has pointed to boards' "lack of information about the corporation's business and…risks"[9] as one of the most important inadequacies leading to the current crises. A healthier model is the timely sharing of important information with the board. The CEO needs to trust his or her board, and the board should adopt the Reaganesque policy of "trust but verify." This process will include challenging the financial policies of the company. This has not been a widespread practice, and many CEOs and boards are not sure how or where to begin. As an aid in this regard, the following subsections provide some helpful questions and examples for managers to consider concerning each of these high-risk activities.

Aggressive Revenue Recognition

Are revenues matched to expenses and free of any contingencies? The answer was no for the sales of fiber optics and other services at Qwest Communications. Qwest recently stated that it incorrectly accounted for more than $1.1 billion in transactions between 1999 and 2001. Revenues were contingent on the purchase of capacity or future services, but they were improperly booked as earned. Unify Corporation went even further when, in 2000, it boosted revenue by loaning money to customers, who then bought Unify products with no reasonable expectation that they would ever repay the company. A $15 million profit was restated as a $7 million loss.

A board member cannot be too careful in asking pointed questions of the company's managers and auditors. Understanding when revenues are recognized is the first step to understanding the quality of the revenue stream. Revenues that are booked after the customer has received and accepted the product or service without any further performance requirement or contingency are of the highest quality. Discussing the methodology and detailed results of sales-confirmation testing with the auditors is not out of line; rather, it is prudent. Inquiring of management whether there are loans to customers or asset-swap agreements is not meddlesome; rather, it communicates to management that the board is serious about proper financial disclosures. Asking a CFO or an auditor whether there are more conservative revenue-recognition methodologies and how they would impact results is not being overbearing; rather, it is exhibiting good governance on behalf of the shareholders.

If a company is not using conservative revenue-recognition policies, a director must ask why. The most common defense is that everyone in the industry applies the same methodology. As the recent disclosures at Qwest, WorldCom, and Global Crossing illustrate, this defense is not good enough. "Everybody else does it" is an excuse you expect to hear from your teenager, not a CFO. The revenue policy applied must have a sound business rationale, one that is easily understood by senior management and directors.

Nonrecurring Charges

Companies are continually making provisions for costs, to be realized in the future, even if they are not sure exactly how much they will be. Merger costs, product returns, lawsuits, obsolete inventory, and bad loans all are expenses that usually give rise to reserves, or nonrecurring, charges. The Center for Business Innovation reports that the number of S&P 500 firms declaring special losses has grown from 68 in 1982 to 233 in 2000. In other words, 47 percent of the S&P 500 had nonrecurring charges. The Center for Business Innovation also found that, over time, those companies that did not declare special items or took minor charges performed better than those that did—even if you ignore nonrecurring charges so that companies declaring special items would not be penalized.

But there are many legitimate one-off provisions due to acts of nature, mergers, and asset sales, so how does a director or CEO identify the misuse of this accounting method to hide underlying weaknesses in operating results? One clue is when a company regularly takes a reversal of a reserve, such as reorganization expenses, back into operating income. This type of activity creates inflation in reported results. In 1999, the SEC sued W.R. Grace for fraud when the company failed to properly classify a reversal of reserves. To prevent this type of regulatory action, directors should ask probing questions of the CFO and auditors regarding the existence, validity, classification, and disclosure of provisions. Questions might include:

- Why is the charge nonrecurring and not a part of normal operating income?
- How was the amount of the charge determined, and how accurate is it?
- What is the likelihood that all or a portion of the charge will not be utilized?
- What will be disclosed about the charge in the financial statements?

Investigate further confusing or hesitant answers to these questions. Document responses and have them on hand for future meetings. If nonrecurring charges are reversed at a later date, solicit and challenge detailed explanations regarding this occurrence.

Changes to Reserve, Depreciation, Amortization, or Comprehensive Income Policy

Does a company regularly change its accounting policy for bad debt reserves, depreciation and amortization expenses, or components of comprehensive income? Frequent changes in accounting guidance can also mask manipulation of the numbers. One of the "poster children" for bad accounting, WorldCom, recently reported another $3.3 billion in bogus profits, using various techniques, including the reversal of bad debts into income.

It is to be expected that the dollar amount of reserves will change with the business climate, but the methodology should not. If an increase in sales results in an increase in accounts receivable, then a corresponding and proportional increase in reserves and bad debt expenses would be expected. If there does not seem to be a direct correlation, directors should challenge the consistency of the reserve calculation. Likewise, capitalized costs should not increase at a rate greater than revenue over time (there may be a lag in related revenue until after capitalized projects are completed). Directors should question capitalization techniques that appear aggressive.

The waste management industry in particular has been known for aggressive capitalization and amortization policies. In 1989 and 1990, Chambers Development Company, Inc., capitalized significant amounts of landfill development costs based on targeted profit margins. This practice allowed the company to report profits when revised accounting provided by the SEC showed a loss. Another company, Waste Management, Inc., depreciated its fixed assets over too long of a life. This, combined with other accounting adjustments, resulted in a $3.5 billion charge in 1998. Expensing rather than capitalizing operational costs is the more conservative approach leading to higher-quality earnings. Generally, any change in methodology should be justified by long-term trends, not short-term needs. Anything less would lead one to believe that the financial statements are being managed and do not fairly reflect the company's operations.

Related-Party Transactions

Does the company enter into related-party transactions? Adelphia Communications did. Not only did the Rigas family allegedly borrow more than $3 billion using company assets, Adelphia created a Rigas-run investment firm, helped purchase the Buffalo Sabres hockey team, and built a golf course on Rigas-owned land. To compound matters, the Rigas debt was not presented or disclosed in Adelphia's financial statements. Conflicts of interest can be among the most damaging control weaknesses absorbed by a company, particularly if they occur between the company and its founder.

Conflicts of interest can also arise when professional managers enter into related-party arrangements. The fall of 2001 will be remembered not only for the tragic events of September 11, but also for the collapse of the energy trading firm Enron. A star CFO managed the creation of off-balance sheet companies with the effect of creating an unrealistic picture of financial health for Enron. In certain instances, the CFO was also responsible for managing the off-balance sheet companies in which he had a financial interest. This insider dealing resulted in the collapse of one of the world's largest corporations. The truth of what happened at Enron will take years to fully understand due to the complexity of the various entities, the many conflicts of interest involving senior managers, and the contribution of outside financial institutions that enabled the shell game to occur. What is clear is that the chief executives and the audit committee of the boards of directors should have had completeness, as well as presentation and disclosure, controls in place to alert them to these irregularities. Insightful analysis should have been made of asset movements, and incisive questions should have been asked regarding Enron employees who supported affiliated entities. Finally, if it had been company policy for mid-level and senior management to annually attest to their knowledge of any related-party dealings, the true story would have begun to surface. Simply asking the auditors or counsel if they were aware of any related-party activities might have led to a detailed discussion regarding how the CFO was compensated for managing the financing vehicles. It was the auditors and lawyers who worked hard to ensure that certain transactions were completed quickly so that management bonuses could be earned. The senior managers of Enron were extremely well compensated to run the company on behalf of their shareholders. For these managers to say they were unaware of the widespread interdealing is, at a minimum, a declaration of their failure to ensure shareholder assets were properly protected and controlled.

Directors and CEOs need to inquire about any related-party activities within their organization. Where they exist, the conflicts need to be neutralized, or additional controls established. If such transactions are allowed to occur, checks and balances must exist to ensure that the interests of the shareholders are fairly represented.

Complex Products

Does your company provide complex financial products, such as structured financial instruments containing derivatives, or utilize multifaceted hedging strategies that few understand? When complex products are produced by a "star," few want to challenge this success or reveal that they don't understand how the system works. This is evidenced by the Joe Jett story. No one was sure how Jett made his margins, but no one wanted to feel stupid by pressing the question. From supervisors to auditors to finance staff, no one wanted to admit that they did not understand his complex explanations. There are a number of internal controls that should have identified this control break, but simply requiring that the process be documented in detail may have dissolved the mirage of profitability. A manager can insist that a complex strategy be mapped out by his or her employees. Jett's supervisor would not have been able to map the process because he did not know how Jett made money on his trades. Likewise, Jett would not be able to, as the game would have been up.

Even financially sophisticated boards can be confused by complex strategies and transactions. Enron's board contained a former accounting professor, the former executives of an insurance company and a bank, the former head of the Commodity Futures Trading Commission, and a hedge fund manager. Enron's financial transactions were confusing even to this highly knowledgeable board.

In 1993, Gibson Greetings entered into derivative contracts with Bankers Trust that it clearly did not understand. Bankers love to sell these complex instruments, as the margins are high, but so are the risks—to their clients. As 1994 ended, Gibson was left holding significant losses on its derivative transactions while Bankers Trust held significant profits. Several internal control issues surfaced at Gibson Greetings. First, the company was purchasing positions on which it could not place a value. It did not have the internal capability or computer models to price complex structured financial instruments. Furthermore, there was no secondary market to observe the value of these positions. Additionally, the board of directors gave the CFO and the treasurer a free hand to enter into transactions as they saw fit. Step 1 of Smart Links is to identify policies and procedures. Step 6 speaks to asset impairment. Gibson had neither a structured hedging policy nor a method to internally identify whether the positions had suffered impairment. Importantly, Bankers Trust was found to have defrauded Gibson by misleading it as to the value of its positions. The resulting lawsuits, bad press, and weakening business model led to the eventual purchase of Bankers Trust by Deutsche Bank.

Who could forget the bankruptcy of Orange County, California? Robert Citron, the county treasurer, had a free hand in leveraging his $7.5 billion investment portfolio into one worth $20.5 billion. He used reverse-repo transactions (which allows one to use current investments as pledged collateral for a loan) to fund further investments. He further enhanced his investment portfolio by using structured notes. By leveraging his portfolio to nearly a 3 to 1 debt to capital ratio, he amplified any returns, positive or negative. However, when interest rates went up instead of down, his portfolio experienced a $1.6 billion loss. Unfortunately, many of the county's investors relied on this money to fund current operations, money that was suddenly no longer available. Incredibly, local school districts borrowed money just to invest in the fund. Their additional leverage only magnified their losses. The quick and stunning losses pushed one of the nation's wealthiest counties into bankruptcy. The result was that programs were cut, services reduced, and about 3,000 public employees lost their jobs.

Directors need to aggressively question an organization's investment and hedging policies. Strict guidelines must be set in place that define the type of instruments that may be used to invest a company's assets or hedge its exposure. It is also crucial that the organization monitor the value of its financial instruments. Loss tolerance levels should be implemented and enforced. Tools such as value at risk (VAR) can assess financial and liquidity risk associated with these financial instruments, using standard statistical techniques. VAR computes the maximum dollar loss over a target horizon (a week, month, or year) such that there is a low, prespecified probability (normally 1 to 5 percent) that the actual loss will be larger. For instance, Orange County might have specified that the VAR of its trading portfolio not exceed $375 million at a 99 percent confidence level over a year. In other words, there would be only one chance in a hundred, under normal market conditions, that a loss greater than $375 million (or 5 percent of the portfolio) could occur over this period. Had VAR been calculated for Orange County, and had it been announced that there was a 5 percent, or 1 in every 20, chance of losing more than $1.1 billion (or approximately 15 percent of the portfolio) over the course of a year, many participants and taxpayers might have voiced concern and enforced change. (VAR is used more and more frequently as a financial and liquidity risk control tool, but its detailed exploration is beyond the scope of this book. In short, VAR can be a very useful key performance indicator regarding a company's compliance with investment and hedging policies and procedures, and directors should be aware of its availability. Obviously, the tool is dependent on the ability to obtain quality pricing information on the financial instruments analyzed. If the valuation control is not in place, as was the case at Gibson, the tool will not be effective.)

Frequent and Material Topside Entries Affecting Income

Does the company book large topside adjustments to income? These adjustments are not automatically produced from the company's accounting system, rather they are manually booked transactions. Many of these adjustments are appropriate and ensure that business activities are accounted for in the proper period; however, they can be used to increase reported income or hide sins.

John Egan, a managing director and the CFO for ING Baring's Americas region, considers excessive topside entries the monster of red flags. Egan has a reputation of being financially conservative, and his approach to regulatory reporting and finance has saved his employers many headaches over the years. I value his integrity and opinion greatly. His insight laid bare what, in retrospect, my experience supported: Management of the financial reporting numbers most often occurs at the very top.

I already discussed the topside entries made at WorldCom, to which its London-based controller objected. Those adjustments reduced expenses and added millions to the bottom line. Another interesting example comes from our own U.S. government, the very institution charged with oversight of financial reporting on behalf of the public. In a recent *New York Times* article, it was revealed that nearly all of the federal agencies audited by the White House Budget Office do not have a financial accounting system that can generate auditable financial statements. As a result, the financial records of the federal government are so bad that the agencies cannot account for billions of dollars. How do they make the books balance? "When many agencies realize that they have made major accounting errors, rather than looking back to see where the money went, they simply enter multibillion-dollar balance adjustments, writing off the money."[10]

The Forest Service, a division of the Department of Agriculture, tried to balance its books at the end of the 2001 fiscal year. It booked more than 15,337 adjusting entries, debits, and credits, totaling over $11 billion gross.

The "auditors examined 144 of those adjustments, totaling $7.9 billion, and found that 73 percent were unsupported."[11]

The Department of Defense (DOD) alone entered an unsubstantiated balance adjustment totaling $1.1 trillion in 2000, down from a $2.3 trillion the prior year. *Trillion*, not billion. To put this into perspective, the budget for the DOD was estimated to be $333 billion in 2002, so the topside adjustment was in excess of the department's *combined* budgets for three years.

Granted, these examples are so egregious and massive as to defy explanation. Mitchell E. Daniels Jr., the director of the budget office, correctly pointed out that the federal government's accounts would "never be tolerated in the private sector."[12] But public companies can learn from the failings of the government. Material topside entries need to be carefully examined and the business purpose understood. Directors and the CEO can request the disclosure and supporting rationale for material topside adjustments from the CFO and then validate these with the auditors. And because finance professionals can easily bury a person with data, insist that they keep it simple. If they cannot easily explain an entry, then the adjustment is likely aggressive or improper.

Underfunded Defined Benefit Plans

It is my belief that the next financial scandals could involve underfunded pension plans. For the most part, defined benefit plans are being replaced by defined contribution programs, such as 401(k) plans. But there are still a large number of defined benefit programs in existence, and these plans can have a massive impact on a corporation's net income.

Under a defined benefit plan, a sponsor guarantees a specific payout to participants. Contributions are made to the plan based on assumed future investment returns. For example, if it is known that in 10 years, when you retire, the company will need to pay you $100, it must contribute $61.39 now, assuming a 5 percent return—or only $46.31, assuming an 8 percent return. If actual gains exceed the assumed returns, they can be reported as income on a company's income statement. During the bull market of the 1990s, many companies adjusted their assumptions of investment returns upward. Such a move would make the pension fund look as if it had more assets than were needed. The companies would then take gains from this financial engineering into income. IBM, for instance, recorded $1.27 billion of net pension income in 2000 and $1.45 billion in 2001.

In 2001 and 2002, however, the markets came nowhere close to meeting those investment assumptions. In fact, those pension surpluses have turned into deficits. How big a problem is this? Credit Suisse First Boston (CSFB) estimates that 240 of the 360 S&P 500 companies with defined benefit plans, or 66 percent, are underfunded. General Motors alone experienced the pain of a $7 billion 1999 pension surplus that turned into a $9 billion deficit by 2001. CSFB estimated that GM was underfunded by as much as $29 billion for 2002. Other pension funds appear to be in even worse shape based on their contributor's ability to pay.

Fitch Ratings estimates that the airline industry's pension funds are underfunded by an astounding $18 billion. Some government projections put the number well north of $25 billion as of September 30, 2003. AMR Corporation, the parent of American Airlines, has a pension fund that is estimated to be underfunded by an amount that represents 600 percent of its entire market capitalization. Similarly, Delta Air Lines is underfunded by over 300 percent of its market capitalization. U.S. Airways recently requested that it be allowed to transfer $500 million of unfunded pilot pension liabilities to the government agency that guarantees pensions. Unfortunately, that agency, the Pension Benefit Guarantee Corporation, is itself experiencing financial difficulties. The agency recently reported a deficit of nearly $6 billion, leading the U.S. Comptroller General to place the agency on a list of "high risk" government operations. U.S. Treasury Secretary John Snow warned that "a financial meltdown similar to the savings and loan collapse of 1989 might be brewing."[13] Even if the agency makes good on its commitments, the pilots stand to lose much. Many have built up retirement benefits of more than $100,000 annually. The top payout available from the government agency is $42,000, and most pilots do not qualify for even that much. To get the maximum payout, an employee must retire at 65. Pilots are forced to retire at 60, and the top agency payout for someone who retires at 60 is approximately $28,000. Therefore, they stand to lose over 70 percent of their annual benefits. For those unfortunate few who are not yet retired, they will be eligible for significantly less. This situation creates a powerful incentive for retirees to take a lump-sum payout from their pension plan, where possible, rather than collecting their benefits over time. If redemptions occur faster than assumed, this also puts further strain on an under-funded plan.

Even with the rebound in the financial markets during 2003, growth projections of many of these companies appear unattainable, and that spells trouble. A substantial number of organizations will have to come up with cash to keep their defined benefit plans credible. General Motors will show a drop of $1 billion or more in its earnings due to its pension plan. General Electric lowered its expected rate of return on plan assets from 9.5 to 8.5 percent. The change will decrease reported earnings between $800 million to $1.2 billion.

Boards of directors, CEOs, and CFOs need to review their plan assumptions. Expected returns in excess of 8 percent should be challenged. Only a plan that's 100 percent invested in stocks would have a chance of exceeding an 8 percent return over time, and that is contingent on past financial performance. The fact is that many pension funds have exposure to bonds and other lower yielding instruments and will do well to earn 8 percent. Berkshire Hathaway's 6.5 percent projection is a conservative benchmark that may prove too cautious over time. But at least it's known that Warren Buffett will report earnings of high quality for Berkshire, unsoiled by poor investment projections.

Management Compensation

If there is one area boards of directors have spent considerable time managing, it is determining the compensation of senior management. Some boards do this better than others. Smart shareholders recognize that they'll need to enrich good management that has played a key role in increasing an organization's value. Owners of companies whose stock continues to outperform the market over time are willing to pay an executive management team handsomely without complaint. Unfortunately, many senior managers seem to obtain ever higher compensation packages regardless of how well their companies perform. For most of us, performance below standard would mean a reduction in bonus and option grants, not an increase. The lack of a causal link between pay and performance can be an important red flag for investors, signaling that there may be a lack of independence on the company's board. The SEC is trying to provide more transparency to the selection of directors by proposing disclosure requirements regarding how nominees are identified, evaluated, and chosen. Even with these disclosures, however, there is no guarantee of director independence. Company executives will still control the selection process. And even if there is independence, some management teams will manipulate the financial reports without board knowledge in order to obtain greater bonuses and option awards.

For example, a report by Tyco International's outside counsel claims that the company reported a profit of $79.4 million on the purchase of a small company called Flag Telecom. Based on this outcome, Tyco paid its top managers $15 million in bonuses. The report indicates that the acquisition actually resulted in a $24 million economic loss by the time the deal closed. The report also reveals that management kept the board in the dark about the bonuses for many months. Eventually, the board's compensation committee did approve them, but the sharp decline in Flag's stock (which undermined the basis for any kind of financial reward) had not been properly communicated to the committee.

Assuming that the board did not have time to investigate the value of Flag's stock, it would still be clear that paying a cash bonus to management on the consummation of the deal would create a conflict between what was best for the company and what was best for management. If the board members truly wanted to link the interests of management to the deal, they should have set aside Flag stock that could be vested by management over a two- or three-year period based on the performance of Tyco. Instead of simply being rewarded for closing the deal, management would have had some incentive to negotiate the best price possible and realize value by actually running the company for profit. Less than a year and a half later, Flag was in bankruptcy and its stock was worth less than a penny. Nevertheless, Tyco managers kept their million-dollar bonuses.

The problem with compensation is that board members may not know what "normal pay" is in a particular industry. They may perceive a limited market in CEOs and want to ensure that their leader is not lured away, but don't know how to design a good reward system. Outside advisors can add a great deal of value to board oversight, and compensation experts are often retained (if none are already on the board) to design and administer executive packages. This is not a cop-out, but smart management. Specialists have seen many different pay and incentive structures and have access to data regarding the pay of senior management for specific industries. Using experts not only can improve the composition and terms of the pay package, but can also help demonstrate that the board takes seriously its fiduciary responsibility to shareholders. The result can be better motivated senior management and a measure of protection for the board.

Arnold Ross, an executive compensation expert with a long and successful track record, believes that a good compensation process serves both the company and the executive equally well. "The process must build from two directions: the needs of the executive and the requirements of and inherent limitations of the company. It requires looking into the future and, then, in a sense, backing up to make that future a reality for the executive and the company."[14]

All that said, compensation specialists are not a panacea; in fact, they may have actually contributed to the current lack of correlation between pay and performance. The National Association of Stock Plan Professionals, one of the associations whose members design and administer corporate pay plans, admits that specialists bear some responsibility for excessive executive pay. George B. Paulin, president of Fredrick W. Cook & Company, a leading pay consultant, was recently quoted as saying that "consultants bore part of the responsibility for excesses because they did not fully warn of how stock options, restricted stock, and other devices could be exploited by executives. . . . [T]he focus now should be on adopting best practices to make sure shareholders do not pay more than necessary for executive talent."[15] Corporate boards need to challenge experts regarding the incentives and expected outcomes of any compensation package. The future must be equitably built from both directions, and poor performance should be reflected in total compensation. As the Tyco example illustrates, poorly structured plans can actually damage a company.

Another pattern directors should look for is the selling of stock by executives just before the release of bad news. If such an event occurs, even if the executive may not have had knowledge of the news at the time he or she placed the order, the board should conduct an independent investigation. If for no other reason, it should be commenced to reassure the investor community and put the issue to bed.

The clouds hanging over HealthSouth Corporation and Imclone Systems are two cases in point. HealthSouth, the nation's largest chain of rehabilitation hospitals, is fighting concurrent battles with regulators over the company's Medicare billings and the sale of stock by its former chairman, Richard M. Scrushy, who was one of the nation's highest-paid executives. Investors have punished the stock, pushing it down over 95 percent since last year over these issues, as well as further concerns regarding the independence of HealthSouth's board. Understandably, analysts have concerns about management's credibility given these revelations. These issues will undoubtedly consume much of managers' time when they should be focused on the critical job of righting their business.

Imclone's former CEO, Sam Waksal, was convicted for acting on insider information. He not only sold his stock but also tipped off family members prior to the FDA's rejection of the company's cancer drug Erbitux. The revelations forced the resignations of senior executives and continue to weigh heavily on the company at a time when it should be concentrating its efforts on correcting its application and getting its drug approved. Waksal was eventually sentenced to seven-plus years in prison for his actions.

CEOs need to avoid any hint of unfair dealing. Such issues, at best, can consume senior management time and, at worst case, end a career and even a company. The board of directors should institute a policy to automatically investigate any sale of stock by senior management if it precedes the release of bad news. Such a policy will cause senior managers to ensure they consider all legal and ethical requirements before they issue a sell order.

General Auditor Reporting Lines

One final concern to explore is the reporting line of the general auditor. This is not necessarily a red flag or a pattern indicative of major fraud or operational risk, but the reporting lines of general auditors can serve to either greatly improve or detract from effective communication with the board. Does the head of internal audit report directly to the audit committee as well as the CEO? Does the audit committee have a hand in determining compensation for the general auditor? Are significant control issues discussed at each meeting? If the answer to any of these questions is no, then the board of directors should review its governance model to ensure that information can flow freely to its members.

Many organizations have their general auditor report to the CFO. The theory is that the CFO understands finance and control, so this reporting line makes sense. However, the general auditor must feel free to report issues to the board without reprisal. The CFO has such an important role in the control structure of a company that he or she can easily be conflicted regarding audit findings. CEOs and audit committees must take responsibility for guaranteeing that auditors can report material issues freely. Direct, uninhibited communication to the CEO and audit committee is a key component of a strong control culture. The fraud at WorldCom came to light due to the courageous actions by the internal auditor. She exposed and reported the false accounting, over the pleadings and objections of the CFO, who wanted to take a charge (one of the red flags discussed earlier) in the next quarter to remedy the problem.

Providing a direct reporting line to the audit committee will not, however, guarantee auditor competence; the committee has to challenge them to objectively evaluate the job being performed. To that end, every audit committee should have a control expert to perform this role. Current or former CFOs, public accountants, and general auditors from other companies best fit this profile.

Summary

The pitfalls described in the preceding sections represent just a few of the most common; the list is not meant to be exhaustive. The point is, nothing replaces the hard work of senior managers and board members to obtain a detailed understanding of what is being reported in their financial statements. It starts with setting the right cultural tone from the top and ends with challenging a company's CFO and auditor regarding a company's financial reporting, and rewarding management for compliance with proper accounting standards.

CASE STUDY

The Cynthia Cooper Story

On June 11, 2002, Scott Sullivan summoned Cynthia Cooper, the general auditor of WorldCom to his office, and gave her 10 minutes to get there. Sullivan was a legend, not only within the ranks of WorldCom, but also on Wall Street. In 1997, he engineered the takeover of MCI, a company nearly three times the size of the upstart would-be acquirer. In 1998, he received an excellence award from *CFO magazine* in the mergers and acquisitions category and, at age 37, was earning well over $19 million a year.

In contrast, Cynthia Cooper led a small, underfunded group of auditors who continually had to prove their worth to senior management. When she entered the room, Sullivan got right to the point: He asked her what her group was up to. She let him know that she was reviewing the capitalized expenses of WorldCom. Calmly, Sullivan asked her to delay the audit. In one of the most important decisions ever made by a general auditor, she rebuffed the former CFO of the Year by politely declining his request. In doing so, she set the stage for an epic battle for the company's soul.

Case Study (continued)

Cynthia Cooper was 38 years old, remarried with two children, and the sole wage earner for her family. She knew that taking on Sullivan was, once embarked upon, a path of no return. She would be isolated both in the company and small community; her job would be imperiled; and tremendous pressure would be placed on her family. Many whistle-blowers end up lonely, depressed, and alcoholic. With so much at stake, why would she risk standing up to such a powerful executive? The answer can be found in concepts as simple as good versus evil and the willingness to speak truth to power. The battlefield may be different, but the bravery required is just as great. It calls for an innate belief that one should care not only for oneself, but also for those not able to defend themselves. Cooper put herself at risk for others, while all those around her put themselves first, looting and plundering a corporation, carrying away all they could.

In retrospect, it is easy to see that Sullivan was outmatched. Throughout her life, Cooper was a fighter. She came from a home life where money was tight. As soon as she was able, she began working at fast food restaurants, including a stint at the Golden Corral, known as the supermarket of fast food and a waitress's nightmare. At the Golden Corral, she started slow, struggling with the volume of heavy plates. Rather than quit, she quickly built up her strength, learned the business, and thrived. In college, she would unrelentingly shower her accounting professors with questions, extracting every bit of knowledge she could from them. Her tenaciousness carried over to WorldCom. During the go-go growth years, senior executives had little time for the nitpicking internal audit department. Growth covers over a lot of sins, and management did not understand how audit could add to its bottom line or protect the franchise. This did not stop Cooper. She called a meeting, which included Bernie Ebbers, the chairman of WorldCom. In true Cooper fashion, she refused to start the meeting for over 30 minutes until Ebbers showed up. She was intent on demonstrating what internal audit could do to improve the financial performance of the company, and did just that. Sullivan would have been wise to take note of this persistence.

Cooper first became aware that something might be amiss at the company when a senior executive complained to her that a reserve he established had been reversed to boost income by $400 million. Normally, internal auditors do not conduct financial audits, as it would only duplicate the work of the external auditors—in this case, Arthur Andersen. More commonly, internal auditors focus on operational audits, testing the effectiveness of the control structure. But Cooper was not your run-of-the-mill

Case Study (continued)

internal auditor. When something troubled her, she was determined to satisfy herself that the risk to the company was properly mitigated. She contacted Arthur Andersen regarding the reversal of the reserve. Andersen told her it was appropriate. Recognizing that Andersen also blessed the dicey accounting at Enron, Cooper then approached Sullivan. Furious at her questions, he told her to back off. That was when her character and intuition kicked in. In a recent interview, Cooper commented, "When someone is hostile, my instincts are to find out why."[16] Recognizing she was embarking on that path of no return, she removed her personal items from her office and secretly began an after-hours investigation of WorldCom's accounting practices. Her team worked late hours, kept quiet about the investigation and their findings, and took precautions (such as burning financial information onto CDs in case management later tried to destroy it).

By the June 11 meeting with Sullivan, Cooper's team had uncovered billions of dollars of operating fees paid to local telephone companies that were capitalized—in effect, moving expenses from the income statement and putting them on the balance sheet. This had the effect of turning a loss into a multibillion-dollar profit. After her meeting with Sullivan, Cooper took her findings to the audit committee chair. At a June 20 meeting of the audit committee, Sullivan was effectively terminated.

Cooper is still paying the price for her courage. Many in the company and community still blame her for WorldCom's collapse, naively believing that the company could have borrowed its way out of trouble had it been given more time. These people would put their trust in a management team that lied to them, to their investors, and to the public to save them. Amazingly, Cooper has received no promotion and has not been publicly embraced by the new management team. The rest of the investing public does, however, recognize her story as a profile in courage, even if she does not. In 2002, *Time* magazine named her one of their "Persons of the Year." According to Cooper, "I am not a hero; I'm just doing my job."[17]

STEP 13: KNOWING THE BEST AND BRIGHTEST

Steps 11 and 12 of Smart Links established feedback loops for management, investors, and regulators. No less important is the feedback we provide to our employees. They are the ones who provide labor, and most have a psychological need to be recognized for their efforts. While pay is one reward, it is not the only method of recognizing their vital contributions.

Some businesses look at employees as a commodity. As mentioned earlier, they are not a commodity, but rather a splendid resource, a key component to quality output and control. High employee turnover generates training costs, impedes the development of a corporate culture, contributes to regression of productivity gains, and weakens the health of the control structure. Well-run companies experience turnover rates two to four times lower than poorly run companies. Good employees can be worth up to five times as much as average ones. Simply put, the quality of a company's operations is only as good as the quality of the people doing the operating.

Even great companies struggle to implement and link performance to compensation. One of the biggest mistakes many of them make is linking pay directly to performance without any other major determining factors. If a salesperson is paid only on sales, his or her incentive is to push as much product as possible through as many channels as possible. The fact that certain channels are inappropriate or that he or she knows a certain channel is stuffed with product will make little difference to the salesperson. He or she will continue to push product, sacrificing future sales for today's commissions. If a wide range of aspects are not taken into account, the salesperson may be well compensated, but at the expense of the company's overall profitability.

So how does a manager get the salesperson to consider these factors and do the right thing for both the customer and the company? As noted by Stephen George and Arnold Weimerskirch in their book *Total Quality Management*,[18] many management experts believe performance appraisals support quality improvement under the following conditions:

- "The performance appraisal must be separate from the compensation system."[19] The focus must be changed to improve performance because it is the right thing to do rather than because it is more profitable for the individual. While performance appraisals should be frequent and separate from the compensation process, this is not to say that chronically poor behavior will not result in reduced incentive compensation or even dismissal. Rather, the processes should be distinct from one another. The idea is to frequently evaluate and redirect undesired behavior and pay based on the achievement of corporate objectives.

- "The performance appraisal must be based on observable, measurable behaviors and results."[20] The identification of key performance indicators should be recognized as being as important in measuring the health of the operating or control environment as it is in measuring the performance of employees.

- "The performance appraisal must include timely feedback. Annual evaluations are too infrequent to support continuous improvement."[21]
- "The performance appraisal must encourage employee participation."[22] In order for an evaluation to be effective, the employee must be a participant in the process.

Goals and actions must be owned by the employee and encouraged by management. The SMART acronym (no relation to Control Smart) has often been used as a guide to developing goals and objectives. They must be *S*pecific, *M*easurable, *A*chievable, *R*elevant, and *T*imely to be useful for assessment. By having employees set their own objectives and perform self-assessments against these goals, management has an active tool to evaluate and counsel them. This continuous feedback loop between manager and subordinate will help management make sure that employees understand corporate objectives and guide them to optimal team performance.

An effective performance evaluation program will have clear, measurable attributes that are known to the employee and are regularly reinforced. An objective to comply with the company's policies and procedures and its statement of shared values should be an integral component of any performance evaluation. Many companies do not put these objectives out in front until a control break has occurred. Then an employee is promptly punished. This is backward logic and is the type of management activity that leads to employee dissatisfaction and turnover. With the exception of illegal behavior, it is likely that there are plenty of opportunities to address procedural issues in a positive manner *prior* to a control break. If management has the right indicators, and continuous feedback loops are operating, behavior can be corrected without harm to the company or employee.

Key performance indicators are indispensable tools for measuring compliance with policies, procedures, and values. Good, timely information will not only protect the company, but will provide management the opportunity to interact and direct employees in a proactive and fair fashion. We will spend more time on the concept of monitoring indicators in Chapter 8, but for now, be aware that performance evaluations are an important tool that requires a manager's special consideration, effort and time. To be effective, this feedback has to be acted on before significant damage is done to the enterprise.

Let's examine how the evaluation process can work to the advantage of both the company and the employee. Let's eavesdrop on a performance evaluation meeting between Sarah, an IT development manager, and Matt, a programmer who reports to Sarah. Early in the year, Matt and Sarah set as his primary objective the completion of a new order entry system for the sales staff of their office products distribution company. The project was completed on time and on budget, with users giving high marks for the implementation. But Matt had some problems during the year working with other members of the development team. Sarah also had to speak with him about his attempted access to an unauthorized application:

Matt: Hi Sarah, is now a good time?

Sarah: Hi Matt. Sure, please sit. I've been going over your self-evaluation marks. I noticed that you rated yourself high on technological skill, control awareness, and efficiency—giving yourself a "substantially exceeds standard"—but somewhat lower on teamwork and project management, with a "meets standard." Why don't you explain your thinking behind your ratings?

Matt: Well, as you know, my main objective for the year was the implementation of the order entry system, which was completed on time and underbudget.

Sarah: Yes, everyone sees the project as a success. Your technical expertise certainly contributed to that success, and I agree with your technical and efficiency marks. But you rated yourself lower on teamwork, and your peer reviews were a little low.

Matt: Yeah, well, there was certainly some friction between me and the other team members.

Sarah: Why do you think that was?

Matt: Honestly, I think they are jealous of my technical capability. It just seems that anything I say they ignore, no matter how right I am.

Sarah: There may be truth to that. I could see the team getting defensive if they perceived you as much brighter then they are, and you constantly show it. You are not exactly a wall-flower. (She chuckles.)

Matt: (Smiling) Yeah, that's true. I guess I can be pretty direct. But that does not change the fact that there are better ways to do things.

Sarah: Exactly. There might also be better ways to interact with the team to get your point across. How might you help the team overcome their fear of you?

Matt: Really, I don't know.

Sarah: Remember when we talked about softer approaches? Perhaps you should ask other team members for their opinion once in a while. You can also pick your battles. If the issue is not that important for the success of the system, perhaps you can let the team make what you perceive as the less optimal call. Maybe even phrase your feedback differently—instead of saying, "The right way would be to..." you could say, "One option is to...."

Matt: Yes, I remember. I'll try harder to use those tactics.

Sarah: Good. I was also curious about your high mark for control awareness. What was your thinking on that?

Matt: Well, I am very aware of how important controls are.

Sarah: I rated you a notch lower, at "meets expectations," based on your unauthorized access attempts on the Peoplesoft system.

Matt: Oh yeah, I forgot about that. You know that I was just trying to find the names of salespeople for user acceptance testing and thought the HR system would have been a good place to get that kind of information.

Sarah: I know, Matt, but you have to follow procedure. That is a core value. You should have asked me for permission. Instead, you repeatedly tried to access a system containing sensitive information over a period of days. I did not rate you as "does not meet" because I have noted no other attempts since then.

Matt: No, and you won't. I learned my lesson.

Sarah: Okay. Enough on that subject. On the bright side, I did mark you higher on project management. Your task-tracking skills and work ethic are qualities that really helped bring in the project.

Matt: Thanks. I marked myself lower because of the issues I had with the team.

Sarah: Well, we handled that in the teamwork section. I think that once you master the personal skills you need to work well with the staff, you will make a tremendous manager one day.

Matt: I appreciate your confidence in me. What do you think about my objectives for the coming year...

Sarah and Matt have had a constructive dialogue, which highlighted both Matt's strengths as well as those traits he still needs to work on. Sarah refrained from being overly authoritative and allowed Matt to explain his rational for his self-evaluation. As is often the case, Matt recognized many of his weaknesses and was able to discuss them. This may be due, in large part, to Sarah's practice of discussing these issues with him during the year, rather than only during the evaluation process. She also helped reduce tension by kidding with Matt about his direct demeanor. Humor can be effective where there is a strong working relationship between a manager and his or her staff. But it can also be dangerous if that rapport does not exist or if there is infrequent communication between a manager and employee. Here it worked to Sarah's advantage and helped Matt open up to different possible courses of action.

A difficult problem arises when an employee rates him- or herself significantly higher than his or her manager. When this happens, a manager must be ready to give the rationale to support the rating. Sarah did not agree with Matt that his control awareness exceeded standard, and she could back this up. While she was firm, she also credited him with improvement in this area. Finally, Sarah finished on an up note, which will help motivate Matt going forward. He is ready to set objectives for next year to prove himself. A key success of the evaluation process was that the objective of completing an order entry system was specific, measurable, achievable, relevant, and timely. Sarah very capably managed this important process and will ensure that the objectives for next year also are SMART.

CHAPTER 7

Protect Yourself

W̲e now know where we are vulnerable. After answering the control questions in each step of Smart Links, a manager will have a list of gaps identified for certain activities. These gaps are like holes in a dike. If not plugged, water will flood our town with the next heavy rains. Our gaps must now be addressed in order to defend our company, employees, and careers. This leads us to our next pathway milestone in Exhibit 7.1, protect yourself. But how do we identify the perfect control that will provide that defense?

EXHIBIT 7.1 CONTROL SMART PATHWAY

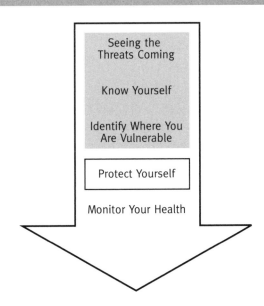

Seeing the
Threats Coming

Know Yourself

Identify Where You
Are Vulnerable

Protect Yourself

Monitor Your Health

In Appendix D is a list of control activities that may comprise the cement that helps plug a gap. The list is sorted by Smart Link step to make it easier to scan activities that might be relevant. Most processes that you can conceive of will have a common control activity that is suitable to the situation. For instance, the common method to make sure cash receipts and payments are properly recorded is to reconcile them to a bank statement. It may take some imagination to properly mold it into a process, but it is worth the effort.

Every process is different, however, and it is possible that a procedure is so complex or unique that common control activities will not easily provide the answer. In the rare case that a manager cannot identify or conceive of a procedure to address a weakness, there are other resources to tap. Management can solicit the opinion of auditors or retain outside consultants who are experts in the field. For the vast majority of gaps, however, a manager can find a solution in Appendix D.

FIND THOSE GAPS: THE DENTEX CASE

Control gaps identify process vulnerabilities which, if unrecognized and/or attacked, can result in a material loss or harm to the enterprise. Vulnerabilities themselves will not cause a material loss; rather, an event or purposeful attack may be the catalyst that surfaces the weakness. An effective control gap template will identify the gap and determine the control objective and the activity necessary to achieve the objective.

To illustrate the assessment process just reviewed, let's perform an assessment for a manufacturing business. To do that, we'll eavesdrop on Dentex, a $300 million manufacturer of dental equipment. Scott Lee, the president of Dentex not only wants to meet the provisions of the Sarbanes-Oxley Act, but he's also very concerned about what has happened to American companies and wants to ensure his control structure is strong. Therefore, he intends to assess all aspects of his operations for good internal control.

Scott runs a profitable plant located near Seattle, which produces and delivers operatory equipment to dealers, who in turn sell to the end users, the dentists. His plant is a subsidiary of Dental Giant, a large European-based company that provides all types of dental instruments and has American Depository Receipts (ADRs) that trade on the NYSE. Sales are consummated with distributors of dental equipment by a centralized team that supports all of Dental Giant's products and is managed out of the company's European and North American headquarters. Scott has an operations manager, Allan Schott, who has decision rights for all manufacturing activity up to and including shipping. There is an IT department, headed by Brent Fall; a finance and administration department led by Susan O'Conner, and an HR department run by Rich Cappelli, who also serves as the part-time mayor of Willow Creek, a very small and quaint town about 30 minutes from the plant. The company culture supports strong controls. Nevertheless, concern about the wave of competitors that experienced devastating, control-related losses has led Scott to call a meeting of his direct reports to initiate an assessment of Dentex's operations. Let's listen in on the meeting:

Scott: Good morning everyone. As you have probably read in the media, a number of our competitors have experienced severe operational and financial pressures due to poor internal controls. Legislation has been passed that will require senior management to sign off on the adequacy of their financial reporting controls. While I believe we have a strong culture that would preclude such losses, I would like us to perform an assessment of our control structure. Today we will embark on a project to evaluate our controls and identify gaps. I would like to introduce Greg Baker, a control expert who has helped other clients execute a control assessment program.

Greg: Hello everyone. I am looking forward to working with each of you.

Scott: Greg has already requested information from me. Many procedures he has identified as core to any good control environment we already perform in the normal course of conducting our business. For instance, he asked me what our objectives are for the coming year and what we perceived the risks to achieving those objectives might be. I gave him a copy of our business plan, which discusses our products and identifies those that are selling particularly well. It also sets our objectives for this year, which include improving productivity by 10 percent as measured by fully loaded cost per unit produced. We all recognize that this is an aggressive, but achievable, target. I also let him know that we have assigned owners to our nonoperational risks. Susan manages financial and liquidity risk, Brent has responsibility for business continuity planning and similar event risk, Rich manages any regulatory and legal issues relating to human resources, and I will take responsibility to manage any other legal threats to our operations. Credit and market risk are managed by headquarters, so we play only a supporting role, by providing information as requested. Greg pointed out to me that each of us is responsible for managing the operational risk inherent in his or her individual departments, and that will be the focus of this project.

Rich: I think the idea is very good, Scott, but I am no control expert. I am not comfortable that I can get this right. I also believe many staff and supervisors might resist this project, as it will highlight problems in their areas that have been present for a long time.

Scott: Point taken. The reason I retained Greg is to facilitate our evaluation and implementation. He can keep track of our progress as well as help us identify and address any gaps. Regarding employee resistance, I firmly believe this will work only if it is perceived in a positive light. We must make it clear that there is an amnesty regarding any control weaknesses identified. We should also put together a recognition program for those employees who identify the most gaps, are most energetic in supporting the assessment process, and so on. Rich, can you put together a couple of recognition options for this team to consider, along with a draft communication to the organization?

Rich: Sure. When do you need it?

Scott: How about the end of business tomorrow? Will that work?

Rich: That's fine.

Susan: I'm not sure this applies to me. I am trained in controls, and besides, headquarters prepares the financial statements. They are responsible for the accuracy of the numbers and for ensuring there are proper disclosures.

Scott: I recognize your expertise in this area, Susan, but it is always helpful to have a new set of eyes look at a process. I would also point out that this business can be material to the operations of our parent, so we want to make sure we have a belts-and-suspenders approach to reporting our numbers.

Brent: I understand from Greg that we need to assign business owners to each user application and to review access levels. When do we do that?

Greg: We can actually start on that right away. I can sit with you to determine who the most logical business owner of each system is. We can then have each owner review and approve the access levels of users.

Brent: Great, I appreciate the help.

Scott: Any questions, Allan?

Allan: No, sounds great.

Scott: Okay, if there are no more questions, let's begin identifying and documenting all processes for which we have responsibility. Let's plan to meet every week at this time to assess our progress. Remember to keep Greg in the loop. He will keep track of all areas and help you set target dates for completion of each task. Let's set a goal of having all of our processes identified and at least one major process documented and evaluated by next week.

Scott has done a great job of establishing structure, creating goals, and setting a positive tone for the project. By setting regular meetings and requiring that certain tasks be accomplished before the next meeting, he has given the project a sense of urgency. The amnesty and recognition program will also break down resistance and provide momentum. By making Greg available, he has also provided confidence to those without control training that they can succeed, and lets everyone know that the program will be continually monitored and reported to the president. At this point, everyone seems onboard—though Scott did notice some hesitation from Susan, and made a mental note to check in on her later to make certain she is moving forward with her assessment.

APPLYING SMART LINKS

Allan Schott, the operations manager, was actually ahead of the process. In previous discussions with Scott, Allan had recognized his concern about the control structure—Scott had been going on about the losses experienced by other companies and asking pointed questions about Allan's procedures.

Allan read the writing on the wall and already had his shipping supervisor, inventory manager, and shop foreman busy documenting their procedures. He knew that they would have to work with Greg to get them into good form, but he wanted to be on top of any gaps that might exist. The first document Allan wanted to present to Greg was the overview of the production process (see Exhibit 7.2).

Armed with the preliminary document, Allan sat down with Greg to go over the procedures. Once again, let's eavesdrop on their conversation:

> Greg: Allan, I think it's great that you have taken the initiative and have already documented your processes. I will use an efficient 13-step tool to help us analyze these processes. Let's start from the beginning of Smart Links: culture and documentation.

> Allan: Greg, we are more like a family on the floor, so I believe the right culture is present. People want to do the right thing. We just need to make our focus on controls more apparent and link them to our overall goal of intelligently increasing productivity 10 percent. We don't want to burn our guys out; we need to work smarter, not necessarily harder.

> Greg: I've noticed the family atmosphere you refer to. The strong culture of doing the right thing for the company is definitely present. Employees are aware of both the plant's mission and statement of values. As managers, we need to be cognizant that values need to be continually reinforced by visible actions.
>
> Step 2, has to do with clients. Clients can be different for every one of your processes. For instance, the floor supervisor is the customer for the inventory manager, as he depends on him to have material on hand and have it delivered to the floor on a timely basis. The inventory manager is the customer for receiving as he depends on an accurate count and delivery of incoming inventory. Let's stick with production for now. Who do you consider your clients? I guess one would be the sales department, as once an order gets to you, it has already been approved and you need to fill it.

> Allan: That's right. We use the orders to plan our production and order our materials. When filled, the orders are marked as such in the system. We notify sales if we have any problem with delivery dates.

EXHIBIT 7.2 PRODUCTION PROCESS

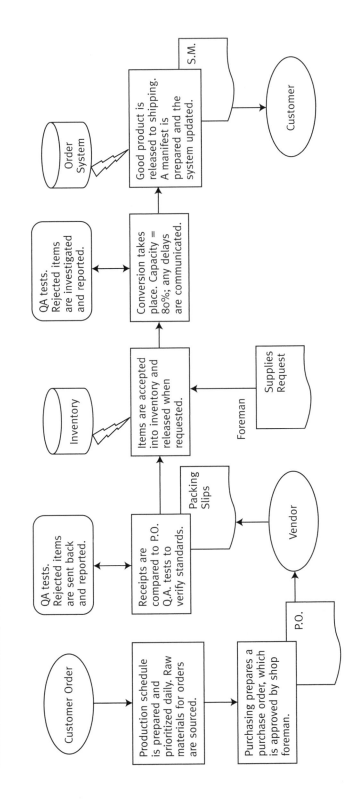

Greg and Allan are off to a good start. They agree that the culture is positive and that this contributes to an effective control environment. Allan has had his managers prepare documentation so that he and Greg can subject it to the Smart Links process together. Greg has been careful to separate the various processes for which Allan exercises responsibility and decision rights. These initially include inventory, receiving, and production. By identifying the various customers of each department, he has effectively distinguished between each function and helped Allan focus on production. They can subject production to Smart Links, which will naturally interface with inventory and receiving, and, when completed, they can repeat the process focusing specifically on these other processes. Let's return to the evaluation.

> Allan: Step 3 has to do with sourcing materials, which we are very involved with. To answer the specific question, we know whether items are all received in good form because we note quantities of receipts against a copy of the purchase order. The quantity column is left blank for a blind count, and we then conduct a second tally to verify the first. Each dock worker signs it and then we send it to accounts payable. Every once in a while, they will check with us to see if we made a counting mistake. Generally, the vendor has sent a partial shipment or made a mistake. We also test key materials before we use them. Occasionally, something has to be returned. We complete a form, send a copy to finance, and notify the vendor that we are returning the material for credit.

> Greg: The blind and verifying count are great controls. They will help accounts payable staff make sure that they only pay for what has been received. It seems that they serve as another control point since they follow up on differences. The component testing is a great way to ensure that bad inputs do not make it to manufacturing and cost the company even more money. I don't see either that or the returned merchandise procedure here.

> Allan: I will have to follow up with quality assurance and shipping procedures.

At this point, Greg and Allan have identified several important controls and some missing procedures. Greg makes certain that Allan understands where the control points are by repeating them and explaining how they contribute. For example, the segregation of the count in receiving and verification of receipts by accounts payable is a strong control. Additionally, Greg noticed that Allan did not provide testing documentation. It is easy to overlook certain procedures that a manager does not recognize as a standalone process.

Allan: Step 4, system access is next. I believe that is where we look at who has which IT capabilities. Well, I guess from today's meeting I will be sitting down with Brent's people to go through access to inventory, shipping, and production systems.

Greg: Yes, that should be done soon. I will join you to go through that process. Let's move on to Step 5, which is designed to make certain that manufacturing defects, aged inventory, or poor data is surfaced. Is there a method to identify defects?

Allan: You bet. My quality assurance guys can be a pain to the foreman, but they are great at identifying problems. Every defect is categorized, investigated, and reported to executive management. As I mentioned earlier, I will get the Q&A department procedures to you.

Greg: That's fine. What about inventory? How do you know it is all properly recorded and valued?

Allan: Our vendors are key partners. They shoulder much of the responsibility for keeping us supplied. We keep a perpetual inventory record, but we also conduct an inventory every quarter with our vendors and agree on stocking targets. I also have a materials aging procedure that identifies old product. I give this to finance and, together, we agree on a number to put against the old stuff.

Greg: That's excellent. The inventory counts and the support for the inventory reserve are also excellent controls. But I noticed that the reserves seem a little light when compared to inventory over six months old.

Allan: Well, last quarter was particularly tough financially for the company. Susan and I agreed that I would try to work down some of the older inventory or find a buyer. Truthfully, I have had mixed success. We will probably have to take a larger write-down this quarter.

Greg: Does Scott know about this?

Allan: I don't know. I assume Susan has kept him posted.

Greg: You might mention this to Scott. You do not want him surprised by a last-minute write-off.

Allan: That's a good point. I will talk to him today.

It is not unusual that employees will take an action that they believe is in the best interests of the company, but that actually could do more damage down the line. Inadequate reserves can lead to a growing, unrecognized problem that will surface at the most inopportune time for management. Although aging metrics exist, Allan does not know whether Scott is aware of the reserve deficiency or its impact. Greg points out to Allan that he should make certain that Scott is aware of the problem before it grows into a larger issue. Greg will also note these issues when helping Scott identify key performance indicators that he should follow as president.

Greg: You know, manufacturing operations in the Seattle area often have a tough time keeping well-trained employees, and even a tougher time hiring more when the economy is good.

Allan: We have some turnover, but it is lower than many of our peers. We do have a well-trained staff with adequate backup at every position in the event we lose key people. We should be alright unless growth really takes off, but expansion isn't in the plan. We figure that we can handle maybe a 20 percent increase in volume without any new investment, so we should be okay. We actually tested our capacity utilization thresholds last spring by purposely putting through an order in excess of our stated capacity, which proved our assumptions.

Greg: Are your primary and secondary employees documented in a depth chart for every position?

Allan: No, I suppose we should do that.

Greg: Okay. What about information backup? You should make sure everything you need can be obtained in case you lose access to the system. It might also be wise to think about your vendor relationships and the impact a strike or other event at a supplier might have on your ability to continue production.

Allan: I'm not sure how our information is backed up. I will have to ask Brent about that. I'll let you know what he says. We do maintain secondary vendors for all hard-to-source items. It is probably a good time to revisit that; I will have procurement formalize that list.

Capacity and labor constraints are important factors in capital allocation and hiring plans. A manager needs to know how much product a machine can produce as well as how deep his or her labor pool is. Capacity utilization should periodically be tested to validate constraints and identify bottlenecks. The amount of time it takes to hire and train a new employee and have him or her working effectively on the line should also be known. Allan's response to Greg's pointed question tells him that Allan is very cognizant of this key indicator.

Contingency planning is a primary responsibility of every manager. It is not enough to simply think through various threats such as the replacement of a sick or injured employee; a continuity plan and related depth chart need to be documented. If an event rendered the foreperson and other floor labor unavailable, then properly trained backup employees may not be easily identified, thereby retarding recovery. Likewise, a loss of systems would have an impact on operations, so Allan should understand what Brent's recovery capabilities are and what he will have to do without. While investment in an off-site recovery facility is not a decision over which Allan exerts control, he nevertheless should understand not only the recovery capability of the company, but how he would continue to operate without systems or loss of a key supplier. Hard copies of orders and alternative vendors may need to be maintained to ensure he can continue production for a period of time should the systems become unavailable or merchandise deliveries disrupted.

Allan: Steps 7 and 8 ask whether all product is delivered in good form and whether there is an independent evaluation of defects. We usually find out that there is a problem when a return shows up at the dock or customer service calls telling us we did not ship a complete order. Of course, they are usually wrong; most shorts are a result of client mistakes. More often than not, the full shipment was received and an error was made in the receiving department of our customer. I know that a common control is to keep an open order aging for product deliveries. We have that. But it would be great to get better notification and more detail regarding why items are returned.

I noticed that another common control mentioned is that we should track defect percentage. Most of this stuff is fine and we are able to resell it, but we really don't track that. It would be better to formalize both return notification and testing of returned merchandise. I will mention this to Scott.

Greg: Very good. I agree that it would be a great improvement. Maybe Scott can do something to bring greater control and more feedback to this process—like getting the VP of customer service to agree to set up a committee with a mandate to improve the return process. It is often hard for separate departments in different cities to coordinate customer queries and returns. Traditionally, cross-functional teams are effective at improving these types of processes. Regardless, it is important that defects be categorized and investigated. Typically, I have seen companies log a returned product, assign an investigator who will analyze the defect, and determine the cause. When he or she is assured that the cause has been corrected, he or she will then report back to client service and agree with them that the case can be closed.

Greg is right. Intercompany handoffs between departments and functions are the Bermuda Triangle of business. Transactions, nonstandard processes, and related controls all fall off the radar screen in this netherworld. One department believes it has handed off a transaction to another, and the other believes that the first department is still working on it or, worse, may not be aware of it at all. When identified, cross-functional teams are usually a good approach to addressing interdepartmental problems.

Greg: Step 9 addresses payment. Do you ever receive anything into shipping in trade for product sales?

Allan: No, I do not recall any instances of this, and all payments are booked at headquarters. We simply tell finance what has been shipped and they ensure that we get paid. I know they do that reconciliation there, which is the focus of Step 10.

The next is Step 11, cost controls and metrics. Scott follows our productivity and defect numbers. He is always asking me why they went up or down.

Greg: Given the focus on productivity, that is understandable. That means Scott is also a client as far the management reporting product is concerned. We will want to come back to the management reporting process and subject it to Smart Links separately.

Allan: Definitely. Step 12 does not apply to me; I will let Susan wrestle with that one.

Greg: Well, your departments do have an impact on financial reporting. Do you have cutoff procedures at the end of the month?

Allan: Oh that. Yeah, we get instructions from finance that tell us the day and time of the cutoff. They usually come by to identify the last sales shipment and inventory receipt on that day.

Greg: That control helps finance ensure the financial information is reported consistently and in the right period.

A manager often will not fully understand his or her role in the overall function of the firm. In this case, Allan knew he was required to follow cutoff procedures, but did not identify it as a control for financial reporting purposes. Greg did a great job pointing out this interrelationship to Allan. He also delineated the management reporting function from production. So, again, he has surfaced another area for which Allan has decision rights and responsibilities, which should be separately subjected to Smart Links.

Greg: The last step has to do with performance evaluations.

Allan: Yeah, we use a standard 360-degree process developed by Rich. It's his baby and he is on top of us at year-end to get them done. We tie corporate objectives to individual goals. This seems to work pretty well.

Greg: Take me through how that works.

Allan: It all starts with Scott. He sets the corporate objectives for the year. For instance, this year, the main objective is to increase productivity by 10 percent. We then set our goals, which must somehow contribute to corporate objectives. We use the SMART format meaning that they must be specific, measurable, achievable, relevant, and timely. My goal is to automate our packaging process, which is highly manual. This target meets the SMART profile; and, for little investment, I can achieve most of the productivity increase Scott is looking for from my department. At the end of the year, Scott will ask me to perform a self-evaluation on my performance. He will also solicit feedback from Susan, Rich, and Brent to make certain I am a team player; and from subordinates to ensure I am adhering to corporate values. We discuss any differences in perception between my self-assessment and how others view me.

Greg: What do you think of the process?

Allan: It works, but honestly, I would rather that subordinates not have a say.

Greg: Why is that?

Allan: It just makes my interaction with them uncomfortable during this period. None of the operations guys are touchy-feely types, you know? But we have to sit down and discuss our relationships with each other. I think they dislike it as much as I do.

Greg: But you said it works.

Allan: Yes, we do identify better ways to do things and, from time to time, clear up some miscommunications.

Greg: Maybe you and your team could benefit from better training regarding how to conduct these evaluations. The focus should be primarily on performance. Sometimes, the approach can be altered to make the interactions more businesslike, which might help eliminate that uncomfortable feeling.

Not all employees will be thrilled with every control procedure, but they will be more likely to comply if they understand the rationale for the process. Allan's reaction to the performance evaluation process is understandable. Fortunately, Allan recognizes that despite being uncomfortable, this course of action is important for meeting corporate objectives and identifying operational improvements. Greg also has put forth a solution that may help Allan and his subordinates better execute this vital step.

Allan: Wow! Done already, that was pretty easy. It looks like I need to close the loop regarding returned items.

Greg: Yes, you also need to prepare your Q&A procedures, prepare a depth chart, and meet with Brent to assess access levels and determine how your information is backed up. But this is an excellent start. You are way ahead of everyone else. I will get the project plan updated and the gaps you identified documented. Good work!

Allan: Thanks. We wanted to get out in front of this project. I will get you these other items ASAP. Let's schedule some time to go through the other procedures.

Greg: Great. There will be some overlap in the other areas with production, so they should go much faster.

This interaction between Greg and Allan did not take a lot of time because Allan was prepared. Greg was able to walk through Allan's processes and easily identify issues because they were documented and easy to follow. Allan identified certain weaknesses such as the process for returned merchandise, and Greg aided the process by pointing out that the quality assurance procedures were not documented, and that there was no depth chart to help management analyze coverage for each position. He also reminded Allan that it is his responsibility to ensure critical data is backed up and system access supervised. A manager cannot rely on IT without confirming procedures and implementing a method to ensure compliance. The plans may need work to standardize, but the basic information is available and gaps can be immediately identified and addressed. Greg can take the documents Allan gave him to update the project plan and the control and gap template for Allan's department.

But not all of the work is going so well.

INTERRUPTING AN EMBEZZLEMENT

Greg next sits down with Brent, the IT director, and Susan, the head of finance, to go through system access levels.

Susan: Well, let's get through this. I have things to do.

Greg: Should we reschedule? This could take a bit of time. We need to understand the system capabilities each of your staff has been awarded.

Susan: I really do not think it will take long. I am very familiar with system controls.

Brent: I brought the access report for Susan's department.

Greg: Let's start with accounts payable. I noticed something on the report that we should look at. It appears that the supervisor, Jason, has the capability to set up and approve a vendor payment. Normally, these two functions are segregated.

Susan: Well, he used to be the accounts payable clerk. We just did not remember to take away his recording capability when he was promoted.

Greg: We should probably remove that capability immediately. You might also want to review recent payments as an additional check that these powers were not abused.

Susan: I'll do that. Let's move on.

Greg: Okay. Well, that will be one feather in your cap, Susan. Scott sees the identification and correction of these types of control gaps very positively.

Clearly, Susan is not fully onboard with the assessment program, but Greg did a good job keeping to business and forging ahead. The identification of conflicting recording and authorization powers is not by itself a problem. In fact, the identification of the conflict and the applied solution of restricting Jason's capability strengthen the organization and should be encouraged. Greg did a good job reminding Susan that there is a sort of amnesty on control gaps found and that she will be rewarded for addressing them.

A week later, however, Susan enters Scott's office with troubling news.

Susan: Scott, do you have a moment?

Scott: Sure, is everything all right? You look troubled.

Susan: We have a problem. I admit, I initially did not think that a review of controls in my area was necessary, but in working with Brent and Greg, we discovered that Jason, our accounting supervisor, had system access to both the preparation and supervisory functions for procurement payments. If you remember, he used to be the accounts payable clerk before his promotion. When he became a supervisor, we provided him with supervisory access so that he could release checks for vendor payments, but we never eliminated his ability to set up a payment.

Scott: Okay, that seems simple enough; we just restrict his access.

Susan: Well, there's more. When we discovered this, Greg recommended that we review vendor payments for the last few months. I normally review payments made at the end of the month to ensure I have approved all checks over $5,000, in accordance with policy. But, honestly, there are so many payments that I only focus on those over the limit. In reviewing the payments for last month, I saw a check made out to SouthFork Bank.

Scott: Well, that's our bank.

Susan: Right, but it usually credits our account for any bank charges, and debt payments are usually well over $5,000. I could not think of a reason why we would send them a check for more than $3,000 last month. In looking at the vendor file, the payment address was not to the corporate clearing center we normally send loan payments to. When I pulled the canceled check, the endorsement mark was from SouthFork Bancard Services.

Scott: A payment on a credit card?

Susan: That's right. Here's the canceled check. And, Scott, there are more. I went back 10 months, and there are similar checks every month, totaling almost $20,000. I will need to pull records from the warehouse to determine how long this has been going on.

Scott: Well, when was Jason promoted? That is when he was granted supervisory access.

Susan: Believe it or not, it has been almost four years. You know he has been with us for over 12 years now. I just don't understand what he is thinking. I thought we were friends.

Scott: Let's quietly pull all of the records and get our lawyers and accountants to look at them.

While the purpose of a control assessment is to deter fraud, it is possible that the process may interrupt a current embezzlement. The profile of an effective embezzler is often similar to Jason's: an educated male who is a long-term employee in a trusted position. Jason will likely be arrested on the advice of counsel and end a long career with a good company.

FINISHING THE JOB

Once Greg has met with the other members of Scott's management team, he will combine the templates to provide Scott with the overall view of the major controls protecting his business. The template Greg prepared can be seen in Exhibit 7.3.

EXHIBIT 7.3   SMART LINKS PRIMARY CONTROL
SUMMARY

Dentex Corporation
Primary Control Structure
February 15, 2004

Smart Link Step	Analysis/GAP	Control Implemented
1	Boundaries	Documented policies and procedures (P&P) and Statement of Values.
2	Customer credit and regulatory restrictions	All products are paid for prior to shipping by credit card or check at headquarters.
3	All materials received and independently validated	All purchases received are matched to a purchase order and invoiced by person independent of purchasing and receiving/inventory. Customer orders are scheduled for production and personnel scheduled by floor foreman and approved by the operations manager.
4	Access restrictions	Shipping/receiving, inventory, accounts payable, accounts receivable, sales are all electronically segregated and restricted. Supervisors have read-only and approval functions only. A report of all changes is received by the technology manager daily. Firewalls are in place and tested regularly. Information sent over the Internet is encrypted. Access to the data room is electronically restricted to the database administrator and programmers. Audit trails are electronically maintained and backed up automatically off-site every day.
5	Identify product defects and report in a timely manner prior to shipping	Quality assurance independently reports defect percent daily to the operations manager. Aged inventory report sent by inventory cage to Operations Manager and Controller monthly.
6	Capacity constraints	Plant capacity and system utilization reports prepared weekly and reviewed by the Operations Manager. Plant and systems stress-tested and bottlenecks identified. Manual backup plans prepared and volume benchmarks set for additional investment in plant and systems. Safety, overtime, and illness monitored. Turnover metrics, depth charts, career planning process are operational.
7	Complete and timely shipments sent in good form	Shipping manifests matched to open orders. Aged open and partial order report sent to operations manager, controller, and to headquarters daily.
8	Detection of defective items shipped	Customer service directs defect complaints directly to floor foreman, operations manager, and president.
9	Customer payment	All payment received prior to shipping. Payments are processed by accounts receivable and credited to a customer order. Only items paid in full can be released by the system for shipping.

EXHIBIT 7.3   (CONTINUED)

Smart Link Step	Analysis/GAP	Control Implemented
10	Cash account is reconciled	Cash account is reconciled daily in finance by a person independent of the accounts receivable function. The reconciliation is reviewed daily by the controller.
11	Financial cost controls	Budget to actual reports, manufacturing efficiency variances, margin percent, performance reviews.
12	Government regulations	Internal OSHA compliance reviews, safety metrics, and so on
13	Staff reviews	Include policy and procedures compliance in staff reviews.

Now that Scott has addressed control gaps, it would be prudent for him to make certain that policies and procedures are updated to reflect additions and changes to processes. Further review of the revised procedures by internal or external auditors would provide further assurance that the changes are sound and adequately address control objectives. Most managers avoid frequent contact with their auditors. This is a basic human reaction, as no one enjoys being critiqued and, worse, having it reported to others. Get over it. By being proactive, managers can develop good rapport with auditors and control experts, and benefit from frequent, informal communication regarding best practices. Smart managers will reach out to internal audit every time they take on a new assignment.

By getting feedback upfront, you can address control issues before you take ownership of them. If internal audit does not have the time to address your concerns (due to risk priorities), or the audit culture is too cold for comfort, then it would be appropriate to retain control consultants to provide necessary feedback. There are a number of added benefits to using consultants: You'll obtain an outsider's point of view; the consultants will report results solely to you, the manager; and the report can be used in future audits to effectively demonstrate the integrity of the control structure.

APPLYING SMART LINKS TO FINANCIAL REPORTING PROCESSES

The purpose of Section 404 of the Sarbanes-Oxley Act is to improve internal controls over financial reporting. The primacy of financial reporting requirements of the act makes these processes the highest priority for documentation and evaluation. As we now know, terminal risks can migrate from almost anywhere in an organization to the financial statements. This is why all managers, not just financial managers, must assess their internal control structure and the impact that their operations have on their company. Most managers are not trained in internal control, a shortcoming this book hopes to remedy. Most financial managers do, however, have some internal control training. Even for these managers, Smart Links can serve as an additional reinforcing tool to evaluate their accounting and financial reporting processes.

The process for applying Smart Links to a financial manager's operations is the same as for other processes. The most important starting point is for a financial manager to know which accounts, group of accounts, or reporting classifications he or she has responsibility over. Depending on the size of the organization, a controller or CFO will generally ensure that there is an "account owner" for every general ledger account. That owner is responsible to deliver the financial product attributable to that account. For most accounting and financial reporting processes, the end deliverable will be financial information that is valid, accurate, properly classified, and timely. This deliverable is a financial product that has been manufactured from raw material inputs taking the form of information originating in other systems, hard copy sources such as vendor invoices, subledgers, management estimates, and so on. The conversion of information into reportable financial data, including the sources of the raw numbers, must be documented and mapped (Smart Link Step 1). The relevant accounting standards and policies for these accounts must be well understood so that misclassified transactions can be identified (Step 2). Completeness and validity controls must be present to ensure that all information was captured in good form (Step 3). Access to accounts and related systems must be safeguarded from unauthorized access (Step 4). Quality control procedures such as supervisory review, analytical review, account and systems reconciliations, impairment evaluations, and so on must be present to ensure that the information is properly valued, directed and compiled (Step 5). Human and system constraints must also be known, to ensure the job can be completed in a timely manner and to meet regulatory deadlines (Step 6). There must be a completeness control to ensure that the deliverable (financial data) made it to its destination in good form (Step 7). Proper segregation and detective controls will be needed to discourage undetected manipulation (Step 8). Controls are needed to verify and validate liquid assets (Steps 9 and 10), if applicable to your area. Metrics that help you monitor your account activity should be available. For instance, do sales volume and trends support the receivables balance in your account (Step 11)? Obviously, controls to ensure that financial statements and regulatory filings have been properly completed are critical to financial managers (Step 12). Above and beyond handing information off to your internal customer, you must ensure it is properly reflected in the final product if the accounts are significant. Good senior management will also have entity level controls, such as committee review of disclosures, management estimates, and accounting policies; but as a financial manager, I would want to know that my accounts were being reported properly. Finally, financial staff should be evaluated for compliance with accounting policies and standards, as well as the company's code of ethics (Step 13).

While the Control Smart approach for financial managers is essentially the same as for other managers, there are some unique aspects to their operations, and additional measures are available to these managers to help them identify where risk resides in their financial processes. These processes normally handle a high volume of financial transactions from multiple sources, which must be captured, classified, and reported. Distinguishing between routine transactions and nonroutine transactions or estimates can help a manager focus on those areas that are at greater risk for error. In distinguishing between these classes of transactions, routine transactions are generally subjected to a more formalized control structure in order to handle the anticipated volume efficiently and accurately. Routine transactions might include payroll, cash disbursements, procurement, and so on. Nonroutine data and estimates tend to be less common and more subjective, such as the calculation of income tax expense and estimating the allowance for doubtful accounts. Controls over these types of transactions are typically less formal. More care needs to be given to the nonroutine and estimation transaction control structure. Not only should the sources of data be mapped and evaluated, but assumptions, models, and advisors used to develop the estimates should be challenged and the results documented.

While covered in Smart Links Step 3 for incoming information, and Steps 7 and 8 for outgoing information, financial managers should nevertheless pay more attention to data interfaces both within their processes and external links. Data lost between system, departmental, or branch interfaces occurs more frequently than you think. As an auditor, I cannot tell you the number of times I have found a situation where one department sent a transaction to another department or branch, only to have it hang out there indefinitely (commonly in an intercompany, suspense, or other "unowned" account). Either the sender did not notify the receiver of the transaction, or the recipient did not properly pick it up. As illustrated in Exhibit 7.4, these handoffs can occur anywhere within the financial reporting process, but primarily can be found between the sources of information and financial accounts, as well as between the general ledger accounts and the reporting classifications found in the financial reports.

EXHIBIT 7.4   FINANCIAL PROCESS INTERFACES

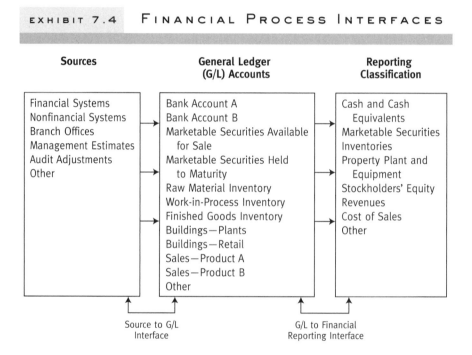

Even systems that worked perfectly in the past will fail to hand off information from time to time. This could be due to system upgrades, new transactions not properly mapped, unknown software bugs, and so on. A recent case in point involves a Connecticut money manager who recently reported that he bought tens of millions of dollars of stock over a period of several months without knowing it. His unknown buying spree accumulated stakes in two companies that required disclosure via regulatory filings, but were not made. While the details are not yet known, the money manager has inferred that three layers of software had failed. If true, this implies that trades were being executed and settled, but that the transactions did not flow upstream to the management information used to run the business. If position and dollar reconciliations had been performed between the trading systems or the financial systems and management reports, or a simple reconciliation had been made of the firm's positions to depository or broker statements, such errors would have been caught months ago. This manager now faces upset investors and angry company boards, and he could face SEC action over his failure to make timely disclosures of his controlling ownership in these companies.

So the importance of documenting and mapping the financial reporting processes is clear. Exhibit 7.5 reviews graphically a simplified single source of information, a payroll system for a partnership, as an example of how to map accounts to their sources. Note that the payment processes for salaried and hourly employees are highly automated, but the payments to partners, which consist of advances and periodic distributions of profits, are nonroutine. That is because the amounts can vary with results as well as from changes in each partner's ownership percentage. These variables require manual intervention and introduce a greater chance for error. Since partners are not employees, rather owners of the business, activity will be booked to the partners' capital account, rather than an expense account. Additionally, partners pay their own taxes based on profits, so payroll tax is unaffected, whereas the firm must pay employment taxes on their salaried and hourly workers.

Now let's look at how the general ledger accounts will map to the financial reports; that is shown in Exhibit 7.6. In this example, the treasurer of the partnership is responsible for maintaining liquidity and ensuring that the reported balance in the bank account is correct. The payroll manager is responsible for the accounts that roll up into employee expenses. The CFO is responsible for ensuring the partner accounts are correct. Therefore, every account has an owner and is mapped to the consolidated financial reports.

These additional documentation tools will help a financial manager identify and apply Smart Links to those processes critical to significant accounts. The application of Smart Links to each process impacting these accounts will help the manager identify and assess controls. The appeal of Smart Links is its flexibility. The tool can be applied to almost any process: operations, finance, human resources, and so on. All can be subjected to the Control Smart Approach and Smart Links. The results will provide a viable action plan to implement controls and prepare a reporting mechanism for your key performance indicators.

EXHIBIT 7.5 MAPPING SOURCES TO ACCOUNTS

	Payroll Process			General Ledger Accounts						
Source	Process Type	Owner	Transaction Types	Bank Account	Salaries Expense	Hourly Expense	Overtime Expenses	Payroll Taxes	Partner A	Partner B
Payroll System	Salaried Payroll	Payroll Manager	Routine	X	X			X		
	Hourly Payroll	Payroll Manager	Routine	X		X	X	X		
	Partner Distributions	Payroll Manager	Nonroutine	X					X	X

EXHIBIT 7.6 MAPPING ACCOUNTS TO FINANCIAL REPORTS

General Ledger Accounts		Financial Reporting Classifications			
Account	Owner	Cash and Cash Equivalents	Employee Expenses	Partners' Capital
Bank Account	Treasurer	X		
Salary Expense	Payroll Manager		X	
Hourly Expense	Payroll Manager		X	
Overtime Expense	Payroll Manager		X	
Payroll Taxes	Payroll Manager		X	
Partner A Distribution	CFO			X
Partner B Distribution	CFO			X

CHAPTER 8

Monitor Your Health

Many deadly physical conditions do not produce any outward signs of trouble. The president of Albertson College, a gifted visionary and leader, took a leave of absence from his career to fight prostate cancer. As he put it to me, "Everyone needs to get a regular checkup; I felt fine and had no idea I was sick."

Fortunately, he did get regular checkups to monitor his health and he caught the problem early. Unlike many who are diagnosed with cancer, the president went public with his illness in order to raise awareness and counsel others to get an annual physical. The importance of watching your health also applies to monitoring the condition of your control structure.

EXHIBIT 8.1   CONTROL SMART PATHWAY

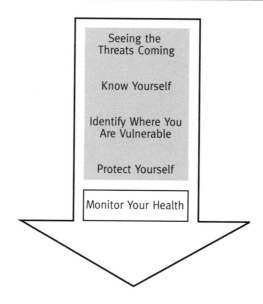

Seeing the
Threats Coming

Know Yourself

Identify Where You
Are Vulnerable

Protect Yourself

Monitor Your Health

The next and last step in the Control Smart approach, as shown in Exhibit 8.1, is to monitor the control environment through the regular reporting of key performance indicators (KPIs). Good KPIs are used not only to communicate the health of the control structure, but also the health of the business. They tell the rest of the story the financial numbers alone can't. These indicators can also be used to educate investors, outside analysts, and employees about the drivers of success. For instance, we now know that buying trends is a key indicator for Wal-Mart. These trends do not tell Wal-Mart how successful it has been, but the company's ability to spot and react quickly to them is widely recognized as one of its competitive advantages.

What Is Driving Your Business?

The Smart Links analysis performed earlier identified key control points. With the control points identified and evaluated, some managers might close the gaps and call it a day. But controls have a way of failing if no one is watching. For every major control point, there should be an indicator, automated alert, or other procedure designed to help a manager determine how well it is working. The indicator might be a simple factor, such as the number of days lost to injury; a metric, such as the percentage of product defects; a list that details unavailable materials; an exception report that points out threats to a system, such as when an attempt is made to circumvent system controls; or even periodic reviews and testing in which an inventory count is made or system capacity tests are performed.

The Control Activities table (Appendix D) that was used earlier to identify control gap solutions also provides some suggestions for key performance indicators. Appendix C provides a list of key performance indicators sorted by financial, operational, and exception-reporting characteristics. If you are having difficulty identifying an indicator, one of the generic KPIs presented in these appendices may help. Regardless of the source, the KPI you develop has to be relevant to the objective you are trying to achieve and should resonate with those who use the indicator as feedback.

For example, the New York City Police Department has identified response time as a key indicator. It is used as a measure of efficiency in reaching a crime scene. Obviously, a quick response improves the chances that a criminal will be apprehended, and can help limit the severity of injuries to victims. According to the mayor's office, as of June 2002, the police response time improved 29 percent over the same period from the year before. This occurred even though the number of police declined. This indicator is relevant feedback to patrol officers, city managers, and the community at large. It is clear that the police force has been able to do better with fewer resources, and all stakeholders can find good news in this metric. Police can be proud that their efforts resulted in this improvement; the community can perceive the police as more responsive and the streets safer; and the city government can report productivity gains to the tax-payers. A declining number would indicate to the city and community that there might be a problem that should be addressed.

Certain indicators are self-evident and will tell the whole story. For instance, an exception report will tell you that a boundary has been tested or breached. Other indicators are more meaningful when put into context. The establishment of goals or comparisons in the form of benchmarks can help managers to understand the full meaning of the information available.

WE KNOW WE ARE BETTER!

Benchmarking is a terrific management tool that helps give perspective to raw data. There are many sources on which you can draw, both internal and external to your organization. Traditional external sources would include industry association statistics; statistics compiled and reported regularly by accounting, consulting, and service firms such as PricewaterhouseCoopers and the Gartner Group; and now there are Internet participation groups from which to glean data.

The advantages of going the extra mile to develop external benchmarks are significant. External benchmarks help identify best practice, highlight performance gaps, and can help management identify sources of competitive advantage. Data that is developed independent of your company can provide a litmus test to the success of your organization. At ING Barings, we liked to compare the effectiveness of our activities to industry data published by the National Securities Clearing Corporation and the Depository Trust Company. We knew we had an effective operation when our operating statistics beat the industry averages by a wide margin. ABN Amro cited ING Barings' well-controlled and efficient operating platform as one of the main reasons they purchased its New York operations.

Internally developed benchmarks may be all that are available or relevant for certain KPIs. The strengths of internal data are that it is relatively easy to access and tend to come from common systems. By adding trend analysis and comparative data, additional perspectives can be gained regarding the health of the operation. For instance, a report may tell management that it has the same dollar amount of aged receivables outstanding as it had over the last three months. This is helpful as it is clear that the company's maximum dollar risk is not increasing. But if management combines that data with sales and understands that revenues have fallen significantly, then the risk of loss has actually increased. The company has more aged receivables per sales dollar than in prior months.

Benchmarking can also be used as a continuous tool for improvement. Periodically, it's a good idea to revisit and brainstorm certain benchmarks to determine whether they need to be revised to reflect best practice. If results are falling well short of best practice, then management time and resources need to be spent studying this process with an eye toward reengineering.

ARE WE THERE YET?

Anyone who is a parent understands the frustration of driving to a vacation destination with a young child. No matter how many times you explain that the trip will take several hours, the child will invariably ask the same question over and over again: "Are we there yet?" The child is not at fault. He or she is likely too young to understand how long an hour is or be able to gauge the miles traveled. As the child matures, he or she develops a sense of time and distance. The same is true of a young, undeveloped enterprise. Until unique key performance indicators are identified, it has nothing to gauge performance against. Management and staff will never know if or when they have arrived at their destination.

We have identified our KPIs and established benchmarks to help put our metrics into context. We are now ready to determine the method and timing of our review. Each manager will determine the best method of reporting KPIs. The frequency and method of reporting will likely depend on the importance of the KPI, the source of the information, and the delivery systems available.

Most businesses will rely on more than a single indicator to communicate the health of the enterprise. As an example, Appendix B lists the key performance indicators for a Fortune 500 manufacturer of consumer goods. The company clearly states that its objective is to "track business performance and drive continuous improvement in the supply chain." It communicates to its employees what is being measured, how it is calculated, the business purpose, and how to interpret the metrics. The goal of each metric is clear. Each is designed to:

- Measure and control unnecessary inventory fluctuations.
- Measure working capital effectiveness.
- Drive down total inventory carrying costs and share savings with customers and vendors.
- Reduce the amount of equipment required to service sales.
- Reduce complexity and supply chain costs.
- Determine which product lines are shipped efficiently.

While not disclosed, the company has established benchmarks or goals for each of these indicators so that it can measure progress. It will know when they have arrived.

While a single, simplified report is the most preferable method for oversight, some businesses are too complex to easily simplify into a single document. Furthermore, certain departments may track metrics that are not relevant to the entire operation, but nevertheless are important to the department and the organization. Determining what information to track is one of the most important decisions a manager will make, and it will be different depending on what is being managed. A CEO will likely identify high-level KPIs that will tell him or her how his or her business is performing, and flag any future threats to the health of that business. He or she might use these KPIs to motivate and direct the firm's employees and resources. A lower-level manager, in contrast, might track a single KPI that is key for his or her department and that is not reported to anyone outside that department.

As a managing director of operations for a broker/dealer, I received a daily flash report with the most critical and risk-sensitive information, a weekly and monthly report with detailed KPIs, a monthly financial report that included financial benchmarks and metrics, and a detailed report of operating information sent to regulators. Given the complexity and risk of the business, no single report was relevant to all of the departments or could be used to manage the entire area supervised.

One tool we employed as a management team was a well-developed culture of "no surprises." This helped us keep our "arms around" the massive operational risks involved in the securities trading business. Managers were expected to report any problems or potential issues immediately. I would make sure everyone understood that our policy was not to shoot the messenger, but to encourage full disclosure. Knowing of a problem but not reporting it was not acceptable. My employees would be evaluated on the "surprise quotient" as a part of their year-end performance evaluation. Daily flash reports were delivered by e-mail and provided me with early warning of operational risks in the event that one of my managers did not pick up the phone and notify me of a problem. I could then address these issues immediately before they had a chance to grow into larger problems.

The daily, weekly, and monthly reports described may sound like a lot to handle, but actually, they did not take much time to review unless there was a concern with one of the metrics. Once I became comfortable with the information and knew what to expect, exceptions would spring off of the page. As our culture took hold, potential problems were known before they showed up in any report. Overall, I had an efficient and effective way to know that the organization was well controlled and that the operational risk was normal and within a tolerable range.

The frequency and format of KPIs is up to each manager. Using the control assessment example performed earlier for Dentex, a basic template has been prepared (see Exhibit 8.2). It effectively captures and monitors metrics for the Dentex management. (Note: For brevity, not all of the metrics identified in our example have been included. In practice, you will have more than one KPI for most steps; and for those steps over which you do not have decision rights, you may have none.)

WHAT HAPPENS NOW?

We now have a way to monitor our control environment, and can take comfort that the controls we identified or installed are operating. So what happens now? The principal executive officer and principal financial officer must evaluate these results in conjunction with other assessments made by specialists such as risk managers, treasurers, actuaries, general counsel, internal auditors, and so on, together with any other entity-level controls so that they can prepare a report on internal control and certify the company's internal control over financial reporting. Section 404 of the Sarbanes-Oxley Act is fairly specific regarding what is required for management's report on internal control. The final rules "require a company's annual report to include an internal control report of management that contains:

EXHIBIT 8.2   KEY PERFORMANCE INDICATOR REPORTING*

Dentex Corporation
February 15, 2004

Smart Link Step	KPI Description	Frequency	KPI Source	Delivery Method	KPI	Benchmark/ Threshold
1	Policy and procedure updates	Annually, as needed	Direct reports	Formal review	All policies and procedures updated annually	100 percent compliance
2	Customer credit and regulatory restrictions	Exception reporting	IT	Printout	Items shipped without payment override	Zero
3	All materials received and independently validated	Weekly	IT	Printout	Number open/aged P.O.s	Aged P.O.s and shipments received without a P.O. are assigned for investigation and tracked. Purchase agent comments documented in report.
4	Access restrictions	Exception reporting	IT	Printout	System access change report	Number of changes = number of approved change requests.
4	Access restrictions	Exception reporting	IT	Printout	Unauthorized attempts report	Any attempt by users to access unauthorized modules
5	Identify product defects and report prior to shipping	Daily	Quality assurance report	E-mail	Number of defects	Six Sigma—3.4 defects per million
6	Capacity constraints	Weekly	Floor manager	Report	Utilization percentage by manufacturing function	Manufacturer's stated capacity
7	All shipments sent in timely manner, complete and in good form	Daily	Sales	E-mail	Number aged customer orders	All orders shipped on time

continues

EXHIBIT 8.2   (CONTINUED)

Smart Link Step	KPI Description	Frequency	KPI Source	Delivery Method	KPI	Benchmark/ Threshold
8	Detection of defective items shipped	Daily	Customer service	E-mail	Number items returned due to operational error	Six Sigma
10	Reconciled cash accounts	Monthly	Accounting	Report	Unexplained reconciling items	Zero
11	Financial cost controls— cost per unit	Monthly	Finance	Report	Total cost of each unit produced by product and cost variance by input component	Target cost per unit based on sales target
12	Government regulations	Quarterly	Internal audit	Report	Compliance with OSHA regs	100 percent compliance
13	Staff reviews	Annually, as needed	Operations Manager/ direct reports	Formal review	All employees employed more than 3 months reviewed	100 percent compliance

* "Payments received and applied" (Smart Link Step 9) is performed at headquarters for this example, so it is not included in the exhibit.

- A statement of management's responsibility for establishing and maintaining adequate internal control over financial reporting for the company

- A statement identifying the framework used by management to conduct the required evaluation of the effectiveness of the company's internal control over financial reporting

- Management's assessment of the effectiveness of the company's internal control over financial reporting as of the end of the company's most recent fiscal year, including a statement as to whether or not the company's internal control over financial reporting is effective. The assessment must include disclosure of any "material weaknesses" in the company's internal control over financial reporting identified by management. Management is not permitted to conclude that the company's internal control over financial reporting is effective if there are one or more material weaknesses in the company's internal control over financial reporting

- A statement that the registered public accounting firm that audited the financial statements included in the annual report has issued an attestation report on management's assessment of the registrant's internal control over financial reporting."[1]

Section 302 of the act also requires that the principal executive officer (normally the CEO) and principal financial officer (normally the CFO) certify that they have a control structure that provides reasonable assurance regarding the reliability of financial reporting. (An example of the required certification is provided in Appendix E.) It should be clear to any CEO and CFO making this certification that they are held responsible for the internal control environment over financial reporting and disclosures.

External auditors also must perform procedures to attest to management's report on internal controls. How they will assess it is really no secret; it is pretty well spelled out in the COSO framework. While the emphasis may change depending on the approach and experience of the auditors, as well as for conditions that are unique to the business or industry, auditors will evaluate the company's control environment, risk assessment, information and communication, control activities, and monitoring capabilities as recommended by the COSO framework. While I would recommend that all managers familiarize themselves with their entity-level controls, CEOs and CFOs must be prepared to answer and provide evidence for their activities in these areas. A senior manager can use the checklist in Appendix D, which is based on the COSO framework, to prepare for this assessment at the entity level. While the approach and emphasis of your outside auditors may differ, this list should get you most of the way home. This is not cheating; it is being prepared and proving to the auditors your competence in the area of internal control.

For most of us, the majority of items contained in the checklist will not be directly relevant to our area of responsibility, but will help us think about entity controls that help protect our company. A breakdown in entity-level controls could have a serious impact on all company operations, including our own, so we all need to be vigilant to identify control problems, even if we do not have decision rights over them. Whether we report these to the responsible manager, internal audit, or senior management will largely depend on our relationships and receptiveness of our suggestions. Regardless, they must be reported and corrected to protect our company and our jobs.

CHAPTER 9

Call to Action

The great orator William Jennings Bryan said, "Destiny is no matter of chance. It is a matter of choice. It is not a thing to be waited for, it is a thing to be achieved." Together we have fully explored the Control Smart approach. As illustrated in Exhibit 9.1, we have come to the end of our pathway.

You now know which risks affect your company and how to determine ownership. You can identify the processes over which you have decision rights, and can document each process. You have the ability to subject each

EXHIBIT 9.1   CONTROL SMART PATHWAY

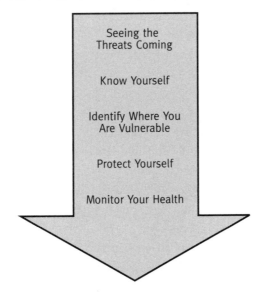

Seeing the
Threats Coming

Know Yourself

Identify Where You
Are Vulnerable

Protect Yourself

Monitor Your Health

process to Smart Links and to address control gaps. Finally, you can capably monitor the health of the environment. Our goal of a strong, well-controlled environment is established—all that is needed is the energy and will to achieve it.

Preventing fraud and operational loss requires diligence and control smarts. If it were simple or easy, there would never be a successful fraud or devastating operational losses. As we have learned, fraud can originate from almost anywhere in an organization. Preventing fraud begins by reinforcing positive values in our schools, our government, our families, and our workplace.

In response to the recent corporate scandals, President George W. Bush signed the Sarbanes-Oxley Act into law. The reforms are far-reaching, the standards high, and the penalties severe. President and CEO of the American Institute of Certified Public Accountants (AICPA) Barry C. Melancon has embraced these important measures. In a recent speech at the Yale Club of New York, he reasserted the need for strong cultural ideals: "Culture must build upon the profession's traditional values. Values like rigorous commitment to integrity. A passion for getting it right. A commitment to rules—not just to their letter, but their spirit—and zero tolerance for those who break them."[1]

Kim Clark, the dean of the Harvard Business School, recently sent out a letter to alumni outlining the school's response to the recent business crises. In addition to the "values and learning initiative" that it began five years ago in an effort to define a new approach to accountability for its students, the school plans to hold ambitious workshops on campus. These will bring together the "faculty, business leaders, government, and academia to examine topics ranging from ethics, values, and leadership to executive compensation."[2]

This is the type of call to action we all must undertake. We may not be in a position to assemble the business leaders of our country like Dean Clark, or mold the accounting profession like Barry Melancon, but we *are* able to set an example for those with whom we come in contact. It begins with our family and our workplace. Our discussion of values and ethics must be public, steadfast, unrelenting, and meaningful—backed up by positive examples and action.

An example close to home that I can relate involves our local school system on the North Shore of Long Island. One night, a group of high school students conducted a scavenger hunt that resulted in damage to homes and businesses in the community. Although not sanctioned by the school, the principal of the school took responsibility, called together the seniors of the school, explained how the actions of a few had hurt the community in which they lived, and called on the students and their parents to make a bad situation right. The students responded as a group; recognizing that they were part of a larger community, they came together to repair all the damage done. The school district then followed up with a letter to the entire community explaining what had happened and that the student class as a whole was committed to mend all that was broken. It is this type of positive value reinforcement that will establish a template for life-long behavior. High school students destroying property is not new or uncommon and will continue to happen, but how a community responds to an incident is what is important. The principal and superintendent are to be commended for their support of the community and taking a leadership role in establishing values in our future leaders.

We can "walk our talk" by taking the culture of our companies seriously. We are able to create positive values as company objectives and appropriately compensate those who uphold the company image. Employees need to feel a part of something they can be proud of and have a hand in nurturing. Control Smart provides an inclusive approach that relies on user-friendly tools to assist in a manager's evaluation and monitoring of the control environment. Managers and employees can work together as partners to improve operations and protect their company. Many illustrative examples have been provided throughout the book to illuminate and aid understanding. You can use these essential tools to evaluate the risks to your company: Determine which risks might impact your operations; document the processes over which you have decision rights; establish controls and key performance indicators; and monitor the health of your operations.

If a positive control culture is nirvana, then key performance monitoring is the lighted path to that coveted place. Over time, good managers develop a feel for their key performance indicators (KPIs) in much the same way a doctor can tell from a chart how a patient is doing. The metrics will focus managers' attention where it is needed most and will alert them if a control break occurs. I've designed these practical methods to apply to almost any process and to be used by almost any manager. While these techniques can help implement fundamental control, nothing takes the place of the judgment of seasoned managers and their ability to truly understand a business, its operations, its culture, and, most importantly, its people. There are many books to help a manager devise strategy, motivate human resources, improve operations, improve selling techniques, and better plan their day. Now, with the Control Smart approach, managers will also have much-needed tools to better control their environment, protect stakeholder assets, and protect their careers and the jobs of their employees. Not a bad ambition. It is now up to us as managers to do our share.

Epilogue

There are inherent limitations to even the best legislation, as represented by the post–Sarbanes-Oxley mutual fund scandals. Despite the fact that the Sarbanes-Oxley Act will not prevent fraud from reoccurring, or market bubbles from bursting and causing investors financial pain, the record of the act since its inception does contain some real accomplishments. Companies are getting their financial houses in order. Restatement of financial statements is at a record high, as companies correct past accounting and disclosure errors or adjust to refined accounting guidance. Financial analysts are reporting improvements in the quality of earnings and financial disclosures.

Independence on public boards of directors is also increasing. According to the American Society of Corporate Secretaries, 62 percent of the corporate boards of its membership now have an independent chairperson, lead director, or presiding outside director. This is up from only 26 percent the year before. Directors are more active, and independent audit committees have been strengthened. They now have real oversight authority, including the ability to retain their own independent counsel.

Much remains to be done under the act, however. As this book goes to press, the New York Stock Exchange and the NASDAQ issued their final rules for corporate governance standards for public companies. Listed companies have until the earlier of either their first annual meeting after January 15, 2004 or October 31, 2004 to comply.

The NYSE rules include:

- A requirement that listed companies must have a board that consists of an independent majority

- That a company's board must make a determination regarding each director's independence and may adopt categorical standards to assist in this determination

- Certain independence guidance that covers not only employees of the listed company, but also business relationships where a director receives more than $100,000 in compensation (other than his compensation from his board service), or where a company he or she is affiliated with pays the listed company more than $1 million or 2% of the of other company's consolidated gross revenues. Internal and external auditors are also not independent. These rules extend to immediate family members and will disqualify a director from being independent until 3 years after the end of the employment, auditing relationship, or affiliation.

- That nonmanagement directors are required to meet at regularly scheduled executive sessions without management

- A requirement that a company have a nominating/corporate governance committee that is composed entirely of independent directors. The committee must have a charter that outlines their responsibilities and that must include director succession, corporate governance principles applicable to the corporation, oversight of the evaluation of management, and annual evaluation of committee workings.

- A requirement that a company have a compensation committee composed entirely of independent directors. The committee must also have a charter that enables it to review and approve corporate objectives and determine executive compensation based on their evaluation, make recommendations to the board regarding nonexecutive compensation, and prepare a compensation report as required by the SEC for inclusion in the annual proxy statement or 10-K filed with the SEC.

- A requirement that a company have an audit committee consisting of at least three directors, all whom must be independent, that are financially literate and at least one member with accounting or related financial management expertise. The committee must have a charter that enables it to assist the board with oversight of the integrity of the financial statements, compliance with legal and regulatory requirements, the independent auditor's qualifications and independence, and the performance of internal and external auditors. The committee must prepare an audit committee report to be included in the company's annual proxy statement as required by the SEC. They must also evaluate the committee's work annually. The committee must also obtain and review an annual report by the independent auditor describing the firm's internal control procedures, any material issues raised, and any steps taken to deal with such issues within the last 5 years. They must discuss the company's quarterly and annual "Management's Discussion and Analysis of Financial Condition and Results of Operations," as well as press releases, earnings guidance, and other information provided to analysts and rating agencies. They must meet regularly with internal and external auditors and discuss any audit problems and management's response to these issues, and set hiring policies for employees of the independent auditor.

- A requirement that each company have an internal audit department
- That companies must adopt and disclose corporate governance guidelines covering director qualification standards, director responsibilities, director access to management and advisors, director compensation, director orientation and continuing education, management succession, and annual performance evaluation of the board
- A requirement that companies adopt and disclose a code of business conduct and ethics for directors, officers, and employees, and promptly disclose any waivers of the code for directors or officers
- That foreign private issuers must disclose any significant ways their corporate governance practices differ from those followed by domestic companies under NYSE listing standards
- That each CEO must certify to the NYSE each year that he or she is not aware of any violation of the NYSE corporate governance listing standards

The NASDAQ rules are similar, although some thresholds for independence are lower with compensation greater than $60,000 or business with the listed company in excess of $200,000 disqualifying a director's independence. The NASDAQ rules also do not require independent compensation or nominating committees; rather, approval of compensation and nominations by a majority of the independent directors is required.

While it is not entirely clear at this early date how these rules will impact sitting directors, there is little doubt that board independence will be improved.

The SEC and Financial Accounting Standards Board (FASB) still face an enormous undertaking in making the move from rules-based standards to a principles-based approach, as mandated by Sarbanes-Oxley. The product of this initiative could have a significant and wide-range impact on companies, not only in the United States, but throughout the world. The Public Company Accounting Oversight Board, the new body established to regulate the accounting profession, is implementing registration requirements for all accounting firms doing business in the United States, including foreign-based firms. It also will be producing final standards the profession must adhere to for maintaining independence and performing audits.

Implementation has not been a bed of roses. Many companies complain of the costs of complying with the act. Some even claim to have gone private in an effort to avoid these costs, but evidence that the act is creating a stampede to privatize is notably absent. Importantly, the number of companies "going private" has not increased markedly when compared to recent years. Furthermore, a survey of costs conducted by PricewaterhouseCoopers found that 61 percent of senior executives surveyed did not believe the initial expense of complying with Sarbanes-Oxley to be particularly costly. Granted, this leaves a good number of executives who believe implementation costs to be burdensome. In fact, the cost to meet the internal control requirements of Sarbanes-Oxley, which are not mandated until June 15, 2004, could be the most expensive element for companies to implement. Some of the largest companies will be billed more than $1 million annually to support the new Public Company Accounting Oversight Board.[1] There are estimates that documentation of systems and procedures used to produce financial data could increase accounting costs from 25 percent to 100 percent. In truth, these practices should have been in place prior to the act, and now companies must spend to catch up to where they should have been all along. And there are less expensive ways to document controls than to hire outsiders. Control self-assessment using tools such as those found in this book can keep costs in check.

While I am concerned about overregulation killing initiative and prudent risk-taking by our public companies, it appears at this early stage that the benefits of the act have been well worth the costs. I often think back to a program I watched on television on which the lawyer for Bernie Ebbers, the former CEO of WorldCom, professed that his client had nothing to do with the decisions made at the bankrupt company. I remember asking myself, "If he had nothing to do with decisions at the company, what were shareholders paying him to do?" Mr. Ebbers was paid more than $70 million the last five years of his tenure for his efforts. For this money, he accepted responsibility to operate the company on behalf of its owners. Is it too much to ask that he have a hand in monitoring the financial reporting of his company to ensure it was materially correct? Unfortunately, corporate malfeasance has risen to the point that CEOs must formally certify their financial statements and controls over financial reporting. Even though most CEOs are hardworking, honest businesspeople, the American people have had enough of certain highly paid CEOs shirking their responsibility to their employees, customers, and investors. They will continue to demand that corporate executives who knowingly deceive the public spend time behind bars. For those who are simply not competent enough to make certain that they have a proper control structure in place and that their published financial information is correct, regulatory fines and dismissal will become the standard.

Corporate America owes it to her employees, to her shareholders, to the free market system that provides for her existence, to take her management responsibilities seriously. We live in the greatest country in the world primarily because we hold ourselves to the highest standards. The free enterprise system depends on good regulatory oversight in order to function. However, this same system can be threatened by excessive government interference. Too many restrictions and oversight will kill the creativity that has been the hallmark of our nation's financial markets. Chairman of the Federal Reserve Alan Greenspan commented directly on this point: "The extent of government intervention in market to control risk-taking beyond the commonly practiced control of system risk is, at the end of the day, a trade-off between economic growth with its associated potential instability and a more civil and less stressful way of life with a lower standard of living. . . . The choices that we make in our societies on these critical issues will importantly shape the opportunities for the unforeseen, but inevitable, innovations that have the capability to advance the economic well-being of the citizens of the United States and our trading partners."[2]

We must strike the right balance between regulation and free enterprise, and taking responsibility for our corporate culture is the place to start. I am certain that with trust in our markets, our corporate leadership, and our means of government, the United States will create and experience broad-based wealth beyond any known in the history of humankind. The country owes it to its children to restore confidence in free enterprise. And, after all, is it not true that each generation owes it to the next to leave the world better than they entered it?

Statement of Values

Many companies have developed value statements, but few truly use them to manage their business. The health care giant Johnson & Johnson, and investment banking goliath Goldman Sachs, are examples of companies that rely on value-based management as a best practice. Their values are ingrained in their organizations, and decisions conform to accepted behaviors and priorities. Both companies have kindly allowed me to reprint their value statements—Johnson & Johnson's credo and Goldman's business principles—in this appendix.

JOHNSON & JOHNSON CREDO

We believe our first responsibility is to the doctors, nurses, and patients, to mothers and fathers and all others who use our products and services. In meeting their needs everything we do must be of high quality. We must constantly strive to reduce our costs in order to maintain reasonable prices. Customers' orders must be serviced promptly and accurately. Our suppliers and distributors must have an opportunity to make a fair profit.

We are responsible to our employees, the men and women who work for us throughout the world. Everyone must be considered as an individual. We must respect their dignity and recognize their merit. They must have a sense of security in their jobs. Compensation must be fair and adequate, and working conditions clean, orderly, and safe. We must be mindful of ways to help our employees fulfill their family responsibilities. Employees must feel free to make suggestions and complaints. There must be equal opportunity for employment, development, and advancement for those qualified. We must provide competent management, and their actions must be just and ethical.

We are responsible to the communities in which we live and work and to the world community as well. We must be good citizens—support good works and charities and bear our fair share of taxes. We must encourage civic improvements and better health and education. We must maintain in good order the property we are privileged to use, protecting the environment and natural resources.

Our final responsibility is to our stockholders. Business must make a sound profit. We must experiment with new ideas. Research must be carried on, innovative programs developed, and mistakes paid for. New equipment must be purchased, new facilities provided, and new products launched. Reserves must be created to provide for adverse times. When we operate according to these principles, the stockholders should realize a fair return.

(Reprinted with permission of Johnson & Johnson.)

GOLDMAN SACHS' BUSINESS PRINCIPLES

1. Our clients' interests always come first. Our experience shows that if we serve our clients well, our own success will follow.

2. Our assets are our people, capital, and reputation. If any of these is ever diminished, the last is the most difficult to restore. We are dedicated to complying fully with the letter and spirit of the laws, rules, and ethical principles that govern us. Our continued success depends upon unswerving adherence to this standard.

3. Our goal is to provide superior returns to our shareholders. Profitability is critical to achieving superior returns, building our capital, and attracting and keeping our best people. Significant employee stock ownership aligns the interests of our employees and our shareholders.

4. We take great pride in the professional quality of our work. We have an uncompromising determination to achieve excellence in everything we undertake. Though we may be involved in a wide variety and heavy volume of activity, we would, if it came to a choice, rather be best than biggest.

5. We stress creativity and imagination in everything we do. While recognizing that the old way may still be the best way, we constantly strive to find a better solution to a client's problems. We pride ourselves on having pioneered many of the practices and techniques that have become standard in the industry.

6. We make an unusual effort to identify and recruit the very best person for every job. Although our activities are measured in billions of dollars, we select our people one by one. In a business, we know that without the best people, we cannot be the best firm.

7. We offer our people the opportunity to move ahead more rapidly than is possible at most other places. Advancement depends on merit, and we have yet to find the limits to the responsibility our best people are able to assume. For us to be successful, our men and women must reflect the diversity of the communities and cultures in which we operate. That means we must attract, retain, and motivate people from many backgrounds and perspectives. Being diverse is not optional; it is what we must be.

8. We stress teamwork in everything we do. While individual creativity is always encouraged, we have found that team effort often produces the best results. We have no room for those who put their personal interests ahead of the interests of the firm and its clients.

9. The dedication of our people to the firm and the intense effort they give their jobs are greater than one finds in most other organizations. We think that this is an important part of our success.

10. We consider our size an asset that we try hard to preserve. We want to be big enough to undertake the largest project that any of our clients could contemplate, yet small enough to maintain the loyalty, the intimacy, and the esprit de corps that we all treasure and that contribute greatly to our success.

11. We constantly strive to anticipate the rapidly changing needs of our clients and to develop new services to meet those needs. We know that the world of finance will not stand still and that complacency can lead to extinction.

12. We regularly receive confidential information as part of our normal client relationships. To breach a confidence or to use confidential information improperly or carelessly would be unthinkable.

13. Our business is highly competitive, and we aggressively seek to expand our client relationships. However, we must always be fair competitors and must never denigrate other firms.

14. Integrity and honesty are at the heart of our business. We expect our people to maintain high ethical standards in everything they do, both in their work for the firm and in their personal lives.

(Reprinted with permission of Goldman Sachs International.)

Key Performance Indicator Reporting

This appendix lists the key performance indicators (KPIs) for a Fortune 500 manufacturer of consumer goods (whose name is not revealed at the request of the company). The company's objective is to "track business performance and drive continuous improvement in the supply chain." The company communicates to its employees what is measured, how it is calculated, the business purpose, and how to interpret the metrics.

Number	What Is Being Measured?	How Is It Calculated?	Business Purpose	Interpretation
1	Variability of demand	Actual versus planned production	Measure and control unnecessary inventory fluctuations.	Greater conformance to plan results in reduced need for safety inventory.
2	Variability of demand	Actual production versus shipments	Measure and control unnecessary inventory fluctuations.	Greater conformance to plan results in reduced need for safety inventory.
3	The time it takes to convert raw material purchases into cash received from sales	Receivable days plus inventory days less payable days	Measure working capital effectiveness.	Shorter cash conversion cycle translates to greater cash availability and less likelihood of losses due to poor receivables collection or obsolete inventory.
4	Total inventory across the supply chain	Average inventory (including customer and supplier) divided by net sales	Drive down total inventory carrying costs; share savings with customers and vendors.	Lower system inventory equals stability in demand. Higher equals less control; unusual circumstances.
5	Manufacturing equipment utilization	Realized capacity equals net production divided by potential at ideal and target speeds	Reduce the amount of equipment required to service sales.	Higher levels indicate effective asset utilization and higher PCE (less capital required).
6	Amount of profit generated proportionate to the number of SKUs managed	Number of SKUs that support 95 percent of sector contribution	Reduce complexity and supply chain costs.	Higher percentage indicates reduced complexity.
7	Cost to deliver product from case packer to retail shelf	Total distribution divided by actual cubic feet shipped	Determine which product lines are shipped efficiently.	Lower $/Actual volume of product shipped indicates greater distribution and handling efficiencies.

Examples of Key Performance Indicators

This table lists common types of key performance indicators. These generic indicators can be applied to a wide range of businesses and operations and may be a helpful tool for identifying KPIs critical to your business.

Operational Metrics	Exception Reporting
• Throughput	• Audit reports
• Throughput as a percent of capacity	• Assets assigned to employees in excess of threshold or benchmark
• Defects as a percent of throughput	• Unauthorized system access attempts
• Number of order deliveries past due	• General ledger accounts without assigned owners
• Rush order percent	
• On-time delivery percent	• Assets without assigned owners
• Customer satisfaction rating	• Unreconciled accounts
• Number of complaints	• Inventory aged over threshold
• Number of complaints to revenue (e.g., 10 per $1 million)	• Wires/checks issued over $ threshold
• Returns as a percent of units delivered	• Deliveries over past-due threshold
• Number of manual journal vouchers (accounting entries) per full-time equivalent employee	• Sales to unapproved customers
	• Sales to customers over established limits
• Ratio of support staff to total number of employees	• Wash or suspense accounts (or other accounts that should have a zero balance) with a balance
• Days of inventory outstanding	
• Inventory turns	• Unavailable materials report
• Market share	• Inventory count differences
• Number of outstanding audit issues	• Purchase orders aged over threshold
• Book-to-bill ratio	• Unmatched receipts
• Days sales outstanding	• Unsigned management representation of financial results
• Overtime percent	
• Days without a workplace injury	
• Number of hours production is off-line	
• Personnel/material requisitions open past threshold or benchmark	

Financial Metrics

- Cost per unit
- Revenue per full-time equivalent
- Employee expenses/headcount
- Accounts receivable turnover
- Write-offs as a percent of sales
- Reserves as a percent of assets
- Reserves as a percent of accounts receivable over 90 days past due
- Budget-to-actual variances
- Value at risk
- Market value to contract value of financial instruments
- Unreconciled accounts exposure
- Accounts payable aging
- Financing costs as a percent of revenue
- Margin percent
- Regulatory capital charges (where applicable)
- Working capital
- Interest coverage
- Sales, general, and administrative (SG&A) expenses as a percent of revenue
- Earnings per share
- Operating cash flow per share
- Risk-adjusted return on capital
- Debt/equity trend

Monitoring

- Internal threat analysis of competitor control incidents
- Evaluation of proposed or pending legislation effects on current operations
- Periodic threat analysis of extremist groups on current ops
- Camera surveillance of key areas to identify illegal activity

Control Activities

It is not always easy for a manager who is not trained in control analysis to identify a control that addresses a specified weakness. A tool that lists generic activities and related control activities can help make that connection. For each Smart Link step, the following table provides examples of control activities that can be found in most generic processes. Additionally, KPIs are identified that can be used to monitor these activities.

Step	Generic Activity	Control Lever	Control Activity	KPIs
1	• Material, personnel and information inputs • Payment for inputs • Customer request • Create deliverable • Deliver to customer • Receive payment • Monitor profitability • Regulatory review	Information processing	Document all processes, determine who is responsible for each process, and ensure appropriate policies govern the processes.	Number of exceptions
2	Customer defines deliverable.	Segregation of credit and sales	Orders are accepted only within credit parameters established independent of sales.	Number of credit exceptions/overrides
2	Customer defines deliverable.	Segregation of contract negotiation and review	Contracts are reviewed by legal prior to execution.	Periodic review and testing of contracts
2	Customer defines deliverable.	Segregation of sales and compliance	Legal or compliance evaluates clients and customers against regulatory requirements. Authorization needed to set up new customer in the sales system.	Number and aging of accounts with missing customer information
3	Information inputs	Information processing	A schedule of information inputs is maintained by due date and source.	On-time performance
3	Information inputs	Segregation of purchase request and execution.	Information sources that need to be purchased are properly authorized and processed by purchasing.	Exception reporting by purchasing; periodic review and testing of payments to P.O.s
3	Material inputs	Information processing	Inputs budgeted and scheduled are compared to material available.	Unavailable materials report
3	Material inputs	Information processing	Manual or automated procedures prevent an invoice from being paid twice.	Periodic review and testing of payments

Step	Generic Activity	Control Lever	Control Activity	KPIs
3	Material inputs	Information processing	Month-end procedures to ensure all receipts are properly recorded into inventory and recorded in the proper period.	Periodic review and testing end-of-period material receipts cutoff
3	Material inputs	Information processing	Material receipts are matched to P.O.s or contracts. Unauthorized purchases are rejected.	Missing or aged P.O.s; unmatched receipts
3	Material inputs	Physical controls	Release of inputs to create deliverables is restricted to appropriate personnel.	Inventory count differences
3	Material inputs	Segregation of purchasing request and execution	Additional inputs required are approved for acquisition at the appropriate level. All prenumbered P.O.s are issued by the purchasing department to approved vendors.	Missing or aged P.O.s
3	Material inputs	Segregation of inventory custody and payment	Only invoices that are matched to a properly authorized P.O. and receipt are processed for payment independent of purchasing and receiving.	Exception reporting of unmatched payments/P.O.s/invoices
3	Material inputs	Segregation of purchase requests and vendor selection	A program of periodic bidding on input items is performed, documented, and reviewed by management. Contracts are approved by legal.	Price variances; clean audits with no material findings
3	Payment for material inputs	Information processing	Access to accounts payable files and cash disbursement files is restricted.	Unauthorized access attempt
3	Payment for material inputs	Physical security/ segregation of check custody and record-keeping	Checks are prenumbered and secured independent of the record-keeping function. Check-signing machine and signature plates are properly secured. A log of checks is maintained, and missing or voided checks are investigated.	Number of missing or voided checks

Step	Generic Activity	Control Lever	Control Activity	KPIs
3	Payment for material inputs	Segregation of purchasing, receiving, and payables	Payments are approved by individuals independent of procurement, receiving, and accounts payable.	Approval of exception report from finance; periodic review and testing
3	Payment for material inputs	Segregation of purchase request and authorization	Authorization levels for check and wire issuance are determined by dollar amount. Confirmation of authority levels is performed in finance independent of authorization and payment request.	Approval exception report from finance; periodic review and testing
3	Payment for material inputs	Segregation of check custody and recording	Payments are mailed independent of accounts payable recording function.	Periodic review
3	Personnel inputs	Information processing	Labor budget and schedule are compared to personnel available.	Overtime percentage
3	Personnel inputs	Segregation of request and authorization	All hires are processed through HR and are approved at the appropriate level.	HR exception reporting: number of payroll employees without applications
3	Personnel inputs	Segregation of approval and recording payroll	The individual in charge of approving time cards or payroll does not have access to the payroll system.	Periodic review and testing
3	Personnel inputs	Segregation of recording and approval	Ensure all time cards are collected and reconciled to approved hires in HR.	Exception reporting by HR
4	Information inputs	Information processing	Computers are password-protected and access rights restricted.	Unauthorized attempts report
4	Information inputs	Physical security	Access to sensitive information is restricted by manual or electronic locks.	Periodic review and testing
4	Material inputs	Segregation of custody and recording inventory	The individual in charge of issuing material does not have access to update raw materials inventory (unless alternative independent reconciling control to authorized release is present), purchasing, or payment systems.	Unauthorized attempts report

Step	Generic Activity	Control Lever	Control Activity	KPIs
4	Payment for material inputs	Segregation of procurement and payment of materials	Bank statements are reconciled to cash in the general ledger independent of accounts payable, purchasing, and physical check custody functions. Differences are investigated and aged.	Unreconciled items
4	Payment for material inputs	Segregation of accounts payable and purchasing	Intercompany accounts are reconciled and confirmed with the counterpart independent of accounts payable and purchasing.	Unreconciled items; confirmation percentage
4	Payment for material inputs	Physical security	Checks are prenumbered, logged, secured, and released independent of the record-keeping function.	Periodic review and testing
4	Payment for material inputs	Physical security	Check-writing machines and signature plates are properly secured.	Periodic review and testing
4	Payment for material inputs	Physical security	Access to payroll systems and files are restricted. Passwords are changed regularly.	Unauthorized access attempts; password aging
4	Payment for material inputs	Segregation of payroll approval and recording functions	Payroll is reviewed and released by a manager independent of employee adds, deletes, and change capability, and payroll setup.	Periodic review and testing
4	Personnel inputs	Information processing	HR performs background checks on all new hires.	Number of hires rejected; periodic review and testing
4	Personnel inputs	Segregation of payroll record and custody functions	Payroll accounts are reconciled regularly independent of the payroll function.	Aged reconciling items
5	Create information deliverable.	Information processing	Run new programming or systems in a test environment parallel to the production environment before implementation.	Number of production problems; number of IT service complaints/outages

Step	Generic Activity	Control Lever	Control Activity	KPIs
5	Create information deliverable.	Information processing	Information is compared to another independent source for confirmation, if available, or reviewed using trend analysis and other techniques. Unexpected results are investigated.	Exception reporting
5	Create product deliverable.	Segregation of production and testing	Procedures are implemented to identify defective inputs, such as independent QA testing and defect reporting.	Defect percentage; inventory aging
5	Create product deliverable.	Segregation of custody and recording assets	Procedures are implemented to confirm asset values, such as physical counts and/or repricing, and so on.	Count and pricing variances
5	Create service deliverable.	Segregation of recording and approval	Senior management compares deliverable to engagement letter.	Exception reporting
6	Create deliverable—IT capacity constraints	Information processing	Backup procedures are executed regularly, and backup files are maintained in a safe, off-site location. Retrieval and preparation of backup information are tested regularly.	Periodic review and testing
6	Create deliverable—IT constraints	Information processing	Prepare and approve an IT plan to address future capacity needs.	Periodic review
6	Create deliverable—personnel	Performance reviews	Safety metrics (worker's compensation, insurance claims, etc.) are monitored. Accidents are fully investigated, violations censored, and safeguards implemented.	Number of injuries; lost days
6	Create deliverable—personnel constraints	Information processing	Procedures to ensure continued operations are prepared and communicated. Alternative procedures to perform tasks are developed, tested, and made available.	Periodic review and testing
6	Create deliverable—material constraints	Performance reviews	Backup vendors and/or sufficient inventory are maintained.	Unavailable materials

Step	Generic Activity	Control Lever	Control Activity	KPIs
6	Create deliverable—operational constraints	Performance reviews	Capacity utilization is monitored, and capital expenditures for upgrades are planned and budgeted. Backup facilities or business-interruption insurance is maintained.	Periodic review and testing
6	Create deliverable—personnel constraints	Physical security	Safety procedures are prepared, reviewed by legal and safety experts, communicated, and tested periodically.	Periodic review and testing
7	Deliver information to customer.	Information processing	Execute a change program, including user-acceptance testing, prior to implementing any change to production.	User sign-off
7	Deliver information to customer.	Information processing	Integrate quality assurance procedures into production processing. Number of batch jobs processed are verified, check numbers are reconciled, delivery versus schedule analysis is conducted for critical path processing.	Defect percentage; unprocessed jobs
7	Deliver product to customer.	Information processing	Orders are reviewed daily, and those nearing delivery dates are evaluated. Orders past delivery dates are investigated and expedited.	Open order aging; rush order percentage
7	Deliver product to customer.	Segregation of production and testing	Quality assurance procedures are independently implemented, and defect analysis is performed and reported.	Defect percentage
8	Deliver information to customer.	Segregation of shipping and customer feedback	Delivery times are independently confirmed. Late or inaccurate delivery of information is investigated.	On-time performance
8	Deliver product to customer.	Segregation of production and customer feedback	Customer complaints/warranty claims are logged, analyzed, and reported independent of production.	Percentage of customer returns

Step	Generic Activity	Control Lever	Control Activity	KPIs
8	Deliver service to customer.	Performance reviews	Independent from the service team, service evaluations are requested from every client, and are evaluated. Compensation is tied to client satisfaction.	Average service level rating
9	Expense allocation	Information processing	Allocation methodologies are agreed on with clients, and all expenses are allocated.	Exception reporting
9	Receipt of payment	Information processing	Aged receivables are investigated, and collection procedures are implemented.	A/R aging
9	Receipt of payment	Physical security	Direct customer payments are made to a bank lockbox or bank wire.	Number of payments not sent to lockbox
9	Receipt of payment	Physical security	Surveillance cameras are used to record thefts or other activity.	Exception reporting
9	Receipt of payment	Segregation of custody and recording of returned goods	The individual responsible for issuing credit memos for returned goods is independent of accounts receivable and sales, both physically and electronically. Returns are tracked by customer and salesperson, and reviewed by senior management.	Return percentage; return dollar amount
9	Receipt of payment	Segregation of custody and recording of cash or checks	Assign opening of mail to an individual who is independent of accounts receivable or cash accounts, physically and systemically. Compare receipts to bank deposits.	Periodic review and testing
10	Expense allocation	Segregation of billing and recording	Internal clients are notified of allocations by individual independent of those calculating the allocations.	Complaints; periodic review and testing

Step	Generic Activity	Control Lever	Control Activity	KPIs
10	Receipt of payment	Segregation of custody and recording of cash	Bank statements are reconciled to cash in the general ledger independent of accounts receivable and sales. Differences are investigated and aged.	Unreconciled items
10	Receipt of payment	Segregation of sales and account charges	Intercompany accounts are reconciled and confirmed with counterpart by someone independent of sales and accounts receivable.	Unreconciled items
11	Evaluate profitability, cost controls, and financial metrics.	Information processing	Management reviews key metrics to evaluate progress toward objectives.	Market share percentage; margin percentage; budget-to-actual performance; price and materials variance; on-time delivery percentage; risk-adjusted return on capital (RAROC); working capital projections, and so on
12	• Regulatory review • Material, personnel, and information inputs • Payment for inputs • Customer request • Create deliverable. • Deliver to customer. • Receive payment. • Monitor profitability.	Segregation of recording and approval of regulatory filings and oversight	Procedures are set up and confirmed with legal counsel to ensure compliance with all applicable laws and regulations, including DOL, SEC, FTC, Treasury (IRS), DOD, FDA, state and local, and so on.	Exception reporting
12	Regulatory review—government filings	Segregation of preparation, custody, and approval oversight	An individual independent of the preparation of regulatory reports reconciles information back to the books and records of the firm.	Unreconciled items

206

Step	Generic Activity	Control Lever	Control Activity	KPIs
12	Regulatory review— financial reporting	Segregation of preparation, custody, and approval oversight	Outside independent accountants evaluate all financial policies and procedures of the company.	Annual report
12	Regulatory review— financial reporting	Performance review	Each senior manager attests to the accuracy and fairness of the financial statements.	Exception reporting
12	Regulatory review	Segregation of custody, recording, and authorization	A hotline is established to outside legal counsel for reporting fraud and regulatory violations.	Number of calls; aging of unresolved issues
13	• Material, personnel, and information inputs • Payment for inputs • Customer request • Create deliverable. • Deliver to customer. • Receive payment. • Monitor profitability. • Regulatory review	Performance reviews	Evaluate employees for compliance with company objectives, laws, and regulations (OSHA, IRS, SEC, etc), control procedures, and risk management objectives.	360 performance reviews; OSHA, IRS, SEC, and other government agencies; external accountants and internal audits; client evaluations

APPENDIX **E**

Example of Section 302 Certification

Each certifying officer must complete the following certification, which clearly articulates the responsibilities of these officers.

I, [identify the certifying individual], certify that:

1. I have reviewed this [specify report] of [identify registrant];

2. Based on my knowledge, this report does not contain any untrue statement of a material fact or omit to state a material fact necessary to make the statements made, in light of the circumstances under which such statements were made, not misleading with respect to the period covered by this report;

3. Based on my knowledge, the financial statements, and other financial information included in this report, fairly present in all material respects the financial condition, results of operations and cash flows of the registrant as of, and for, the periods presented in this report;

4. The registrant's other certifying officer(s) and I are responsible for establishing and maintaining disclosure controls and procedures (as defined in Exchange Act Rule 13a-15(e) and 15d-15(e)) and internal control over financial reporting (as defined in Exchange Act Rules 15(f) and 15d-15(f)) for the registrant and have:

   (a) Designed such disclosure controls and procedures, or caused such disclosure controls and procedures to be designed under our supervision, to ensure that material information relating to the registrant, including its consolidated subsidiaries, is made known to us by others within those entities, particularly during the period in which this report is being prepared;

(b) Designed such internal control over financial reporting, or caused such internal control over financial reporting to be designed under our supervision, to provide reasonable assurance regarding the reliability of financial reporting and the preparation of financial statements for external purposes in accordance with generally accepted accounting principles;

(c) Evaluated the effectiveness of the registrant's disclosure controls and procedures and presented in this report our conclusions about the effectiveness of the disclosure controls and procedures, as of the end of the period covered by this report based on such evaluation; and

(d) Disclosed in this report any change in the registrant's internal control over financial reporting that occurred during the registrant's most recent fiscal quarter (the registrant's fourth fiscal quarter in the case of an annual report) that has materially affected, or is reasonably likely to materially affect, the registrant's internal control over financial reporting; and

5. The registrant's other certifying officer(s) and I have disclosed, based on our most recent evaluation of internal control over financial reporting, to the registrant's auditors and the audit committee of the registrant's board of directors (or persons performing the equivalent functions):

(a) All significant deficiencies and material weaknesses in the design or operation of internal control over financial reporting which are reasonably likely to adversely affect the registrant's ability to record, process, summarize and report financial information; and

(b) Any fraud, whether or not material, that involves management or other employees who have a significant role in the registrant's internal control over financial reporting.

Date:_____

_____

[Signature]
[Title]

Attestation Checklist

This book has focused on controls at the process level that impact most managers. There are, however, entity-level controls designed to address nonoperational risks that most managers will not have decisions rights or responsibility for maintaining. Certain executives, such as the CEO, CFO, and to a lesser extent, their reports, will exercise authority over entity controls, and the Sarbanes-Oxley Act requires that they must assess them. The following checklist will help managers evaluate their entity-level controls and governance processes in much the same way an external auditor will. While each auditing firm will employ its own approach, and audit teams will tailor their analysis to their assessment of unique company and industry risks, this checklist will help a manager prepare for the vast majority of their questions.

Control Environment	Yes	No
Integrity, ethical values, and behavior of key executives:		
• Is there a widely communicated statement of values or other code of conduct that is evident in management's words and actions?	____	____
• Do rewards and incentives support an appropriate ethical tone at the company?	____	____
• Is there evidence that management disciplines departures from proper conduct?	____	____
Management's control consciousness and operating style:		
• Is there effective oversight by the board of directors, and is the management structure appropriate?	____	____
• Are financial reporting policies conservative?	____	____
• Do regular communications support the importance of internal controls?	____	____
• Does management dedicate enough time and resources to internal control assessment and quickly address deficiencies?	____	____

Control Environment (continued)	Yes	No
• Are financial and other targets realistic, and are incentives balanced?	___	___

Commitment to competence:

- Is departmental staffing adequate, and are employees properly prepared for their assigned level of responsibility? ___ ___
- Is management's functional experience broad, and not overly reliant on one or two individuals? ___ ___

Board of directors' participation in governance and oversight:

- Is there sufficient independent representation on the board, as evidenced by diverse backgrounds and expertise, no ties to the company other than as a director, as well as active and significant participation in company matters? ___ ___
- Does the board determine the compensation of executive officers and chief internal auditor? ___ ___
- Is the audit committee independent and vigilant, and does it include at least one financial expert and have the authority and resources to discharge its responsibilities? ___ ___
- Does the audit committee maintain a direct line of communication with internal and external auditors? ___ ___

Organizational structure, operating style, and assignment of authority and responsibility:

- Is the organizational structure appropriate for the size of the company, and does it support the flow of required management information required to run the organization? ___ ___
- Are the responsibilities of individual managers clearly defined? ___ ___
- Is there adequate supervision of decentralized operations? ___ ___
- Is there excessive turnover in key functions such as accounting, data processing, and internal audit? ___ ___
- Is there a structure for assigning ownership of accounts, applications, and databases? ___ ___

Human resources policies and procedures:

- Are there written policies and procedures covering hiring, training, promoting, compensating, and terminating employees? Are they clear, current, and communicated regularly? ___ ___
- Are there written job descriptions or other methods to inform personnel of their duties? ___ ___
- Is employee performance periodically evaluated? ___ ___

Risk Assessment	Yes	No

Objective Setting:

- Is the strategic plan communicated in such a way that all employees have an understanding of the company's strategy? Are company-specific objectives established, communicated, monitored, and consistent with the strategy? ___ ___
- Are relevant, measurable process-level objectives established and linked to entity-level objectives for all major business processes, including information technology? ___ ___

Risk Assessment (continued)	Yes	No

- Are all levels of management involved in the objective-setting process?   ___ ___

Risk analysis and mitigation:

- Is a risk assessment regularly performed for entity and process objectives for both external and internal sources? Does the board of directors address significant risks identified?   ___ ___
- Is there a new product/business committee or approval process that evaluates proposals against objectives and adequately assesses all relevant risks? Are significant initiatives board-approved?   ___ ___
- Are privacy- and data-protection policies in place and operational?   ___ ___
- Does internal audit perform a periodic risk analysis? Are actions taken to address these risks?   ___ ___

Managing change:

- Are contingency plans maintained for changes in market conditions, capacity constraints, business disruptions, or access to the financial markets?   ___ ___
- Are budgets and forecasts used to identify significant changes in the operating environment?   ___ ___
- Are there individuals or groups responsible for updating management regarding changes in accounting standards, legislation, workforce pool, market demographics or spending patterns, competitor movements, foreign political risk, and so on?   ___ ___
- Do new systems and process initiatives go through change control procedures?   ___ ___
- If restructuring a business, department, or process, are the effects on the other businesses and accounting department evaluated? Are transferred or terminated employees' control responsibilities reassigned? Are safeguards implemented to protect the company against disgruntled employees?   ___ ___
- Is there a process to ensure that changes in GAAP are properly applied? Does the board of directors review and approve changes to accounting policies?   ___ ___

Control Activities	Yes	No

Policies and procedures:

- Are policies and procedures periodically evaluated (at least annually) and updated? Is clear ownership assigned for this evaluation at an appropriate level of management?   ___ ___
- Are accounting and closing procedures followed consistently throughout the year? Are transactions booked in a timely fashion and properly documented?   ___ ___
- Does an appropriate level of senior management review significant accounting estimates and supporting documentation for topside journal entries and unusual or nonroutine transactions?   ___ ___

Monitor objectives:

- Does management regularly monitor key performance indicators? Are variances from expected performance investigated and resolved?   ___ ___

Control Activities (continued)	Yes	No
• Are deviations from expected performance discussed with the board of directors at least every quarter?	____	____
• Are financial reports disseminated to management, together with analysis of the performance?	____	____

Organizational structure:

• Do organizational charts exist?	____	____
• Are key functions segregated, such as record-keeping from asset custody, application and system programmers from IT operations and database management, and information risk management oversight from other IT functions?	____	____
• Are appropriate approvals required to allow or adjust individual access profiles for applications, systems, and databases?	____	____
• Is there a process requiring system owners to periodically review and confirm access privileges?	____	____

Safeguards:

• Are there procedures to periodically conduct physical counts to reconcile assets such as securities, inventories, property and equipment, and so on against the accounting records, and to make proper adjustments? Are recurring adjustments investigated?	____	____
• Are liquid and valuable assets such as cash and securities regularly reconciled to the accounting records?	____	____
• Is there a document destruction policy that protects against unauthorized access to, or destruction of, records, including electronic files?	____	____
• Are key documents, such as blank checks, properly restricted and secured?	____	____

System security:

• Are appropriate access safeguards in place to monitor and protect against unauthorized access to applications, operating systems, and databases, both from internal and external threats?	____	____
• Is there a dedicated individual or department responsible for monitoring the IT environment? Are incidents logged and investigated, and is action taken to prevent reoccurrence?	____	____
• Is the data center or other locations (such as telecommunications closets) where important technology systems are kept properly secured?	____	____
• Are the general IT controls periodically reviewed by internal audit or a service provider, and are results communicated to the audit committee?	____	____

Information and Communication	Yes	No

Required information:

• Can the entity currently meet, or is developing, the capability to meet the SEC's new accelerated reporting deadlines for filing timely, accurate reports?	____	____
• Does the board of directors receive timely information in the right amount of detail needed to discharge its responsibilities?	____	____

Information and Communication (continued)	Yes	No

- Are goals, objectives, and key performance indicators measurable, and is actual performance communicated to the board of directors? ____ ____
- Are procedures in place to obtain and report relevant external information, such as regulatory developments, competitor initiatives, market conditions, foreign political risks, and so on? ____ ____
- Is the board of directors satisfied with the timeliness, quantity, and quality of information received? ____ ____
- Do managers have the information they need to carry out their responsibilities? ____ ____

Strategic IT development:

- Is there a technology strategy that supports business objectives and strategies? ____ ____
- Are policies and procedures in place to control the development, modification, conversion, or replacement of accounting and other systems? Do such policies include the thorough testing of new or modified programs (including parallel processing, where possible) and user acceptance, and do they require that appropriate authorizations be obtained before they are introduced into production? ____ ____
- Is financial management involved in systems development to ensure proper controls are resident? ____ ____
- If applicable, are vendor processes and application controls reviewed or are transactions otherwise outsourced? Is this assessment documented and monitored? ____ ____
- Is there a reasonable level of user satisfaction with the functionality of systems provided? Is the satisfaction level monitored by technology management? ____ ____

Financial and human resources:

- Are sufficient resources, with the requisite technical capabilities, provided to develop needed information systems? ____ ____
- Are the board of directors and senior management involved in monitoring major system projects? ____ ____

Business continuity:

- Are programs and data files regularly backed up and stored off-site? ____ ____
- Is there a business continuity/disaster recovery plan that covers critical systems and procedures? Does the plan identify critical users and systems and the time required to deliver needed resources and systems? ____ ____
- Are continuity plans tested at least annually, and updated to reflect changing conditions? ____ ____

Communication:

- Are clear lines of authority and responsibilities widely communicated? ____ ____
- Are internal training processes, job descriptions, and written procedures provided in sufficient detail to ensure that employees understand their duties and responsibilities and how they relate to departmental and corporate objectives? ____ ____

Information and Communication (continued)	Yes	No

- Is there a mechanism for employees to report unethical, illegal, or other behaviors outside of policy to the board of directors? Is this procedure communicated clearly and regularly to the entire organization? Are all such contacts logged, investigated, and addressed in a timely manner? ___ ___
- Are the company's ethical standards communicated extensively and routinely, both internally and externally? ___ ___
- Is there a process to log, investigate, and resolve complaints from customers, vendors, or other external parties? Is top management aware of the nature and volume of complaints? ___ ___
- Are there well-established communication channels that reach all parts of the company, even in foreign lands or remote locations? ___ ___
- Is there a high level of communication and cooperation between accounting and other departments? ___ ___

Monitoring	Yes	No

Evaluation of internal controls:

- Are there procedures that require management to review processes to ensure that internal controls are operating as designed? Are the scope, depth, and frequency of the review adequate? ___ ___
- Are there procedures in place to detect when controls have been overridden? ___ ___
- Are there policies and procedures in place to ensure that control exceptions are addressed? ___ ___
- Do adequate risk management procedures exist to manage risks inherent to the business? (For instance, are there adequate standards and oversight for the credit reviews at financial institutions or position exposures at investment banks?) ___ ___
- Do managers have to sign off or approve the accuracy of their financial statements, and are they held responsible when there is an error? ___ ___

Internal audit:

- Is the size and experience level of the internal audit function appropriate? ___ ___
- Is an annual audit plan developed and based on an assessment of risk? Is it shared with senior management and the board of directors? ___ ___
- Does the general auditor report to the audit committee? Are control deficiencies reported to the audit committee? ___ ___
- Does management address internal audit, external audit, and regulatory audit findings in a timely manner? ___ ___
- Are audit personnel independent, have no operating responsibility, and have the authority to examine any and all company operations? ___ ___

Compliance:

- Do employees have to periodically acknowledge compliance with the code of conduct or similar policies? ___ ___
- Are signatures required to evidence critical control activities such as reconciling accounts? ___ ___

Notes

Chapter 1

1. Ira M. Millstein, "Leading the Board in a New Era of Expectations: Do We 'Get It?'" *Directorship* (July/August 2003), p 1.
2. Ibid.
3. Gary McKenchnie and Nancy Howell, *Million-Dollar Frauds* (Altamonte Springs, FL: The Institute of Internal Auditors, 1998).
4. In Mike Freeman, "Simply No End in Sight to These Transgressions," *New York Times* (August 25, 2002), Sports Section.
5. Patrick M. Lencioni, "Make Your Values Mean Something," *Harvard Business Review* (July 2002), p. 113.
6. In Barnaby J. Feder, "WorldCom Messages Suggest a Silencing Effort," *New York Times* (August 27, 2002).

Chapter 2

1. Adam Smith, *The Wealth of Nations* (H. Regenery & Co., 1909).
2. In Stephen Kinzer, "Military's Sole Supplier of Anthrax Vaccine Still Can't Make It," *New York Times* (October 6, 2001), *www.anthraxvaccine.org\kinzer.html*.

Chapter 4

1. Michael E. Porter, *Competitive Advantage: Creating and Sustaining Superior Performance* (New York: The Free Press, 1985).
2. Global eXchange Services, "Solutions for Your Business," at *www.gxs.com.gxs/solutions*.

Chapter 6

1. Donald F. Hastings, "Lincoln Electric's Harsh Lessons from International Expansion," *Harvard Business Review* 77, no. 3 (May-June 1999), pp. 163–178.
2. Ibid.
3. Ibid.
4. Report of the NACD Blue Ribbon Commission on Risk Oversight: Board Lessons for Turbulent Times (2002), p. 7.
5. David H. Sherman and S. David Young, "Tread Lightly through These Accounting Minefields," *Harvard Business Review* (July–August 2001), p. 129.

6. Charles W. Mulford and Eugene E. Comiskey, *The Financial Numbers Game: Detecting Creative Accounting Practices* (New York: John Wiley & Sons, Inc., 2002).

7. Jeffrey A. Sonnenfeld, "What Makes Great Boards Great," *Harvard Business Review* (September 2002), p. 106.

8. Ibid.

9. Ira M. Millstein, "A Self Correcting Course for Governance," *Directors & Boards* (Spring 2003), p. 27.

10. Joel Brinkley, "Auditors Say U.S. Agencies Lose Track of Billions," *New York Times* (October 14, 2002), p. A17.

11. Ibid.

12. Ibid.

13. In Mary Williams Walsh, "New Rules Urged to Avert Looming Pension Crisis," *New York Times* (July 28, 2003), p. A1.

14. Arnold S. Ross, James E. McKinney, and Charlotte P. Armstrong, *Executive Employment & Compensation* (Los Angeles: Spencer Publishing, 1993).

15. In David Cay Johnston, "Designers of Executive Salary Plans Fear More Abuses," *New York Times* (October 5, 2002), p. C2.

16. In Amanda Ripley, "The Night Detective," *Time* (December 30, 2002/January 6, 2003), pp. 45–50.

17. Ibid.

18. Stephen George and Arnold Weimerskirch, *Total Quality Management*, 2nd ed. (New York: John Wiley & Sons, Inc., 1998).

19. Ibid.

20. Ibid.

21. Ibid.

22. Ibid.

Chapter 8

1. U.S. Securities and Exchange Commission, "Final Rule: Management's Reports on Internal Control over Financial Reporting and Certification of Disclosure in Exchange Act Periodic Reports," at *www.sec.gov/rules/final/33-8238.htm.*

Chapter 9

1. Barry Melancon, "Melancon: New Accounting Culture Necessary," CPA2biz.com (September 4, 2002), at *www.cpa2biz.com/News/Viewpoint/Melancon+New+Accounting+Culture.htm.*

2. Kim Clark, Letter to Business School Alumni, August, 20, 2002.

Epilogue

1. In Floyd Norris, "Accounting Oversight Board Begins Sending Out Its Bills," *New York Times* (August 5, 2003), at *www.nytimes.com\2003\08\05\business\05ACCO.html?.*

2. Alan Greenspan, "Remarks by Chairman Alan Greenspan before the Council on Foreign Relations," Washington, DC, November 19, 2002.

Bibliography

Ableson, Reed, and Milt Freudenheim. "HealthSouth Ex-Executive Is Charged." *New York Times* (April 9, 2003), p. C1.

Abelson, Reed. "HealthSouth Tries to Regain Its Credibility with Investors." *New York Times* (September 30, 2002), p. C1.

Alexander, Delroy, Greg Burns, Robert Manor, and Flunn McRoberts. "The Fall of Andersen." *Chicago Tribune* (September 1, 2002), at *www.chicagotribune.com\business\ showcase\chi-0209=0315sept01.story.*

American Institute of Certified Public Accountants, Inc. *AICPA Audit and Accounting Guide.* New York: Broker and Dealers in Securities, 1997.

Anderson, Jenny, and John Lehmann. "Feds Blast Frank." *New York Post* (April 24, 2003), p. 31.

Anderson, Jenny. "Much Too Koz-Y." *New York Post* (May 29, 2003), p. 35.

Associated Press. "Broker Accused of Fraud Pleads Guilty." *New York Times* (August 29, 2002).

———. "Harvard's Hasty Pudding Members Charged with Embezzlement." CNN Student News (February 6, 2002).

———. "Former Executive Indicted in Accounting Scheme." *New York Times* (June 5, 2003), p. C10.

———. "Ex-Qwest Execs Named in Fraud Indictment." AOL.Com News (February 26, 2003), at *http://my.aol.com/news.*

———. "Enron Directors at a Glance" (September 25, 2002), at *http://abcnews.go.com/ wire/Politics/ap20020925_1857.html.*

———. "Padding of Resume Causes Bonus Loss." *New York Times* (October 31, 2002).

Barack, Lauren. "Martha's $25M Week Spot." *New York Post* (May 20, 2003).

Barboza, David. "Ex-Executives Say Sham Deal Helped Enron." *New York Times* (August 8, 2002), p. A1.

———. "From Enron Fast Track to Total Derailment." *New York Times* (October 3, 2002), p. C1.

Barrionuevo, Alexei. "Crude-Oil Trader Is Indicted in Plains All-American Case." *Wall Street Journal* (September 6, 2002).

Beckett, Paul. "Citigroup May Pay $200 Million in FTC 'Predatory Lending' Case." *Wall Street Journal* (September 6, 2002), p. A1.

Berenson, Alex. "A U.S. Push on Accounting Fraud." *New York Times* (April 9, 2003).

Berkeley, Bill. "A Glimpse into a Recess of International Finance: An Allegation of Money Laundering." *New York Times* (September 12, 2002), p. C1.

Berkowitz, Arthur L. *Enron: A Professional's Guide to the Events, Ethical Issues, and Proposed Reforms.* Chicago: CCH Incorporated, 2002.

Bianco, Anthony, William Symonds, and Nanette Byrnes. "The Rise and Fall of Dennis Kozlowski." *BusinessWeek* (December 23, 2002), pp. 65–77.

Bloomberg News. "Former ABN Amro Official Is Accused." *New York Times* (August 20, 2002).

———. "Rule Offered on Directors." *New York Times* (August 8, 2003)

Bonnette, Cynthia A. "How Are You Managing Technology Risk?" Microbanker Online, at *www.microbanker.com/artarchive02/hallbankopcommHow Are You Managing Techno. . . .*

Brinkley, Joel. "Auditors Say U.S. Agencies Lose Track of Billions." *New York Times* (October 14, 2002), A17.

Byrnes, Jonathan. "Dell Manages Profitability, not Inventory." Harvard Business School Working Knowledge (June 2, 2003), at *http://hbswk.hbs.edu\tools\print_item.jhtml?id=3497&t=dispatch.*

CBS Poll: "Little Faith in Big Biz." CBS News (July 10, 2002) at *www.cbsnews.com\stores\ 2002\07\01\opinion\polls\main514732.shtml.*

Center for Business Innovation. "Perspectives on Business Innovation. Connected Innovation: Issue 8," at *www.cbi.cgey.com/journal/Issue8/Special_Items.html.*

Clark, Kim. Letter to Business School Alumni (August 20, 2002).

Cohen, Laura, and Julia Angwin. "AOL Is Probed for 'Round-Tripping.'" *New York Times* (August 19, 2002).

Colbert, Janet L, and Paul L. Bowen. "A Comparison of Internal Controls: COBIT, SAC, COSO, and SAS 55/78." Accessed at *www.isaca.org\bkr\cbt3.htm.*

Committee of Sponsoring Organizations of the Treadway Commission (COSO). *Internal Control-Integrated Framework.* 2 vols. Harborside, NJ: AICPA, 1994.

Coopers & Lybrand. *GARP: Generally Accepted Risk Principles.* United Kingdom, 1996.

CPSC. News from the CPSC. "Companies to Pay $885,000 Fine for Not Reporting Weed Wizard Hazards and Injuries." *U.S. Consumer Products Commission* (November 11, 2002), at *www.cpsc.gov/cpscpub/prerel/prhtml03/03032.html.*

Deutsch, Claudia H. "Accounting at Xerox Is Under Inquiry." *New York Times* (September 25, 2002).

Doherty, Jacqueline. "Pay Me Later?" *Barrons* (October 21, 2002), p. 22.

Donlan, Thomas G. "Ethical Indifference." *Barrons* (September 30, 2002), p. 35.

Drape, Joe. "Worker Dismissed as Inquiry Widens into Big Racing Bet." *New York Times* (November 1, 2002), p. A1.

———. "Betting Inquiry Widens to Include Possible Dry Run." *New York Times* (November 7, 2002), p. D1.

Drape, Joe, and John Schwartz. "3 Friends and Big Payoff Pose Tough Questions for Racing." *New York Times* (November 10, 2002), p. 1.

Eichenwald, Kurt. "An Ex-Official Faces Charges in Enron Deals." *New York Times* (October 3, 2002), p. A1.

———. "U.S. Indicts 11 Former Enron Executives." *New York Times* (May 2, 2003), p. C1.

———. "Even If Heads Roll, Mistrust Will Live On." *New York Times* (October 6, 2002), Section 3, p. 1.

Ernst & Young LLP. *Evaluating Internal Controls at the Process, Transaction, or Application Level.* Ernst & Young LLP, 2003.

———. *Preparing for Internal Control Reporting: A Guide for Management's Assessment under Section 404 of the Sarbanes-Oxley Act.* Ernst & Young LLP, 2003.

Feder, Barnaby J. "WorldCom Messages Suggest a Silencing Effort." *New York Times* (August 27, 2002).

———. "2 WorldCom Executives, Faulted in Bankruptcy Inquiry Report, Resign." *New York Times* (June 11, 2003).

Fernadez, Tommy. "Awaking to More Sarbanes Pains." *Crain's New York Business* (April 28–May 4, 2003), p. 1.

Fishman, Ted C. "Get a Room." *Worth* (July/August 2002), pp. 23, 24.

Food Safety and Inspection Service, United States Department of Agriculture. "Colorado Firm Recalls Beef Trim and Ground Beef Products For Possible E. coli." Recall Release FSIS-RC_055-2002 (July 16, 2002).

France, Mike. "What about the Lawyers?" *BusinessWeek* (December 23, 2003), pp. 58–62.

Freedman, Richard D., and Velvet V. Mickens. "Salomon Brothers: 'Apologies Are Bullshit.'" NYU Stern School of Business, (rev. March 1998).

Freeman, Mike. "Simply No End in Sight to These Transgressions." *New York Times* (August 25, 2002), Sports section.

George, Stephen, and Arnold Weimerskirch. *Total Quality Management*, 2d ed. New York: John Wiley & Sons, Inc., 1998.

Global eXchange Services. "Solutions for Your Business," at *www.gxs.com.gxs/solutions.*

Greenspan, Alan. "Remarks by Chairman Alan Greenspan before the Council on Foreign Relations," Washington, DC (November 19, 2002).

Gregory, Holly J. and Jason R. Lilien. "The Role of the Audit Committee in Corporate Governance." *In Search of Good Directors, A Guide to Building Corporate Governance in the 21st Century.* International Private Enterprise, 2003.

———. "Comparison of Corporate Governance Guidelines and Codes of Best Practice: The United States," 2003 at *http://www.weil.com/wgm/cwgmhomep.nsf/Files/IntnlCorpGovGuide_US/$file/IntnlCorpGovGuide_US.pdf.*

———. "Director Liability: The Fundamental Things Apply." Director's Monthly (April 1998).

Harvard Management Update promotion. Volume 6, Number 7 (July 2001).

Hastings, Donald F. "Lincoln Electric's Harsh Lessons from International Expansion." *Harvard Business Review* 77, no. 3 (May–June 1999), pp. 163–178.

House Committee on Financial Services. "Rebuilding Investor Confidence, Protecting U.S. Capital Markets. The Sarbanes-Oxley Act: The First Year."

Johnston, David Cay. "Designers of Executive Salary Plans Fear More Abuses." *New York Times* (October 5, 2002), p. C2.

Jorion, Philippe. "Orange County Case: Using Value at Risk to Control Financial Risk" (2001), at *www.gsm.uci.edu/~jorion/oc/case.html.*

Jubak, Jim. "The Pension Bombshell in the Fine Print." The Street.com (May 14, 2002), at *www.thestreet.com/funds/jubak/10022294.html.*

Kaplan, Robert S., and David P. Norton. *The Balanced Scorecard.* Boston: HBS Press, 1996.

Katz, David M. "Defined Benefits, Loose Accounting." CFO.com (May 20, 2002), at *www.cfo.com/printarticle/0,5317,7224\,00.html.*

Kinzer, Stephen. "Military's Sole Supplier of Anthrax Vaccine Still Can't Make It" (October 6, 2001), at *www.anthraxvaccine.org/kinzer.html.*

Kirkpatrick, David D. "From Piranha at Homestore to Key Role in U.S. Inquiry." *New York Times* (September 27, 2002), p. C1.

———. "New Charges against AOL Made in Suit on Homestore." *New York Times* (November 16, 2002), p. C1.

Koniak, Susan P. "Who Gave Lawyers a Pass?" *Forbes* (August 12, 2002), p. 58.

Labaton, Stephen. "Chief of Big Pension Plan Is Choice for Accounting Board." *New York Times* (October 1, 2002).

Lang, R. Todd, and Holly J. Gregory. "The Sounding Board." *Directorship* (November 1996).

Lashinsky, Adam. "For Cisco, Today's Write-Off May Be Tomorrow's Free Ride." The Street.com (April 18, 2001), at *www.thestreet.com\comment\siliconstreet\1394667.html.*

Lencioni, Patrick M. "Make Your Values Mean Something." *Harvard Business Review* (July 2002), p. 113.

Lieberman, David. "Adelphia Plans to File Chapter 11." *USA Today* (June 23, 2002), at *www.usatoday.com\money\telecom\2002-06-021-adelphia.htm.*

Lynch, Gary. "Kidder Peabody & Co. Investigation of Government Bond Trading by Joseph Jett" (August 4, 1994).

MacAvoy, Paul, and Ira M. Millstein. *The Recurrent Crisis in Corporate Governance.* London: Palgrave MacMillan, 2003.

Malone, Michael S. "Welcome to Feedback Universe: Surrender to the Self-Correcting System." *Forbes ASAP* (Fall 2002), pp. 21–25.

McGeehan, Patrick. "States Talk Tough. Wall Street Sweats." *New York Times* (October 20, 2002), Section 3, p.1.

———. "Goldman Wooed A Star Analyst, Documents Show." *New York Times* (October 12, 2002), p. C1.

———. "Spitzer Sues Executives of Telecom Companies Over 'Ill-Gotten' Gains." *New York Times* (October 1, 2002), p. C1.

———. "Chief of Goldman Sachs Apologizes for Remarks on Firm's Productivity." *New York Times* (February 4, 2003), p. C1.

McKenchnie, Gary, and Nancy Howell. *Million-Dollar Frauds.* Altamonte Springs, Florida: The Institute of Internal Auditors, 1998.

McTague, Jim. "House of Con? 800America.com Head Charged with Fraud." *Barron's* (November 25, 2002).

Melancon, Barry. "Melancon: New Accounting Culture Necessary." CPA2biz.com (September 4, 2002), at *www.cpa2biz.com/News/Viewpoint/Melancon+New+Accounting+Culture.htm*.

Millstein, Ira M. and Paul MacAvoy. "The Active Board of Directors and Performance of the Large Publicly Traded Corporation." *Columbia Law Review* (June 1998).

Millstein, Ira M. and Holly J. Gregory. "Corporate Governance Reform: Learning from Our Mistakes." *Corporate Governance and Capital Flows in a Global Economy.* London: Oxford University Press, 2003.

Millstein, Ira M. "A Self Correcting Course for Governance." *Directors & Boards* (Spring 2003).

———. "Leading the Board in a New Era of Expectations: Do We 'Get It?'" *Directorship* (July/August 2003).

Moore, Matt. "The Associated Press." America Online (August 9, 2002).

Morse, Dan. "Tennessee Producer Tries New Tactic In Sofas: Speed." *Wall Street Journal* (November 19, 2002), p. A20.

Morgenson, Gretchen, with Andrew Ross Sorkin. "Tyco Rewarded an Executive During a Grand Jury Inquiry." *New York Times* (September 26, 2002), p. A1.

Mulford, Charles W., and Eugene E. Comiskey. *The Financial Numbers Game: Detecting Creative Accounting Practices.* New York: John Wiley & Sons, Inc., 2002.

Murphy, Bill. "Enron Movers Tackle Life in the Meantime." *Houston Chronicle* (July 8, 2002), at *www.chron.com\cs\CDA\storyhts\special\enron\1486050*.

NACD Blue Ribbon Commission. Report on Director Professionalism (2001).

———. Report on Audit Committees: A Practical Guide (2002).

———. Report on Risk Oversight: Board Lessons for Turbulent Times (2002).

New York Stock Exchange. Final NYSE Corporate Governance Rules. November 4, 2003. Access at *www.nyse.com\pdfs\finalcorpgovrules.pdf*.

Norris, Floyd. "Accounting Oversight Board Begins Sending Out Its Bills." *New York Times* (August 5, 2003), at *www.nytimes.com\2003\08\05\business\05ACCO.html*.

———. "Investor Says He Bought Stock and Didn't Know It." *New York Times* (July 30, 2003), p. C1.

———. "SEC Picks a Fed Banker to Lead Panel." *New York Times* (April 16, 2003), p. C1.

———. "Tyco Ousts Head of Fire and Security Unit." *New York Times* (March 13, 2003), p. C1.

———. "Tyco Took Profit on Bad Deal, Then Paid Bonuses to Executives." *New York Times* (September 25, 2002), p. C1.

———. "Justice Dept. Starts Inquiry at Sunbeam." *New York Times* (September 8, 2002), p. C1.

Oversight Hearing on Corporate Governance Before the Senate Committee on Banking, Housing and Urban Affairs, 107th Congress (2002). Statement of Ira M. Millstein, Senior Partner, Weil, Gotshal & Manges, LLP.

Porter, Michael E. *Competitive Advantage: Creating and Sustaining Superior Performance.* New York: The Free Press, 1985.

Pulliam, Susan, Randall Smith, and Michael Schroeder. "SEC May Punish Some Executives Who Snared IPO's." *The Wall Street Journal* (September 27, 2002), p. C1.

Rashbaum, William K. "Response Time to Police Calls Is 29% Faster." *New York Times* (September 26, 2002), p. B1.

Reddy, Michael T. *Securities Operations*, 2d ed. New York: New York Institute of Finance.

Report and Recommendations of the Blue Ribbon Committee on Improving the Effectiveness of Corporate Audit Committees, 1999.

Reuters. "3 Former Executives Indicted in Fraud." *New York Times* (September 6, 2002).

————. "Homestore Execs Agree to Plead Guilty." NYTimes.com (September 26, 2002), at *www.nytimes.com/cnet/CNET_2100-1017-959380.html*.

————. "Ex-Kmart Execs Accused of Accounting Fraud." Yahoo! News (February 26, 2003), at *http://news.yahoo.com/news*.

————. "Underfunded Pensions Double in U.S." (September 4, 2003).

Ripley, Amanda. "The Night Detective." *Time* (December 30, 2002/January 6, 2003), pp. 45–50.

Roberts, Thomas A., Greg A. Danilow and Stephen A. Radin. "Director Liability Warnings from Delaware." *Business & Securities Litigator.* Weil, Gotshal & Manges LLP, February 2003.

Romero, Simon. "Former Employees of Dynegy Face Charges of Fraud." *New York Times* (June 13, 2003), p. C1.

————. "House Staff to Question Ex-Executive." *New York Times* (September 27, 2002).

————. "Qwest Announces Accounting Flaws." *New York Times* (July 29, 2002), Section A, p. 1.

————. "Qwest Deals Are Added to Inquiry." *New York Times* (September 13, 2002), p. C1.

Ross, Arnold S., James E. McKinney, and Charlotte P. Armstrong. *1992 Executive Employment & Compensation*. Los Angeles: Spencer Publishing, 1993.

Ross, Barbara, Robert Gearty, and Corky Siemaszko. "The Great Tyco Robbery." *Daily News* (September 12, 2002), at *www.nydailynews.com/news/story/18669p-17595c.html*.

Santora, Marc. "U.S. Lab Worker Hired During Strike Had Arrest Record." *New York Times* (November 19, 2002), p. B1.

Seinfeld, David, and Robert Root. North Shore Central School District Letter to the Community (October 24, 2002).

Serrill, Michaels. "Billion Dollar Loser. A Top Trader at Japan's Sumitomo Creates a Disaster. How Did He Hide It for Ten Years?" *Time International* 147, no. 26 (June 24, 1996), at *www.time.com\time\international\1996\960624\Japan.html*.

Sherman, David H., and S. David Young. "Tread Lightly through These Accounting Minefields." *Harvard Business Review* (July–August 2001), p. 129.

Simons, Robert. "How Risky Is Your Company?" *Harvard Business Review* (May–June 1999), p. 85.

Smith, Adam. *The Wealth of Nations*. H. Regenery & Co., 1909.

Sonnenfeld, Jeffrey A. "What Makes Great Boards Great." *Harvard Business Review* (September 2002), p. 106.

Sorkin, Andrew Ross. "Tyco Figure Pays $22.5M in Guilty Plea." *New York Times* (December 18, 2002), p. C1.

———. "Back to School, But This One Is for Top Corporate Officials." *New York Times* (September 3, 2002), p. A1.

Stanford Law School. Gateway, Inc., Case Information. Securities Class Action Clearing-house, Stanford Law School, 2001.

Stevens, Mark. *The Big Six: The Selling Out of America's Top Accounting Firms.* New York: Simon & Schuster, 1991.

Stewart, John; CPA, CFE. "Embezzlement: How to Avoid Every Business Owner's Nightmare." SmartPros (September 10, 2001).

Supreme Court of the State of New York, county of New York, Criminal Term. "The People of the State of New York against L. Dennis Kozlowski and Mark H. Swartz, Defendants." Indictment No. 5259/02.

Taub, Stephen. "Adelphia CFO Arrested." CFO.com (July 25, 2002), at *www.cfo.com/ Article?article=7486.*

"Tyco's History Under Kozlowski." Washingtonpost.com (June 3, 2002), at *www.washing-tonpost.com\ACZ\wp-dyn\A53065-2002Jun3?language=printer.*

U.S. Attorney Southern District of New York. Press Release Announcing Criminal Indictment of Daiwa Bank (November 2, 1995).

U.S. Securities and Exchange Commission. "SEC Proposes Additional Disclosures, Prohibitions to Implement Sarbanes-Oxley Act." U.S. Securities and Exchange Commission release 2002–150 (October 16, 2002).

———. "Final Rule: Management's Reports on Internal Control Over Financial Reporting and Certification of Disclosure in Exchange Act Periodic Reports" (June 6, 2003), at *www.sec.gov/rules/final/33-8238.htm.*

———. U.S. Securities and Exchange Commission Complaint: SEC v L. Dennis Kozlowski, Mark H. Swartz, and Mark A. Belnick (September 11, 2002), at *www.sec.gov/ litigation/complaints/complr17722.htm.*

Valenti, Catherine. "Crime and Punishment." ABC News.com (August 7, 2002), at *http://abcnews.go.com/sections/business/DailyNews/corporatepunishment_020807html.*

Walsh, Mary Williams. "New Rules Urged to Avert Looming Pension Crisis." *New York Times* (July 28, 2003), p. A1.

The Washington Group. SEC Form 10-K (November 30, 2001).

Wayne, Leslie. "The Corridor from Goldman to Washington Is Well Traveled. *New York Times* (December 13, 2002), p. C1.

Wald, Matthew L. "1988 Warning Rejected at Nuclear Plant." *New York Times* (September 30, 2002), Section A.

Welch, Jack, with John A. Byrne. *Jack: Straight from the Gut.* New York: Warner Business Books, 2001.

Zellner, Wendy, Mike France, and Joseph Weber. "The Man behind Enron's Deal Machine." *BusinessWeek Online* (February 4, 2002), at *www.businessweek.com\print\ magazine\content\02-05\b3768015htm?*

Subject Index

Company Index